JAMKHED

A Comprehensive
Rural Health Project

◆

Doctors Mabelle Arole
and Rajanikant Arole

MACMILLAN

First published 1994

Published by THE MACMILLAN PRESS LTD
London and Basingstoke
Associated companies and representatives in Accra,
Auckland, Delhi, Dublin, Gaborone, Hamburg, Harare,
Kong Kong, Kuala Lumpur, Lagos, Manzini, Melbourne,
Mexico City, Nairobi, New York, Singapore, Tokyo.

ISBN 0–333–57736–1

Printed in Hong Kong

A catalogue record for this book is available from the
British Library.

Dedicated
to
Shobha and Ravi

CONTENTS

Foreword   Professor Carl E. Taylor   vi
Acknowledgements   ix
Introduction   We have overcome   1
1   Growing up in India   16
2   Vadala: experiences in a rural hospital   24
3   In search of answers   36
4   Health, bureaucracy and elusive politics   50
5   Community enthusiasm   56
6   From leaders to people   65
7   Team building   78
8   The health centre: discovering village talent   95
9   Community participation: farmers' clubs   105
10   Times of crisis – stepping stones for progress   121
11   The auxiliary health worker   135
12   A worker for the village   146
13   The village health worker training   158
14   The Mahila Vikas Mandal   182
15   Organisation and expansion   201
16   Monitoring, evaluation and achievements   210
17   Leprosy: integration into primary health care   225
18   Resource mobilisation: towards self reliance and sustainability   235
19   Equity, integration and empowerment   246
References and suggested readings   255
Glossary of Indian words and abbreviations   257
Index   258

FOREWORD

This is a book that many people working in the villages around the world have been waiting for. In simple straightforward language, the Aroles tell how they empowered 250 000 people living in the villages around Jamkhed to solve their own problems. This book should take an honoured place with classics of community development such as the Ting Hsien Experiment (John Grant and C. C. Chen), behind Mud Wall (Wisers) and reports of the total village development work sixty years ago of Rabindranath Tagore at Shantiniketan and Gandhiji at Sevagram.

At Jamkhed the Aroles nurtured a process unique in community action in one of the best primary health care projects in the world. When they were young doctors in graduate public health training at Johns Hopkins, they impressed us as their faculty advisers because of their great personal conviction, dedication and overflowing enthusiasm. They seemed very sure in their choice with what to do with their lives. With the innate courtesy Indian students show to a teacher, they would listen to suggestions about alternate life choices but they returned always to the same clear commitment. Having acquired the best clinical and public health skills, they were going back to India to find an area where conditions were worse than anywhere else and simply serve. They were not interested in status, in potential academic positions or teaching students the accepted wisdom. They had no patience with the notion that it might be a good idea to start in an area where chances of success were good so as to learn to how to work in areas of great need. They did not want to do research, only concentrate on service for those in greatest need.

They were right. Those of us advising a more cautious approach were wrong. As true pioneers they achieved far more than any traditional career path could have provided. Long term field research, such as our Johns Hopkins Narangwal project in the Punjab, had shown the potential impact of a university based project in a rapidly developing area. We had evidence that there were technical methods to bring infant mortality and child mortality down by half in only a few years. The Aroles made the next great advance by demonstrating even greater improvement under conditions where progress seemed impossible and people had no hope. They showed that it was in this kind of extreme situation that the most dramatic benefits could be achieved.

More importantly, they went beyond simply improving health conditions for the most deprived and poor. They demonstrated that health could be an entering wedge into total socioeconomic development. Many people had been talking about empowerment and conscientization of people in greatest need, but the Aroles showed it was possible. They believed and demonstrated that the very poor have a great capacity for change and can effectively take positions of leadership if given a chance and some support. Illiterate and outcast women could become leaders who would address international conferences and advise India's Prime Minister. For these women, improving their own lives generated confidence to make changes that would have seemed impossible. The Aroles took risks and shook up the long established social equilibrium by building success on past success. Their gentle and timely stimulation of an accelerating momentum of social change has turned social inequalities upside down. To promote action, people often need only to be told 'You can do it', by someone they trust. Mutual trust as the motive power for social change emerges as people share difficult experiences.

Trust takes time and persistence. The Aroles patiently and with great humility continued their quiet work in the villages for seventeen years. Then the village women themselves said, 'Now we can continue the process of self development, and you can go do this somewhere else where the need is greater.' The ultimate challenge in community development is extension beyond a local project. Others have lived with the poor and shown conditions can be dramatically changed, but there is so much poverty in the world that we need to learn how to stimulate expansion. A new innovative process of spontaneous extension is evolving at Jamkhed. When the village health workers told the Aroles they could go start the work somewhere else, the Aroles came back to Johns Hopkins to write this book about their experiences. For two years they stayed away and the Jamkhed villagers showed they could, indeed, carry on.

In looking for their next challenge, the Aroles found 120 miles north of Jamkhed, a group of over 60 000 tribal people who had been pushed out of the forests their ancestors had inhabited for centuries because they were being protected as a conservation area. They were in desperate condition, trying to subsist in a bleak semi-desert area no one else wanted. They had to learn to live without the forest resources they had nurtured for many generations. As the Aroles began to prepare for this challenge, the village people heard of this plan. Spontaneously, groups of a dozen or so women would go by bus to the new area. They moved in for a couple of weeks at a time with families living in the new village huts. When the Aroles arrived at Bhandardara area, most of the work was already done. Village clubs had been organised, village volunteers had been trained and a pattern of change in living conditions was under way. The question is, can a ripple of change spread across the countryside of India and other countries where the message and methods of Jamkhed can make a difference?

The Aroles are setting up a training centre at Jamkhed, their own version of a school of public health, to provide a base for the expansion process. Rather than starting in an academic centre that is already established, they are building training on field realities discovered with the villagers.

vii

Village people will share in the teaching. As in other social changes, they are turning the customary academic order upside down. Rather than starting with what is considered academic excellence, they are starting with the ultimate truth, which is that the future belongs to the people.

A remarkable quality of the Aroles and their work is their deep humility. While promoting change that most revolutionaries would not attempt, they do it in a way that empowers and gives recognition to the people. In spite of this innate sense of trying not to take credit, their country and the world have discovered Jamkhed and the Aroles. In a time when authentic heroes are desperately needed, they are finally recognised as role models. Honours are added regularly, including the Ramon Magsaysay Award (the Asian Nobel prize) in 1979, the Padma Bhushan (India's equivalent of being knighted) in 1991 and many more.

The most authentic of their personal characteristics is that everything they do is grounded firmly in their Christian faith. They are quoted as having said 'Our religion is what we do.' They are among the best of the models in the world today of religion in action.

Department of International Health   Carl E. Taylor
School of Hygiene and Public Health   Professor Emeritus
The Johns Hopkins University
Baltimore MD, USA

ACKNOWLEDGMENTS

For many years our friends and colleagues have been urging us to document our experiences at Jamkhed. The opportunity came in 1989, when through a grant from the Ford Foundation and a Carnegie Fellowship we were invited as visiting associate professors to the Johns Hopkins School of Hygiene and Public Health at Baltimore MD, USA. For two years we had time to share our experiences, reflect and write. Our thanks to the Ford Foundation, the Carnegie Foundation, and to Professor Robert E. Black, Department of International Health, Johns Hopkins School of Hygiene and Public Health for the opportunity provided to work in the department and all the support given by the faculty and staff while writing this book.

We also thank the Rockefeller Foundation for hosting us at the Villa de Serebelloni, Bellagio, Italy, where in the peaceful and quiet atmosphere we were able to finalise most of the chapters.

Our profound thanks to Professor Carl Taylor for his constant encouragement and guidance. Without his help this book would never have been written.

Our most sincere thanks to Professor David Morley for all his help and suggestions and in making this book a reality.

Our sincere thanks to Ms Radhika Sekri and Ms Nicole Smart for editing the initial drafts. A special thanks to Ms Carol Ames for her encouragement and good word as she edited the book in the final stages of writing.

A special thanks to Ms Cathie Lyons for her valuable suggestions and reassurance in times of despair. We also thank all our friends who have encouraged us and supported us along the way.

At Jamkhed, we thank the hundreds of village people who were interviewed and who volunteered to speak on tape. Our appreciation goes to the people of Ghodegaon, Bavi, Khandvi, the village health workers, members of the farmers' clubs and Mahila Vikas Mandals for their patience as they were interviewed numerous times. Our special thanks to the staff of the Comprehensive Rural Health Project for all their efforts.

Our special thanks to Mr B. K. Kale, the artist who spent many hours drawing the sketches with great enthusiasm. Our thanks to Dr J. M. L. Jerald for the photographs.

Our appreciation goes to the members of the Governing Board of the Society for Comprehensive Rural Health Projects for their support and encouragement.

Our thanks to Ms Shirley Hamber, the editors and the staff of The Macmillan Press for publishing the book. We also thank TALC and Miseriar for helping to make it a low cost edition.

We place on record our deep appreciation and gratitude to all our friends and partners who enabled the work at Jamkhed to become a reality.

Thank you.

INTRODUCTION

We have overcome

May 1988

*In a huge conference hall in Washington DC, over a thousand participants listen with rapt attention to Muktabai Pol, a village health worker from Jamkhed, India. The listeners include officials from WHO and UNICEF, ministers of health, health professionals and representatives of universities from many parts of the world. Muktabai shares her experience of providing primary health care in a remote Indian village. She concludes her speech by pointing to the glittering lights in the hall. 'This is a beautiful hall and the shining chandeliers are a treat to watch,' she says. 'One has to travel thousands of miles to come to see their beauty. The doctors are like these chandeliers, beautiful and exquisite, but expensive and inaccessible.' She then pulls out two wick lamps from her purse. She lights one. 'This lamp is inexpensive and simple, but unlike the chandeliers, it can transfer its light to another lamp.' She lights the other wick lamp with the first. Holding up both lamps in her outstretched hands she says, 'I am like this lamp, lighting the lamp of better health. Workers like me can light another and another and thus encircle the whole earth. This is **Health for All.**'*

The audience rises to its feet in a standing ovation.

In 1970, we were invited by the leaders of Jamkhed, one of the poorest areas in Maharashtra State's Ahmednagar District, to provide health care in their community. That invitation opened a new chapter in our lives. What started as a modest service programme to provide modern health care to impoverished people in Jamkhed grew into a primary health care movement spreading to 175 villages and touching the lives of almost a quarter of a million people. Not only has it brought better health to the people, it has also been a catalyst in the overall development of their lives.

The Comprehensive Rural Health Project (CRHP), as the care

1

We are like these lamps lighting the lamp of better health. Workers like us can light another and another and thus encircle the whole earth

Health for All

programme is known, serves populations not reached by government health workers or private physicians. It reaches the poor, the marginalised, and especially the often neglected women and children. Around Jamkhed, scores of men and women have come forward and acquired knowledge and skills in health and development. This empowerment has resulted in a drastic reduction in infant mortality, and has improved the quality of village life. Significant changes have taken place in the lives of poor, illiterate women in the area. The stories of two village women, Lalanbai and Parubai, and the village of Ghodegaon illustrate what can happen when such people are given knowledge and control.

Lalanbai's story

Lalanbai Kadam was born in Pimpalgaon, a small village of 250 households in Maharashtra State, India. Her parents, being Dalits or 'Outcastes', lived outside the village and eked out their living as farm labourers. Lalanbai never went to school; she remembers working at home or on the farm since early childhood. Her marriage was arranged when she was only ten years old, and in the due course she gave birth to a son who died before he reached his third birthday. That was good enough reason for her husband to throw her out of the house. Since Lalanbai was still quite young, her parents arranged a second marriage for her, this time to a sickly old man, who died leaving Lalanbai with a 2-year-old daughter. Thus, without a husband for the second time, Lalanbai returned to her father's home at Pimpalgaon.

There Lalanbai worked hard on a landlord's farm, took care of farm animals, cleaned the cowshed, and made cow dung cakes for fuel. She cleaned the courtyards and streets in front of the landlord's house, because he was also the village sarpanch, or mayor. She worked daily from dawn to dusk without break and in return she received only leftover food. Since the high caste avoided touching the Dalits, the landlord's wife would deign only to toss leftovers into the outstretched folds of Lalanbai's sari (garment). Her life was constant drudgery.

One day, the Sarpanch sent for Lalanbai. Her immediate reaction to the summons was, 'Why has he sent for me? I have not done anything wrong.' Reluctantly she came to the village square with her eyes cast down, a fold of her sari entirely covering her head and face. The Sarpanch explained that the village had selected her as a village health worker and that she would have to go to the health centre at Jamkhed to learn about health. She was to assist the doctors and nurses in health activities at Pimpalgaon.

Never having been to school, Lalanbai was not only mistrustful of her ability to learn, but feared she would be rebuked if she failed. She was afraid. Yet, she must obey the Sarpanch. Upon arrival at the CRHP health centre at Jamkhed, she found women from all caste groups sitting together on a carpet, having an animated discussion with the nurses. She was welcomed by the tutor and asked to join the group. However, she was afraid to sit down since Dalits were not allowed to sit on the same carpet as the high caste people. She sat a little apart with her head turned to the wall, afraid that the high caste women would punish her for sitting too close.

Of that first encounter Lalanbai says: 'As a Dalit woman from Pimpalgaon I thought of myself as nobody. I had always been made to feel less than an animal. If by mistake I touched a high caste person carrying food, he would feel polluted and throw the food to the dogs – not even to me. I had no self respect because people addressed me with contempt. Everything was darkness. I expected the

Lalanbai sweeping the cowshed and street

same kind of treatment at the training centre. I was terrified and said to myself "What am I doing here? I am illiterate. I am a Dalit. What can I do?" I was shaking all over. When asked my name, I did not reply but just looked down and wished that I was back in Pimpalgaon doing hard manual labour. I was told that I would try it out for two months. At the end of two months, I could leave if I didn't like it. My two months are still not up as yet.'

Lalanbai found the training so interesting that she regularly attended the weekly training sessions. At the CRHP, she was being told for the first time that she was a human being with a great potential. She was treated kindly. The loving atmosphere shed her fears. Now she was even hearing that she was made in the image of God. Her self image improved; not only did she learn to read and write, but she also learned a great deal about health. Whatever she learned she tried to teach other mothers. She soon realised that there were many things that women could do themselves to prevent disease and death in children, so she resolved to bring about change in her village.

In the beginning, as a Dalit, Lalanbai had problems in the village. She was not allowed to enter the homes of high caste women and they refused to take medicines touched by her. However, she made use of many opportunities to get over these hurdles.

One day, the Sarpanch's daughter was in labour for many hours.

4

The landlord's wife would deign only to toss leftovers

Her mother could no longer bear her daughter's screaming and pain. The women in attendance had tried everything. Reluctantly, they decided to call Lalanbai.

To enter where the woman lay, Lalanbai had to pass through several rooms. The women of the house quickly cleared a passage so that she would not touch anything in the house as she passed. Lalanbai wondered how she could conduct the delivery or do anything without touching the patient in this caste-conscious household. Her training at Jamkhed had made her bold and confident, so she went ahead and examined the patient. She found that the woman was exhausted and she told the mother that some food should be given to the daughter. Some porridge was prepared and the mother asked Lalanbai to feed it to the daughter. Lalanbai hesitated. Was she hearing correctly? She, a Dalit, should feed this high caste woman? After the nourishment, the daughter regained her strength and delivered normally. Thereafter the high caste villagers readily allowed Lalanbai into their homes and from that point on, her popularity grew.

Then came the day when a young man in the village died of a stroke. The whole village was upset. Some felt that they were cursed because they had allowed Lalanbai into their homes to pollute them. Some wanted to do away with her. Scared that they would harm her, she stopped work and returned the medical kit to CRHP. When sick children or mothers in labour needed her help, she was no longer available. Soon, however, the people began to miss her services. They apologised publicly and she was reinstated as village health worker.

Lalanbai tells of the changes in Pimpalgaon over seventeen years. 'In the first year, 1972–3, I did a house-to-house health survey in Pimpalgaon, which has a population of about one thousand people. I found that many children were malnourished and during that year, forty babies were born and eight babies died from diarrhea, fever and measles. After I had worked for a couple of years, I saw many changes. I was able to get mothers to accept regular prenatal care. Mothers started giving solid foods to the children and they had all their children immunised. They would come to me for every small illness, and the modern yet simple remedies for diarrhea and fever proved to be effective. There was hardly a death among the children. In the last ten years there were only three child deaths. One child fell into a well and drowned, the second was a premature baby and the third baby had an imperforate anus, was operated on in Bombay but did not survive.

'In the first few years, I had to struggle to get people to accept family planning. Today, they undergo a sterilisation operation after one male child. Women readily accept oral contraceptives.

'There used to be many graves of small children around my village. For the past ten years, there have been only two. Only a few months ago, a young mother came back from her parents' house. Her 3-month-old baby weighed 2.5 kg. She had no breast milk, and the doctor in her mother's village had advised her to give the baby very diluted milk. For over two weeks, I visited the baby every day and showed the mother how to feed the baby properly. The baby thrived and doubled its weight to 5 kg in a couple of months so that I knew it was out of danger. This baby would surely have died if it was not for me.

'Many old people become blind because of cataracts. I find out when the cataracts are ready for an operation and refer them to CRHP for this. These blind people thank me for the sight they have received.

'Some of the children whom I fed and weighed regularly as babies have grown up to be healthy, smart adults. They go to school and college in the nearby town. During their holidays they return to Pimpalgaon and greet me and address me respectfully. It is joy to see these young people. Many of them would not have been alive if it was not for me.

'I have learned many skills for my livelihood. I lease orchards from farmers and make plenty of money selling fruit. I have built a house for myself and planted five hundred fruit trees around the house. I have helped women in the village to start their own income-generating activities.'

As she served the village, Lalanbai became very popular. In fact, the village people once wanted her to become the Sarpanch. The incumbent Sarpanch, the very same landlord for whom Lalanbai had been a servant, knew that she would definitely be elected and so he pleaded with Mabelle to persuade Lalanbai not to contest the election. When she heard about the Sarpanch's request, Lalanbai laughed and said, 'I already rule the hearts of the people of Pimpalgaon. Let him continue to be the Sarpanch! As I have changed, I have changed the world around me, even this backward village of Pimpalgaon, and that is the best reward for me.'

In the past twenty years, hundreds of village women have taken leadership roles not only in their own families but in their villages as well. Parubai Chande is one such woman. They have had influences reaching far beyond their own communities.

Parubai's story

Parubai Chande is a shepherdess from Goyakarwada, a tiny settlement of six hundred people situated on a hill about 35 kilometres from Jamkhed. Her husband kept a flock of goats and sheep and every summer he migrated with the sheep in search of grass and water. It was difficult to find grazing grounds because the grasslands were becoming depleted. Parubai, the mother of three children, farmed a two acre plot of land during the monsoon season and worked as a farm labourer during the rest of the year.

One afternoon Parubai appeared at the CRHP subcentre at Chincholi, 5 kilometres from her settlement. While working, she had injured her foot. The doctor sutured the laceration. Parubai was bold and inquisitive and she asked the social worker if CRHP would visit their settlement regularly. At the invitation of the leaders, the CRHP team visited the settlement and discussed health and other concerns of the people. During this meeting, the people nominated Parubai as their village health worker.

Like Lalanbai, Parubai assumed health responsibilities ranging from simple medical treatment to a safe water supply. One problem faced by women was access to drinking water. The nearest well was 3.5 kilometres away down a hill. One day, a young woman slipped, fell into the well and drowned. The village men approached the government officials to give them a well but without much success. The local politicians did not help much. So Parubai organised the women and told them that it was no use expecting the Government or anyone else to help them. 'We need the water. Let us get together and find water ourselves.' Men, women and children all joined together to dig a well in the valley. At 20 metres they found plenty of water. They then collected contributions and constructed a pipeline to the top, built a water tank, and installed a diesel pump set to pump the water up.

Parubai and a few other women decided to request a government official to inaugurate their drinking water programme and to see what the women had done for the village. They had to pluck up courage to approach the highly influential chief government official of the entire district of Ahmednagar, which has a population of three million people. This chief official or District Collector, Mr Nanasaheb Patil, was quite taken aback that three illiterate village women dared to walk unannounced into his office with such a request. Perhaps out of curiosity, he agreed to visit the settlement. When the collector and his entourage of dignitaries came, he was extremely impressed with the well at the bottom of the hill. The whole village was clean, children robust and healthy, and women bold and confident. He saw chimneys over the thatched roofs, indicating the presence of smokeless stoves and thousands of tree saplings thriving on the hillside.

The collector was surprised at the practical health knowledge that the women and children had. Parubai had organised informal

Parubai Chande with the District Collector

8

education classes for women and children and they had a library. The women were knowledgeable about farming, dairy animals, poultry and trees.

Parubai requested the collector to recognise this settlement as an independent village so that it would appear on the map and be eligible for such amenities as electricity, a school and a road. The collector not only declared this settlement as a village, but he also sanctioned grants for a community hall. Goyakarwada now became Goyakarwadi; a village on the map of India.

Mr Nanasaheb Patil shared his experience at Goyakarwada with the Prime Minister, Mr Rajiv Gandhi. A few months later, Parubai received an invitation to have breakfast with the Prime Minister at his residence in New Delhi. When she arrived, she was greeted by Mr Rajiv Gandhi, some of his cabinet colleagues, and officials involved in health and development. The health minister who spoke Parubai's language, Marathi, translated for her.

This group of thirty of the nation's top planners asked her many questions. She shared her ideas of village health and development with them for over two hours. Of the incident Parubai says, 'The Prime Minister of our country invited me for a twenty minute breakfast with him. I am an illiterate woman. Yet he spoke to me for over two hours in spite of his busy schedule! I was able to share my ideas of good health with him. I was happy that a person like me, who was considered a stone, had become wise enough to advise the Prime Minister on village work. We shepherds are usually considered stupid and if someone shows lack of intelligence he is called a shepherd.

'The Prime Minister asked me how did I come to Delhi. "Was I not afraid?"'

I replied, "Delhi is one thousand miles away from my village. I spent twenty four hours in the train. Since I was your guest, I was not afraid of other people."

"What is your advice to me?" he asked.

I replied, "Women should be given 50 per cent representation at all levels of government; from the village Panchayat (village council) to the Lok Sabha (Parliament)!"'

The story of Ghodegaon, a village

It is not only women who have been empowered, but entire villages have been transformed. Ghodegaon was one of the first villages to invite CRHP to work with them. The people of Ghodegaon describe the changes that have occurred in their village.

Shahaji Patil, a local farmer says, 'It was only twenty years ago

9

Ghodegaon was one of the poorest villages in this area. The hills were bare and the fields barren. Every year, the monsoon rain swept away the topsoil, leaving us the dry parched earth full of gullies and eroded land. Few of us had enough water to cultivate the land.

'The social workers of CRHP understood that we could not have good health unless we had good agriculture. They helped us to come together. We forgot our caste differences and our social status. All of us, rich and poor, joined together and we terraced and levelled the land. We built twenty three dams and dug forty irrigation wells. We planted over two hundred thousand trees on the hillside and on our farms. We prevailed on the Government to give land to those who did not have any land. Everyone in the village has land today. We got together and with CRHP's help brought those barren lands under cultivation and so have enough food to feed all our children. There is no need to go out of the village in search of food.'

For the past fifteen years Angadrao Gavhale, a Dalit, has been the Sarpanch of Ghodegaon village. He says, 'Twenty years ago, we Dalits could not come to the centre of the village. As a child, I could not go anywhere near the temple. Now I have built my house close to the temple. Yes, many changes have taken place. My family was landless, but today I have land and irrigated fields. I have planted an orchard and raised a plant nursery. Some of the Dalits now own choice land in the valley. Our children are healthy and all the girls and boys in my community go to school. We all have land and have built good homes. Formerly we were made to live outside the village in thatched huts separated by a wall from the main village.'

A high caste man interrupted, 'Yes, today we all from different castes are sitting together, drinking tea and eating snacks. Traditionally we did not socialise with the low caste, rather we who are twice born (high caste) have exploited the poor for centuries. We made them work day and night on our farms and often paid them with leftover food and grain. We would boycott them if they did not obey our orders.'

'We Dalits would be simmering with anger and would take revenge in our own way. We used to poison your prize bullocks and cows,' replied Angadrao.

Shahaji replied, 'Then we punished you by burning your huts.'

Then they all laughed together, remembering their actions, and in a more serious vein Shahaji said, 'Yes, the high caste often behaved like animals and treated the Dalits and other low castes in an unjust way. Now we have learnt how to behave like human beings. Yes, we have our differences. But we have learnt to respect and appreciate each other.'

Dalit huts outside the village wall

Shahaji continues, 'Years of drought had left us frustrated. Every year half the young people of the village would migrate for a few months to sugar factories to keep themselves from starving. Poverty and frustration led to drinking and gambling. There were twelve illegal breweries and a few gambling dens in the village. Anyone who came to Ghodegaon would see drunken brawls. People from surrounding villages also came to join in the drinking and have their luck with cards. It was a common sight to see men lazing around in this front square of the village. Added to this misery was sickness. Children were emaciated, many had swollen limbs and pot-bellies. Many children died before they reached school age and women died in childbirth because there was no doctor around. Well-to-do people went to the doctor in Jamkhed, but the poor depended on the devrushis (the magicians). Then we heard that a doctor and his wife had come to Jamkhed to work in the villages. We invited them to Ghodegaon.'

Yamunabai Kulkarni, the village health worker, animatedly speaks about herself and her experiences. 'Twenty years ago, it was unheard of for a Brahmin woman like me to sit with men or socialise with Dalit women. As a woman I was confined to my home and sometimes I worked on our ancestral farm. Now I am free and serving the entire village as a health volunteer. In the beginning it was difficult for me to visit Dalit women and especially to deliver their babies.

11

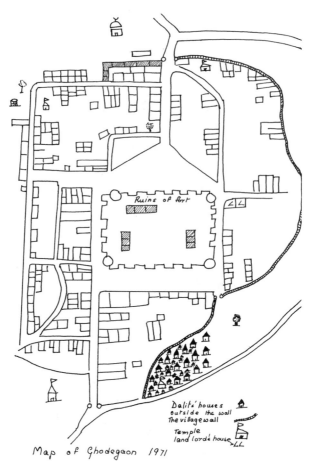

Map of Ghodegaon 1971

Dalits' houses
outside the wall
The village wall
Temple
land lord's house

Two maps of Ghodegaon village drawn by the people of Ghodegaon

'I have been a village health worker for the past seventeen years. I have never been to school. I look after the health of the mothers and children. I have conducted over 550 deliveries and have not lost a single mother during this time. This village has about 250 couples and 150 of them practise family planning. Many women have undergone sterilisation and some take oral contraceptives. I visit all the families in my village and follow up the children.

'Ghodegaon was a different village before I became a village health worker. Most adults suffered from guinea worm infection. We still have scars of this infestation on our ankles, knees and backs. Now it is no longer a problem. We were superstitious and thought that most diseases were curses of a goddess. There used to be repeated epidemics of cholera. We used to sacrifice goats and chickens to appease the particular goddess. The cholera did not disappear. Now since I became

12

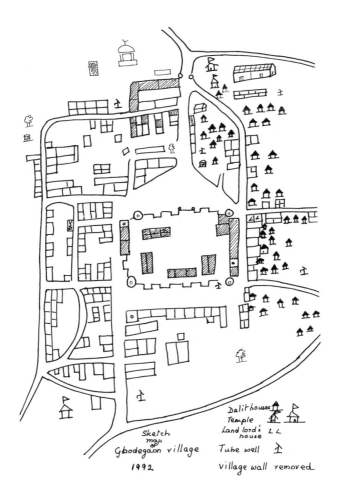

Sketch
map
of
Ghodegaon village
1992.

Dalit houses
Temple
Land lord's
house
Tube well
Village wall removed

a village health worker, the cholera is no more. Every year ten to fifteen children used to die in the village. Now hardly a baby dies.'

One village woman says of Yamunabai. 'Doctors only give medicine when people are sick. Yamunabai is more than a doctor to us. She has taught us simple home remedies for day to day illnesses like coughs, fever and diarrhea. But more than that, she teaches us how to keep from falling sick.'

'My friend here had leprosy,' said Kisanrao Sole, pointing to the man sitting next to him. 'He lives next to me. We drove him out of the village because he had leprosy but now we are not afraid of leprosy. He lives in the village again and Yamunabai treats him like any other patient. In fact, all thirty five of our leprosy patients are almost cured by Yamunabai. Some of them are active in the village. Their children are also married and settled in life.'

13

Angad, the Sarpanch, talks about Yamunabai. 'Ghodegaon people are healthy because of Yamunabai. She is very enthusiastic about her training and her work. One day she was returning to Ghodegaon from Jamkhed. It was raining hard and the stream was flooded. With a baby in her arms she was trying to cross the swollen stream and she slipped and fell into the water. Both mother and baby were swept away by the strong current. A couple of men rescued them. They scolded her for leaving the house in the rain and endangering her own life and that of the baby. She replied, "My training has saved many lives in my village. For the sake of the village I am willing to take the risk."'

Shahaji concludes, 'We villagers have worked together, improved our farms and farm animals. This has ensured adequate and nutritious food. Clean water and sanitation have eliminated many illnesses.

'The whole village worked towards the removal of caste differences and have learned to treat women and girls as equals of men. We can proudly say that Health for All has become a reality in Ghodegaon. CRHP has shown us the way and we have learned to work together for the betterment of our village. Now we do not need to depend on the Aroles or CRHP. As we continue to develop, we are not alone; scores of villages around Ghodegaon are taking part in this movement. Each village develops at its own pace as some take more advantage of their new-found knowledge and some do not.'

Spirituality is alive and active in these people and in this land. This spirituality transcends barriers set by narrow confines of religion. When people are shown the meaning and purpose in their lives, and that they can bring about justice, these miracles happen. All nature is programmed to work for the harmony and balance of the earth. Only human beings have turned it to disharmony and imbalance and injustice. But when heightened awareness changes their perception, they are free and empowered to bring justice and peace among the people.

One sensitive and accurate indicator of the development of a society or a nation is the status of its women and children. In most countries of the world, women and children are exploited both socially and economically. Rural women who live in abject poverty, bear the burden of childbearing and child rearing. Women have to do backbreaking work in the fields as well as in the households. Worse still, these tasks are performed under severe social restrictions and oppression which keep women and female children the most nutritionally deprived and deny them access to education. They have little or no decision-making power or self esteem, even when they are the main wage earners.

Illness and mortality in developing countries are closely related

14

to basic health problems created by inadequate food, polluted water supplies, poor sanitation and the absence of distributive justice. Health services, no matter how efficient, cannot change the condition of the marginalised people unless they are helped to become self-reliant and the root problems are addressed. The traditional role of the people as passive recipients of medical and other help needs to be transformed by involving them in leadership. The liberating effect of education and consciousness-raising of the disenfranchised is well documented.

People who are poor and illiterate are like uncut gems hidden under the dirt and stone. Given the opportunity, they can reach their full human potential and live as responsible, sensitive human beings, possessing self-reliance and the liberty to shed those old customs and traditions that impede health and development.

The examples of Lalanbai, Parubai and Ghodegaon demonstrate that equity, empowerment and integration are central to a sustainable primary health care movement. These are the principles of primary health care that we have learned and used in our work in the Jamkhed area. Although there are no exact blueprints, no organisational development chart that can be transferred from one area or society to another, we believe that the principles can be put to use wherever people take them seriously enough to put them into practice.

In our work with people in the villages, we have been reminded over and over that communication in traditional societies is primarily oral. Stories, dramas and songs, with lots of opportunities for discussion and questions, are effective ways of learning and teaching. So our account of discerning the principles of primary health care and of how we put them into practice, often with much trial and error, can best be communicated by telling our story. Along the way, the stories of others; villagers, bureaucrats, helpers, detractors, ordinary people who emerged into creative leaders, become part of the tale. Parts of our own stories; families, influences, training, are here also. The chapters are organised by topic, but as in a simple story, the development is chronological. Thus, those most central to the primary health care model, the poorer women of the villages, take their full place only more than halfway through this book. That is because the path to those who are most marginalised is long and beset by many obstacles – the very barriers that have so long kept them powerless.

We have shared in the telling of this story as we have shared throughout the work of the project, indeed ever since working in the villages became the shared dream of two medical students, Rajanikant and Mabelle Arole.

CHAPTER 1

Growing up in India

RAJ

Summer, 1935 Kharda, a village in Jamkhed Block in India.

It is evening as the only bus from Ahmednagar rolls to a stop. People around the bus stand look curiously at the strangers getting off the bus. One does not often see a young woman with a child travelling alone in these parts. A new school teacher is expected one of these days. Perhaps she is the one. They shake their heads disapprovingly. They have already found out that she does not follow their religion or caste rituals.

The mother clutches her child protectively. She is tired and worried. She has come from Rahuri, a village 130 kilometres away. What she has heard of Jamkhed is forbidding. The people are known to be poor, illiterate, suspicious and superstitious. They are deeply entrenched in the caste system and therefore intolerant of outsiders. Jamkhed is also notorious for the gangs of dacoits which raid the village.

The child in her arms stirs and begins to cry. He is thirsty. She must hurry and find water and shelter for the night. She hurries to the school supervisor's house to report for duty and to ask for help in finding a house.

'You will not get a house in this village,' the supervisor tells her. 'If you want, you can live in the schoolroom.'

The woman, thankful for the schoolroom, hurries out in search of water. The child's lips are parched. There is a well nearby but as a Christian, she is not allowed to draw from it. She waits in vain for a kind soul to take pity on her child and give him at least a sip of water. The child eventually falls asleep, still thirsty, tired and crying.

The next morning, after a long hot night in the schoolroom, the woman applies for a transfer back to the more developed and tolerant

16

village of Rahuri. The incident, forever etched in the mother's memory, is soon forgotten by the people of Jamkhed. The child back in Rahuri, is too young to understand or remember.

The years went by. One day there was festivity in the air. Two young doctors were welcomed and congratulated for providing drinking water to scores of villages in the Jamkhed area. Little did they know that the man was the baby they had denied water to almost forty years before.

That is how I came to grow up in Rahuri, a village 130 kilometres north of Jamkhed with a population of five thousand. My love for village life and my desire to be a doctor date back to childhood. Life in the village could be blissful. Situated on the banks of the river Mula, Rahuri was surrounded by lush green fields. Oranges were grown in many farms, and twice a year, the fragrance of citrus blossoms filled the air. In summertime my two brothers, three sisters and numerous village friends gathered berries, mangoes and plums. We collected beetles, leaves and brightly coloured seeds from the forest on the river bank. Sometimes we had so much fun that we would forget to go to school!

But life in the village, while simple, was also harsh. The villagers will always remember November 19, 1946, when a flood devastated the village. The destruction of both human and animal lives was immeasurable. Worse than the flood was the aftermath; epidemics of cholera and plague. Health workers frantically sprayed chemicals over the ruined houses and decaying matter but disease spread quickly and the poorest people, living in huts, were affected the most. I remember some of my playmates and schoolmates lying sick and dying in their homes. The suffering and helplessness of the villagers stunned me and I knew from this point on that I really wanted to be a doctor and work in the villages where no medical help was available.

My parents were school teachers in the government elementary school in Rahuri. Teachers in those days were among the few knowledgeable people in villages. My parents were warm and hospitable and active in many community activities. My father helped young men get jobs, found brides for prospective grooms and helped villagers with legal problems. People from all castes came to him for help and advice.

My father was particularly interested in the education of village children. Since many villages around Rahuri did not have schools, he went out of his way to persuade the parents to send their children to the school at Rahuri. Some villagers agreed to send their sons. These boys had to walk 8–10 kilometres to school, wading through streams and muddy fields. During the monsoon season, they got drenched and often had to stay overnight with us. My father helped them with their school work and procured books for them.

My mother also worked hard. After school, she came home, cleaned the house, fixed the meals and took care of all the children. She never complained about her duties, for as an Indian woman, it was the life she had expected.

Indeed the hardships of rural women left a deep impression on me. Every vacation I stayed with my friends on the farm. Early in the morning, I woke to the melodious songs sung by their mothers. They made up lyrics while they ground sorghum between two heavy stones, rotating the stones with their hands. When they had done this, they cooked breakfast and fed the children. After collecting water from a stream or nearby well, they took care of the animals and set out to the fields, returning at sunset to cook the evening meal in smoky little kitchens. From five in the morning until nine at night, these women worked without any rest. While women laboured, men enjoyed positions of power. They either drove the bullocks to irrigate the fields or simply followed the women, overseeing their work. Men had plenty of time to visit the nearby town and attend wedding parties and festivals, all the while giving little or no credit to the women for their hard work.

Like any other village boy, at the age of ten I began helping the family in daily chores; plucking oranges, cleaning and packing them to send to the nearby city for sale. I also took care of a couple of goats, milked them daily and collected fodder for them from the farm. I went to the weekly market and bought vegetables, grains and groceries for my family. I was fortunate to continue my studies. Many of my village friends had so much farm work that they were forced to drop out after only three or four years of schooling.

The one trained doctor in Rahuri worked in the government dispensary, where long lines of patients used to wait for him. One day I went to this doctor with fever. After waiting for over an hour, I reached his table and stood in front of him. A strong smell of phenol filled the air. Looking tired and irritable, the doctor asked me what was wrong. While I talked, he momentarily put his stethoscope on my chest and his hand on my abdomen. He scribbled something on a paper. When I picked up the paper, he called for the next patient.

I took the paper to the pharmacist sitting in the next room who stood behind a few glass jars filled with coloured solutions. He filled the bottle with the same red liquid that many other patients seemed to be getting.

Our family usually turned to Dr Panjabi, a retired army paramedic.

Although he did not have official qualifications or an academic degree, he had a government licence to practise medicine. He was kind, and softly spoken. Once I was taken to Dr Panjabi with malaria. His remedy was an injection that resulted in a painful abscess. Yet our family continually forgave Dr Panjabi's poor technique because of his kind, caring attitude. He was available to us at all times.

These doctors in our village were consulted only for serious ill-health. Illnesses were generally treated at home by our mother or neighbours. For an upset stomach, my mother rolled herbs in a newspaper and made us smoke it. For cuts and scratches, she applied a paste made of leaves. Inflamed eyes were treated with the juice from a thorny bush, and latex from the calatropis plant was used to draw out the broken thorns that often pierced our bare feet.

Like any village child, I had my share of childhood illnesses, including measles, mumps, chicken pox and whooping cough. I survived hepatitis and bouts of diarrhea and malaria. I had to obey many taboos when I was ill, for example, not being allowed to drink water during a bout of malaria chill, because water was thought to enlarge the spleen. This made me so thirsty that I had to bribe the maidservant to give me a glass of cold water.

Once my ambition was born, my father encouraged me to be a doctor. He taught me early in the morning under the kerosene lamp. He realised that I needed a proper background if I wanted to continue on to professional training. Aside from the government school, there was an English medium school with classes up to the eighth grade. My father worked to send me to this private English school although it was rather expensive. I was a good student and stayed at the top of my class. The school principal, who considered himself superior, did not have kind words for me in spite of my achievement. Once, he asked me what my ambitions were. I replied that I wanted to be a doctor. He laughed sarcastically and said, 'That profession is not for the likes of you. You should be content with being a clerk.' I looked him straight in the eyes and replied, 'I will surely be a doctor.' Fortunately, other teachers helped me, encouraged me and were proud of my scholarship.

Upon finishing college, my ambition was insatiable. I wanted to go to the best medical school. The Christian Medical College at Vellore in South India had such a great reputation, that when I was offered seats in three government medical colleges, I forfeited them in the hope that I would be admitted to Vellore.

When acceptance to the Christian Medical College came in 1954, I was overjoyed because the medical college was famous for its international teaching and excellence in medical treatment. The college atmosphere was conducive to serious study and research. The teaching hospital was known for its high technology and excellent facilities. Yet these very strengths created equally strong limits. The teaching made little reference to the deprivation and illness in the rural areas of our country. Like most medical schools around the world, Western high technology, academic medicine was impressed on students and there was little reference to the practice of medicine in rural areas. Despite these restrictive pressures, during my vacations I tested out my knowledge and its relevance to the poor patients at Vadala, a mission hospital not far from my home village of Rahuri. This helped me to focus my clinical learning.

In 1959, I graduated from medical school with excellent academic qualifications. This increased the pressure to continue in a high technology academic setting, and perhaps become a professor myself. My repeated visits to Vadala Mission hospital strengthened my resolve to work in poor rural areas.

Although Mabelle and I were classmates, we seldom met socially. We each had our own circle of friends. But I was becoming curious about Mabelle. Throughout my school and college career, I had always been awarded first rank. But in medical college, no matter how hard I tried, Mabelle kept getting first rank. During final examinations, she walked away with the gold medal and I trailed behind in second place.

During our internship year, we were posted together in a surgical unit. Often we both stayed with seriously ill patients throughout the night. Soon we began taking an interest in each other. For the first time, I realised that Mabelle was also interested in working in the villages. This common interest brought us closer day by day.

MABELLE

I grew up in the secluded, secure atmosphere of a college campus far removed from the harsh realities of life in India. My father taught New Testament Greek and Indian philosophy in a theological college at Jabalpur in central India. He had done his doctoral studies at Boston University and returned to India. He was a true scholar and always surrounded by his books. Most of his time was spent reading, writing and contemplating. My father saw good in every person; rarely did a sharp word escape his lips and he seldom spoke ill of others.

My mother was quite the opposite. A dominating woman, her word was the law in our family. My retreat and escape was my father. I was his favourite daughter and spent hours listening to his philosophy. Even as a small child, he shared with me his ideals and values. It was through him I received a deeper spiritual understanding of the teachings of Jesus Christ, which influenced me to dedicate myself to the service of the poor in the villages. We had a comfortable home, and my family belonged to a prominent South Indian clan. Many of my uncles, aunts and cousins were doctors, lawyers, and academics. I therefore did not come face to face with poverty. My knowledge of poverty and discrimination came only from what I read and what my father told me. He had written books on Indian philosophy and culture, and he was troubled by the way the average woman was treated in India. Women, he felt should be able to enter professional life and become part of the mainstream of society. Perhaps it was from my father that I learned about the lot of Indian village women. His teaching instilled in me a desire to better their quality of life and overall self image.

My father had wanted to become a doctor but could not accomplish his ambition. As a young man, he had worked among the leprosy patients in Madras. His unspoken mandate was that at least one of his children fulfil his dreams by becoming a doctor and working for leprosy patients or poor village people.

As I look back, my childhood seems rather uneventful. There were not many children of my age in the campus and so I hardly had any friends. With a sister nine years older and a brother nine years younger, I was mostly left to my own devices, spending much of my time in corners reading books from my father's library, or making things with anything and everything I could find. I studied music, needlework and craft.

Finishing high school with excellent grades, at fourteen, I could not get admission to any college, since fifteen was the minimum age for entrance. Finally a college in Trichy in South India gave me admission. After completing my premedical studies, I was still too young to enter medical college, so I decided to complete my college studies. I earned a degree in nutrition that I thought would be helpful for village work. At last I was eighteen and old enough to attend Christian Medical College. My sister was in the last year of medical school by this time and my mother was not keen that both daughters do medicine. She arranged for me to be accepted as a teacher in a local school, a job I was not interested in. My father and sister were eventually able to prevail upon her to change her mind, and so in 1954, the same year as Raj, I joined the Christian Medical College at Vellore. It was not a typical medical college, but had originally been started as a school exclusively for women and had only later opened its doors to men. There were almost an equal number of women professors, and men and women were treated alike. There was keen competition between men and women students.

At medical college there was a small circle of friends with whom I socialised, and I took my studies seriously, topping the class in most subjects. My classmates often came to me for help with their studies. I loved to teach and always took time to help them, often finding innovative ways to explain a point. I was also involved in extracurricular activities such as dramatics, and acted in plays staged at least twice a year. This helped me overcome my shyness and I learned to speak in public.

Some professors then at Vellore left a lasting impression on me. Dr Somervell, who had worked in South India for many years, was not only a pioneering surgeon but also a good scientist. He had no qualms about status and examined patients anywhere, for example in the hallways, and under the trees. He mingled easily with the masses, and taught a great lesson about removing barriers of hierarchy and scheduling.

Dr Paul Brand did pioneering work in reconstructive surgery on feet and fingers deformed by leprosy. His lectures, whether he spoke on leprosy, religion or surgery, attracted large crowds. His clear-cut thinking and candid presentation made the subject simple. Even today as I scrub for an operation, I still recall all the steps that he taught me. Dr Brand also introduced me to appropriate technology. He did part of his leprosy research in a hut under mango trees 6 kilometres from the hospital. He knew some of us were going to work in the villages. He taught us to do surgery in a mud house, where there was no electricity or running water. He guided us in surgical procedures as he showed us how to administer open drop ether anesthesia.

Dr P. Kutumbiah was a well known medical educationist and an even better known physician. He practised simple clinical methods and keen observation in making a diagnosis. Laboratory tests, he taught, were only to confirm a diagnosis, and not a substitute for painstaking examination of the patient. Dr Kutumbiah's skill and demystification of high technology, his candid ways and humour were a true source of inspiration to us.

Such people as Dr Bhat and Dr Macpherson also influenced us greatly by their simplicity, humility and service. I had often seen Dr H. H. Bhat visiting patients late at night and enquiring about their welfare; if they had enough to eat, what was their financial difficulty. He taught us to look beyond physical suffering to the human being with his family and environment.

Like Raj, I too was encouraged to take up an academic career and become a clinical specialist. I enjoyed my studies, but my com-

The young doctors Mabelle and Rajanikant Arole

mitment to working in rural India was stronger and I had no desire to stay on and pursue an academic career.

It was towards the end of my internship that Raj and I found we had common ambitions. As classmates we had competed with each other throughout medical college, but had never seriously talked to each other. Although from completely different backgrounds, we found ourselves sharing the same goals. Above all we shared the same ideology and inspiration we had learned from Jesus Christ.

Raj was concerned that I had never experienced village life and feared that I might find it too difficult. He repeatedly told me about its hardships. He explained to me that to a poor person, widow or an untouchable, village life was a living hell. He told me how difficult village life would be for a person used to such amenities of city life as running water from a tap and electricity. These were but trivial inconveniences as far as I was concerned.

We were married in April of 1960 and on our wedding day, we took a vow to work together and devote our life to the marginalised and disenfranchised people living in the villages.

CHAPTER 2

Vadala: Experiences in
a rural hospital

MABELLE

1962–1966

Vadala was a day's oxcart journey from Ahmednagar city in the Maharashtra State of India, approximately 320 kilometres east of Bombay. In 1935 the Marathi Mission had responded to the lack of complete local medical facilities by starting a hospital. The hospital flourished and patients came from miles around.

In 1960, Dr Hale Cook, an American missionary of the United Church of Christ, USA, was in charge of the hospital. An experienced surgeon, Dr Cook also had a Masters degree in Public Health from Harvard. He had spent many years in India and was known for his skill and dedication. The villagers around Vadala almost worshipped him.

Raj's home town was not far from Vadala and Raj frequently went to Vadala during his medical school vacations to work in the hospital. He hoped that after graduating he would be able to work there more permanently. Soon after graduation Raj and I were married and decided to gain some practical experience before going to Vadala. We went to a large hospital at Kolar in South India for two years to gain experience in surgery and obstetrics. By 1962 we felt ready to work in the villages around Vadala. At last our childhood dreams of serving the rural poor people were to be realised.

The day after we arrived, Dr Cook officially welcomed us. He introduced us to the sixty-five staff members, who included everyone from the nurses, midwives, laboratory staff, X-ray technicians and pharmacists to the aides, receptionists and drivers. We had expected to work as doctors in the hospital, with Dr Cook as chief physician. Imagine our surprise when he dramatically pulled a bunch of keys

24

from his pocket and placed them in our hands with the words, 'You are in charge of this hospital. I shall enter it only if you need me.' He went on to explain that he had more work to do in the villages around Vadala.

This meant that the two of us were to manage the whole hospital alone! In those few minutes, Dr Cook taught us an important principle: **Trust leads to trust.** We were overwhelmed by Dr Cook's confidence in us but were also afraid that we might not meet his expectations. Raj and I plunged into the work in earnest. I soon discovered that medical practice in rural areas was very different from working in big medical centres where specialists are readily available for consultation. Yet I found the hospital work both intellectually stimulating and challenging. With limited technology and no specialists to refer to, we often had to be innovative and learn to overcome difficult situations. Because of the hospital's reputation, patients came from the surrounding villages, some travelling more than 80 kilometres by bus or oxcart. Many were often in late stages of illness upon arrival, having previously tried witchcraft. Often we saw patients with problems not generally seen in urban clinics.

The nurse in charge of the operating room was Miss Helenbai Ghodke, called 'Akka' ('Older sister,' in many Indian languages), by everyone. Efficient and experienced, she often guided us in difficult problems using treatments and procedures more appropriate to the village conditions. These treatments and observations had never found their way into textbooks, but were vital for a rural medical practice.

Many surgical emergencies were related to the hazards of village life and farming occupations. Fractures resulted from falling from trees, and hand injuries were caused by farm implements. When bulls ran amok they gored their horns into the abdomen of anyone who came in their way. I had never seen this dramatic injury, so was alarmed at my first experience. A man was brought in with his intestines hanging out of his abdomen and wrapped in his loincloth. The blunt horns of the bull had torn the abdominal wall but spared the intestines. I felt the infection would be so overwhelming that the patient would not survive. Akka, however, had seen many such injuries and confidently showed us the surgical procedure. We washed the intestines with saline and replaced them into the abdominal cavity and sutured the abdominal wall. The patient recovered within a week. The sensational effect on the villagers who observed the recovery increased their confidence in us, the 'new doctors'.

Often we had to be resourceful and use what was available. One day a young woman was brought to the hospital with a ruptured ectopic pregnancy. She had lost blood and was in shock. There was no blood available anywhere, yet if we didn't operate, she would die. We decided to open her carefully, collect the blood from the abdominal cavity, filter it and transfuse it back to her. Then, we proceeded with the surgery. She had an uneventful recovery and went home eight days later. As young doctors, we relished these challenges, and were happy that our training and skills were being used effectively.

So many to help!

The hospital had a reputation for surgery. Sometimes we started at 5 a.m. in order to complete the long list of surgical operations so we could attend the outpatient clinic by 10 a.m. We did hysterectomies, stomach and bowel resections, and even plastic surgery, such as the repair of a cleft lip.

Patients from the surrounding villages attended the outpatient clinic. Almost one-third of them were children with diarrhea or pneumonia. The adults often had typhoid, tuberculosis and other infectious diseases. There were always crowds of people waiting. We insisted on seeing every patient, which meant we usually had to rush through examinations, giving scarcely a few minutes to each patient.

There were always crowds of people waiting

26

Taking the hospital to the villages

It soon became evident many poor patients were not able to come to the hospital at Vadala for their treatment. Villages were remote and public transportation was limited. Raj and I started going to such villages on weekday afternoons to hold outpatient clinics. These were held on weekly market days so that people could do their marketing in addition to attending the clinic. We chose ten villages around the Vadala area; it took well over an hour and a half to reach some of them. Usually, a nurse, a clerk, a pharmacist and other helpers, and Raj or I, piled into a small open jeep loaded with boxes of medicines and supplies. The roads, deep ruts made by oxcarts, crossed barren fields and dry river beds. During the monsoon season, treacherous floods often left us stranded on the roads for hours, waiting for the waters to subside.

On reaching the village, we set up our clinic in a rented room. People from surrounding villages were waiting. As at the hospital clinic, many patients were children. More women came to these clinics because they did not have to depend on someone bringing them to the hospital. When we got back to the hospital, more patients were waiting for us, and of course there were always emergencies that we dealt with during the night.

Raj and I relished hard work and had no problem keeping up this busy schedule. Our small daughter, Shobha, often accompanied us to these village clinics. Our life revolved totally around the hospital and the patients and we treated everyone who came to our doorstep. We went to the villages and treated those who came to the clinics. Those who were seriously ill were admitted to the hospital. Our popularity increased in a short time.

The hospital had meagre resources, and the money to fund it had to be raised through fees from patients who could afford them. Except for family planning, the hospital did not receive any grants from the government but as the number of patients increased, capital grants from the USA helped erect new buildings, and thirty five beds were added. A special tuberculosis ward was also constructed.

Curative versus preventive medicine: a balance

While we were busy with our hospital work, Dr Cook was immersed in outside activities. He was concerned with Mother and Child Health programmes, organising nutrition and immunisation programmes for children and women at Vadala and surrounding villages. He was particularly enthusiastic about family planning, advising villagers on

27

contraception. Many couples were motivated toward family planning and referred to us for sterilisation operations and the insertion of intrauterine devices (IUDs). As he travelled from village to village, Dr Cook encouraged farmers to improve their agriculture, finding credit for farmers to construct wells for irrigation to grow more food, and advising them to grow lentils and vegetables in addition to cereals.

As Dr Cook turned his attention to such programmes in the villages, the hospital staff who had admired his clinical work began to feel that he was wasting his time and lost respect for the work he was doing. They were not willing to leave the hospital and join in his public health activities, so he often had to work alone. While agreeing that preventive programmes were necessary, we saw our own role as efficient doctors doing the utmost to save the lives of those who came to us.

Raj and I were curious that a such an accomplished surgeon and physician had left the glamour of clinical practice and was spending time in rather unattractive activities. We started having long discussions with him. He did not force any of his ideas on us but just helped us to discover for ourselves the inadequacies of the health care system. He asked us to look beyond the disease and its cure to the human face behind it, to the family, the community, the environment, to see what goes on in the villages. Should doctors only cure diseases? Should they not be involved in keeping a community healthy? He often commented that our training had given us a limited, fragmented approach to health care, curing patients rather than looking at health in its totality.

We followed his advice. In the villages we started spending time going beyond the clinic, talking to people and discovering more about what was going on the village.

Society finds its own healers

One Monday evening, Raj was walking through the streets of Salbatpur. He had just finished seeing patients at the village clinic. Noticing a crowd waiting outside a food store, he observed the shopkeeper, with a stethoscope, examining patients. The shopkeeper's assistant was sitting next to him filling syringes with different kinds of medicines. Raj said to himself, 'Surely that crowd is bigger than the one I had! Some of my old patients are in there. Why do these villagers go to these quacks when I come all the way here for a clinic? Don't they know I come from a good medical school and perform operations in the hospital?' As he returned to Vadala, Raj kept wondering what made the shopkeeper so popular. Surely, he thought, patients must be getting well with his medicines. That's why they went to him. Then he recalled his childhood experiences. His parents, too, though educated, preferred to go to Dr Panjabi, the paramedic, rather than the qualified doctor at the government dispensary.

Raj and I decided to find out more about these untrained village practitioners of medicine. We contacted some of them. At first they were reluctant to talk to us, fearing that we would criticise them and take away their business. I found that they prescribed penicillin and similar antibiotics for fevers. So did I. They treated anemia with iron pills. So did I. They gave streptomycin for tuberculosis. So did I. The only difference was that I had the advantage of confirming the diagnosis with laboratory tests and X-rays before starting treatment. I had no definite medicine for infective hepatitis, but their herbal medicine was quite effective. Most important, we were available only once a week at the village clinic. On other days the patients would have to travel long distances to Vadala to see us. These village practitioners were accessible at all times. They lived in the village and were willing to take house calls. They certainly responded to a need.

I discovered that for every eight or ten villages there was a school teacher, a shopkeeper or other enterprising literate person selling Western drugs and injections. Although our egos made it difficult for us to admit, the only difference between those people and Raj and me was that we had been trained in a prestigious medical institution. Medical school had stressed high academic excellence. In fact, even qualified doctors not practising in the environs of academic medicine were scorned. These practitioners were obviously fulfilling a role and they were being appreciated by the people. Like any tradesman in the village, they had been taught their craft from other practitioners. But they practised for profit and were therefore available only to those who could afford their fees. Hence they, too, did not serve the poor, those who had no money to pay. We were both practising the same kind of medicine in the village – temporary treatment of a handful of common illnesses. None of us was getting to the root of the problem. These questions and comparisons led to more questions, more comparisons, which began to shake the basic foundations of our assumptions about and our approach to medical care.

Children were brought to the hospital with fevers, diarrhea, and sore eyes. We treated them and they went back to the same poverty, filth and lack of food and safe drinking water. Inevitably, they fell sick again and returned. Not all our patients returned. Many recognised that we had no lasting cure and went back to the traditional healers or witch doctors. We were finding that our medicines, however modern, did not provide a permanent cure for common illnesses.

Typhoid, measles, whooping cough, hepatitis and polio were seen commonly in our clinic. We felt that the villagers had given us a chance and we had disappointed them. The failure was not that of modern medicine. Rather, we were failing to deal with the root causes of disease; lack of food and adequate nutrition, unsafe water, and bad sanitation. Many of the illnesses we were treating could be prevented if we addressed these core problems. There was clearly a need to integrate curative and preventive medicine. This was exactly what Dr Cook was trying to do quietly without much fanfare. We began to see how really shortsighted we had been. We were too busy running an ambulance service at the bottom of a cliff rather than preventing accidents by putting up a fence at the top. We were sure that we needed to be doing much more preventive work, the kind our training had not prepared us to do.

Dr Cook pointed out that Vadala was the only hospital for an area with a population of 200 000. He estimated that approximately 400 women delivered in the hospital every year. Only those who had difficulty came to us. Of these 50 per cent needed a Caesarian section and the use of forceps or other interventions for delivery. Many arrived with ruptured or grossly infected uteri due to interventions at home. Many of these complications could have been prevented by proper prenatal care. Government nurses and other trained midwives, Dr Cook found out, provided care for another 100 women a year. Given the population of 100 000 and a crude birth rate of 40 per 1000, there would have been 4000 births every year. Only 500 of these deliveries received some kind of professional care. What happened to the other 3500? Who were they? Who attended their deliveries? We were doing too much for too few people. Only those who came to the hospital were treated. But what about the others? Why didn't they come?

As I walked in the marketplace I saw that the poor went to the traditional healers, herbalists, and others who could provide comfort and solace at a cost they could afford. The poorest of the poor did not come to us. They had no money to pay for transportation to the hospital and no one to take care of their children at home. Their relatives could not afford to lose a day's wages to come with them. Often, there was simply no extra sari to wrap themselves in. Most did not feel the need to come since they had never heard of prenatal care. Maternal mortality was high. Many of the women we saw had anemia, and infection during childbirth was common. Women and babies with tetanus were admitted at times. All this could be prevented. We had the knowledge to prevent so much morbidity and mortality among women and children, but by staying in the narrow confines of curative care were we not doing a disservice to those very people we had vowed to help?

On an average we treated about 300 tuberculosis patients every year. Dr Cook had estimated that in his experience, for every 1000 people, 15 had tuberculosis. So there were about 1500 tuberculosis patients in the area we served. What happened to those who did not come to us? Most could not afford costly medicines and could not take time off from work to go to a hospital for injections of strepto-mycin. High costs prevented many patients from completing the course of treatment, leaving them likely to infect family and neighbours.

When we went to the villages we would enter the clinic building, see the patients and return to the hospital. Now we started talking to village people and finding out more about their lives. As we walked around in the villages, well-to-do people recognised us and greeted us. However, when we visited the poorest sections, we saw no familiar faces. They were too poor to come to us. The health system inad-vertently becomes an exploitative apparatus by being expensive. Although we were committed to work for the poor and needy, the major source of financing the hospital was fees for the services we provided. Al-though staff salaries were low, many patients still could not afford the services.

Mabelle sees village bondage face to face

The longer we stayed at Vadala, the more we began to realise the importance of social and economic factors that affected the health of the poor. We were idealistic and wanted to provide the best care without consideration of cost, for those who sought our help. That such care was expensive both for the institution as well as for the people was another aspect we had to consider. Sometimes, unwit-tingly we are parties to exploitation. For example, one day as Raj and I were walking across the fields, we saw a couple digging trenches in the field. Both came running to greet us.

'I'm Namdev,' said the man, 'Last year, I was very sick and came to your hospital. You saved my life.'

'Yes, I remember, Namdev had a perforated peptic ulcer,' I said to Raj. 'We operated on him. I remember they were poor people. Bhikuseth, the community leader, pleaded with us to treat Namdev almost free of cost and we did so. What are you doing in this field?' I asked Namdev.

'My wife and I are bonded for one year to Bhikuseth. We're working on his farm.'

'But why?' I asked.

31

'I had to pay a large hospital bill, it would have been even more had not Bhikuseth pleaded on my behalf. Bhikuseth was kind enough to bring me to the hospital and lend me money when I needed it most. Now I have to pay it back by working for him. Where would I be if it was not for Bhikuseth's timely help? Bhikuseth is like a god to me.'

Raj said, 'Namdev, because you are poor, we reduced the charges to nothing. You did not have to pay the hospital bill. I did the operation free of cost. The hospital does not charge poor people like you.'

Namdev did not seem impressed. 'Sir, nothing comes free for us poor people.' Namdev could not believe that he had been cheated. I was shocked and angry with myself for being so naive. Angry at the injustice and exploitation. I wondered how many times I had been party to such exploitation and cheating. This incident really opened my eyes to the reality of life in the villages. Raj had often explained the problems of exploitation in the village. Now I was encountering it face to face.

In later years we discovered that there were many Bhikuseths and many Namdevs. As we probed deeper, we found that the money-lenders were always looking for the poor to have calamities, so that they could lend money at exorbitant rates of interest. We saw that, in order to come to the hospital, the poor often pawned the tin roofs of their houses, their cooking vessels or, like Namdev, sold themselves. This dimension had not occurred to me. In our enthusiasm to treat the disease we sometimes quite forget the stark realities of life and the ways our decisions affect the lives of our patients and their families. Another lesson was forever etched in my mind.

Our discussions with Dr Cook continued. We were beginning to feel the need to change our own attitudes. Dr Cook had many new and unconventional ideas. Because it is too expensive to have medical specialists for every little job, we need to multiply our hands by training people and delegating responsibilities to them. He had trained high school graduates as technicians to diagnose and treat leprosy and tuberculosis. I saw nurses and ward aides take on more responsibilities, particularly in the operating room. Often they rose to meet an emergency situation and gave timely help.

People are capable of much more responsibility

One afternoon, I was finishing up an operation. The nurses came rushing in, saying that over forty sick patients had inundated the outpatient clinic. As I came out of the operating room I saw the terrible sight of men, women and children, cold and clammy with sunken eyes. Most were in shock with the copious loss of fluid associated with cholera. There was no time for systematic examination of each person. There was no space in the hospital. I asked the staff to pitch tents and start intravenous fluids as fast as possible. Everyone joined in. Ward aides, helpers, and nurses were all starting the fluids as fast as the patients were being brought in. We didn't lose a single patient that day. In the evening, as we sat exhausted, talking about the day's events, we realised that had we stuck to our strict protocol of every patient being seen by the doctor, many would have died before we had a chance to see them.

That day, many had been saved because simple village helpers had been able to insert intravenous fluids into the veins on time. That incident was never forgotten. If these villagers, without real training, could provide basic medical care, then how many other services could they perform? Was medical care the sole prerogative of the medical profession? Of doctors?

When we learned to put our trust in people and to give them responsibilities, we found that they rose to the occasion and did their best. We therefore continued to delegate responsibility to the nurses and other staff. They have proved worthy of our trust. This principle of trust and delegation became the basis of our work in Jamkhed years later.

By the time Dr Cook's term in India ended, we were convinced of a more holistic approach to medical care. We felt that preventive activities should be emphasised and an integrated approach of prevention and curative services be developed.

We were also convinced of the need for family planning programmes. Here was something we could do immediately. Most village women did not want to have many children. The only method of family planning available to them was abortion and it was practised freely in the villages and performed by village women under unhygienic conditions. We made different methods of family planning available. I took an active interest in advocating IUDs and the village women accepted it. A year later, in 1965, the state government decided to hold camps for insertion of IUDs and the district officials requested me to participate in their programme. I went round Ahmednagar district and helped in the IUD insertion camps organised by the District Health Authorities. I toured the whole district, covering hundreds of miles, teaching other doctors how to insert IUDs. It was at these camps I met Mr Bansilalji Kothari, the chairman of the District Health Committee. Mr Kothari was from Jamkhed and he was a zealous family planning advocate. He was quite knowledgeable about different health issues and Raj and I had many discussions with him about rural health care.

In 1965, after we had been in Vadala three years, Dr Cook handed over the work to us and left. After his departure, we carried on his programmes of maternal and child health, family planning, nutrition education and hygiene. But we felt inadequate. Our basic medical training at Vellore medical college was too curative oriented. The training was provided in a tertiary care hospital where the common problems of the majority of the people were not seen. We needed to know more in the areas of social medicine, medical economics and epidemiology in order to be more effective.

Four years at Vadala opened our eyes to many realities of the health of the people. We had gone thinking that through a good hospital in a rural area we would reach the poor and marginalised people with health care. Taking the hospital culture to the village, holding village clinics and maternal and child health clinics there, was not adequate. More than a change of venue is needed. We saw that it was difficult for medical staff to change their attitudes towards public health.

Was it possible to find ways and means of making health care easily available to the poorest of the poor in a form that was acceptable? The traditional healers were certainly doing it to the best of their ability. But how could we bring modern medical knowledge and services to the doorsteps of the people? Health programmes alone would not make an impact. Could they be integrated into other aspects of development? We needed answers to these questions.

In 1966 we decided to leave Vadala and go in search of answers, to find out how best we could bring good health care to the village people in India. We enquired about public health training in India. Practically all public health persons we met were government bureaucrats. The public health institutes were training doctors to administer the government health system. We visited a few hospitals. Everywhere, the pattern was the same. The emphasis was on hospital-orientated practice. Such training was not suitable for us.

American universities appeared attractive because there was intellectual freedom to look at health systems dispassionately. Universities like Johns Hopkins were involved in national health programmes in developing countries. They had faculties with international experience and students drawn from all over the world, as well as good information systems and excellent libraries. Sharing experiences with students from other developing countries was an attractive prospect to us. Raj obtained a Fulbright scholarship to travel to the USA. We decided to do broadbased residency programmes in medicine and surgery for three to four years before doing Masters degrees in Public Health at Johns Hopkins in Baltimore.

Just before we left, Mr Bansilalji Kothari arranged for a farewell meeting with us at Bhandardara, the site of a dam in a tribal block in Ahmednagar District. He promised to keep in contact with us and hoped that when we returned to India we would think of working in Jamkhed.

In summer of 1966 we sailed for the USA with our 5-year-old daughter Shobha.

CHAPTER 3

In search of answers

RAJ

At Cleveland

Mabelle and I spent four years in the United States, preparing ourselves to work effectively in the rural areas of India. Since we believed that good curative services were important, we first spent three years at Cleveland doing our residencies in medicine and surgery. The programme provided access to both the private community hospital and the city hospital. Our experience at the hospital was educative; we were particularly impressed with the standard of individual care, the respect and value for life and the meticulous care given to individual patients.

The administrators, sensing our enthusiasm to go back to India, arranged for us to cover a wide range of specialties that would be of use to us there. Arrangements were made for us to have special training in tuberculosis at the National Jewish Hospital in Denver, Colorado, and training in leprosy at the Leprosy Research in Carville, Louisiana.

The experience at Cleveland was rewarding and gave us further insights into various aspects of health care in the USA. Hospitals in America treated different kinds of patients from those in India. The crowds of women and children suffering from malnutrition and infection were almost absent. Most patients were elderly, suffering from cancer, hypertension or other illnesses that occur with advancing age. We realised that the differences were due to less high technology medicine. We soon discovered that, in addition to the factors of a relatively small population, industrialisation and other socioeconomic factors, the fall in infant mortality and increase in longevity were due to good basic public health measures such as sanitation, safe drinking water and health education.

Another aspect of curative care which was new to us was the

high cost involved. Dependence on laboratory tests and specialised personnel made hospital care expensive. Even in a wealthy country like the USA, poor people without insurance could not afford this complex hospital care. We saw this problem first hand, when our babysitter's husband contracted pneumonia. Needing hospitalisation, but without health insurance, he received treatment that wiped out his savings and drove the family deep into debt.

At the same time we personally experienced the wonders of modern medicine. Our son, Ravi, had a Rhesus incompatibility when he was born because Mabelle was Rhesus negative, and were it not for modern technology, available in Cleveland, he perhaps might not have survived. Our years in Cleveland taught us the benefits of modern technology and public health. We understood that in the Indian context, the emphasis desperately needed to be on public health measures.

The health system on the Navajo Indian Reservation

While in the USA, we also had an interesting summer studying the health care system of the Navajo Indians on a reservation in Arizona. The Navajo Indians lived in hogans (circular huts) located far apart from one another, and the population was sparse. Poverty, water shortage and poor sanitation contributed to many of their health problems. They were obliged to haul water in trucks from long distances and store it in open barrels. Many homes had no toilets.

We learned several lessons from our stay there. Many children went to boarding school where they had toilet facilities and access to clean water. When they returned home for the vacation, they demanded the same facilities, so many homes added toilets and proper water storage facilities. The effective way in which children changed the attitudes and practice of adults helped us understand the role of children in health education.

We also saw traditional medicine integrated with modern medicine. Traditional healers, performed ceremonies to care for the sick. These healers were allowed to visit the modern hospitals on the reservation and offer their services to the patients.

The Navajo attitude to family planning was interesting. Often the women would come to the hospital for the tenth or twelfth delivery and they were advised to have a sterilisation operation for family planning. They confided to us that they wanted to have a big Navajo nation and therefore needed to increase their population. This reminded us of arguments that some of India's caste and religious groups put forward against the practice of family planning, and we understood how universal this problem is.

Johns Hopkins School of Hygiene and Public Health

In 1969 we made our way to the Johns Hopkins School of Hygiene and Public Health in Baltimore, Maryland. This is one of the oldest public health schools in the country and is famous for its international health department. The faculty had done pioneering work in the field of public health and development of health services in different countries.

At the School of Public Health we learned as much from fellow students as from the faculty. Many students either belonged to or had served in developing countries. They brought considerable experience and ideas on how to improve health services. Extensive literature on aspects of health care in the developing countries was also available.

The Masters degree course in Public Health helped us to focus on the issues involved in providing health to currently unreached populations. Many concepts of health care later embodied in the Alma Ata declaration on Primary Health Care (1978) were already being discussed.

Origins of primary health care

In modern times, many pioneers in different areas of the world had demonstrated how to make health care available to all. Their efforts influenced us greatly as we planned our primary health care project in India.

Community diagnosis

Conceptualising the community as the patient and finding remedies affecting the community as a whole led to the development of community health. The most prominent international leader in public health and the innovator of the present movement was Dr John Grant. He not only contributed to the founding of national public health training institutes in China and India, but also influenced public health policy in Asia and South America.

Dr Grant tirelessly advocated health care for the poor. In his work and writings he emphasised regionalisation, popularising the idea of regional health centres. Believing that health is part of total development, he maintained that the organisation of medicine cannot be separated from the socioeconomic organisation of the community.

As well as stressing that good health ultimately depended on people themselves having the awareness and knowledge to practise preventive measures, Dr Grant also believed that community volunteers and community health workers should be involved in planning and implementing health at the grass roots. His principles of how to organise health services with his emphasis on community participation, the integration of health services and an intersectoral approach broadened our horizons about health care. Another such pioneer was Mr James Y. C. Yen of China, born into an urban Chinese elite family and educated at Yale University. James Yen was appalled at the illiteracy and poverty of Chinese peasants. In the 1920s he initiated the Mass Education Movement to teach thousands of peasants to read and write. Ting Hsien (Ding Xian), a county with 400 000 people, became his laboratory for social change. Education, livelihood, health and self government were four components of his People's School programme. The concept that health and development should be a people's programme appealed to us. We, too, believed in mobilising village people to participate in health programmes. Ten years later, in 1979, we had an opportunity to meet Mr Yen and listen as he recounted events from his vast experience. He spoke of his visit to India and of the ways in which he had shared his vision for people's development with India's first minister for Community Development Mr A. K. Dey.[1]

Dr C. C. Chen, a graduate of Peking Union Medical College, joined James Yen to take charge of health work in Ting Hsien. To our knowledge he was one of the first doctors to teach villagers simple first aid. Village elders were encouraged to recruit local residents to take a ten-day health training course, followed by periodic refresher training. The health worker had a small medicine kit and kept a record of births and deaths.

Dr Grant drew his innovations from this Ting Hsien experience of C.C. Chen and the wisdom of the people. He, along with Dr Andreja Stampar of Yugoslavia, saw the need for a shift to make health services more equitable. Dr Stampar foresaw that advances in medical technology and continued emphasis on individual therapy would help only the fewer and fewer people who can afford such care. He pointed out that the British were the first to realise this connection and to introduce such reforms as hygienic housing, which later led to widespread improvement in health.[2]

Dr Grant persuaded others like Dr Sydney Kark to try new approaches. Dr Kark went on to introduce a rural health project in a rural area in South Africa. There he introduced the team approach and family and community diagnosis leading to comprehensive health care. Other innovative programmes were started in Indonesia (Hydrick) and elsewhere.

Role of auxiliaries

In many developing countries, the most educated people do not like to stay in the villages, so usually only people with less basic education live there. Early primary health programmes learned that such people can be trained to perform certain specific tasks. Since these workers do not find jobs elsewhere in the city, they stay in the villages and continue to work.

Many countries had introduced these trained auxiliaries in health care. Through his work in Kenya, and other parts of Africa and Southeast Asia, Dr N.R.E. Fendall demonstrated that training and maintaining health auxiliaries was less expensive than training doctors. The auxiliaries could work in simple surroundings without sophisticated equipment, yet perform important tasks in nursing care, environmental health, pharmacy and laboratory work. The key was that this training could be legally undertaken by people with minimal education. It provides opportunities for semi-educated young people to acquire skills and do meaningful jobs.[3]

Integration of health
In Narangwal, Punjab, a research project jointly undertaken by Johns Hopkins University, the Indian Council of Medical Research and the Ministry of Health demonstrated how effective the auxiliaries were in providing health, nutrition and family planning services to rural villagers. There Dr Carl Taylor demonstrated how auxiliaries and health visitors could be trained and supervised to provide an integrated package of health, nutrition and family planning. Nor did each programme require a separate auxiliary worker; instead, auxiliaries could be trained to carry out several related tasks. This integrated approach was cost-effective and convenient. Communities had all services under one roof available at all times through one auxiliary, namely, the Auxiliary Nurse Midwife (ANM). The success of the Narangwal project made us think of providing integrated services and also of using ANMs as 'king pins' in providing health care in the rural areas.[4]

The Under Five Clinics
The crucial years for a child's survival are the first five years of life. The concept of Under Five Clinics for children was developed by Dr David Morley. He trained auxiliaries to work with health professionals in under five clinics in Ilesha in the western region of Nigeria. He expanded the concept of delegating responsibilities, putting nurses in charge of under five clinics to maintain the health of children. He also showed that by the simple technique of weighing the children and keeping growth charts, the first danger sign, failure to gain weight, could be picked up by the mother. We decided to include this as a strategy in our programme.[5]

Today there are many more successful mass programmes. Notable among them are the 'Health at low cost' of Kerala in India and that of Sri Lanka.[6] Chairman Mao drew heavily from the experiences of C. C. Chen in Ting Hsien, which led to the 'Bare foot doctor' programme in China.

Our fellow students and practitioners from Africa, Latin America and different parts of Asia shared their experiences in health care, which affirmed what we had seen in rural India. They shared how they had tried to reach the people. Together we discussed the ideas in **'Medical Care in Developing Countries,'** a book edited by Dr Maurice King on a symposium held at Makerere. Here we read about equity in health care, health team concept, delegation of responsibility and appropriate technology.[7] But we realised what little impact these concepts actually had on the developing world. In these poor countries the government leaders and medical professionals continued to invest precious material and human resources in establishing sophisticated hospitals, mainly to be used by the urban elite. Some countries spent major portions of their budgets in supporting these showpiece hospitals in their capital cities.

The development of primary health care in India

India has a long, ancient heritage in developing medical science and technology. Archeological findings indicate the presence of sanitation in the dwellings of the Indus valley civilisation. Various systems of medicine were developed in India by each set of invaders entering the country. Beginning with Ayurveda, the Unnani and Siddha systems of medicine came into the country. With the British came the Western system of medicine known as Allopathy. However, given the social structure of India, all these systems have in large part remained confined to the elite classes. As a result, the majority of people have their own beliefs and traditions and depend on local healers and herbalists to take care of their health problems.

In 1943 the British Government in India established the Health Survey and Development Committee. This Committee was chaired by Sir Joseph Bhore of the Indian Civil Service and became known as the Bhore Committee. Dr John Grant was one of its prominent members. In 1946 this committee submitted its report, which became the blueprint for India's health planning after independence in 1947.[8]

Almost thirty years before the 1978 Alma Ata Declaration on Primary Health Care, the Bhore Committee recommended that health care should be available to all, irrespective of ability to pay. The Committee recommended that adequate curative, preventive and promotive health services be available to all, with full community participation.

The Committee also suggested the concept of a health worker for each village and a primary health centre for defined rural populations. The Committee regarded the role of the doctor as scientist, social worker and member of the health team.

In 1952 some of the Bhore Committee's recommendations were accepted and gradually implemented by the Government of India. The country was divided into community development blocks each having approximately 80 000 to 100 000. people. At least one primary health centre with one doctor and a staff of approximately 40–45 people was established in every community development block. The primary health centres were further divided into subcentres, each responsible for a population of 10 000. Each primary health centre had six beds for maternity care. The subcentre was in the charge of an auxiliary nurse midwife; her activities were mainly mother and child health, and family planning. By 1970 an additional doctor was posted to each primary health centre to be responsible only for family planning activities, and the other doctor mainly practised curative medicine. The budget allocation for medicines and transport was meagre, and most of the expenditure was on personnel.

In addition to these primary health centres, the central government introduced some national programmes with separate budgets and personnel. Each was administered vertically and not integrated with the other programmes. These programmes were technocentric and based on individual health problems. They included programmes to control and subsequently eradicate such diseases as tuberculosis, small-pox, malaria and leprosy as well as family planning programmes.

Usually state governments spent most of their medical budgets supporting medical colleges and large hospitals in the cities, leaving very little for rural areas, where 70 to 80 per cent of the people actually lived. For example, Maharashtra State was spending 80 per cent of its health budget on maintaining hospitals in its four or five major cities.

Though there were primary health centres in the rural areas, these centres had no budget provision for medicines, equipment and facilities to take care of patients. Lack of experienced personnel and facilities resulted in inadequate care. Simple procedures like a venesection to administer fluids to a dehydrated child or a diagnostic lumbar puncture for convulsions could not be performed. There were no facilities for abnormal deliveries. As a highly placed official said: 'If the untrained traditional birth attendant cannot deliver a baby, neither can the inexperienced young doctor at the PHC without proper training and facilities.'

The Narangwal research had already pointed out that scarcely

10 to 15 per cent of the population utilised the health services and that the influence of the primary health centre did not extend beyond a 4 kilometre radius. The majority of women and children had no access to health care. It is ironic that even today Sir Joseph Bhore's native village in Ahmednagar District still does not have easy access to health care.

For every one doctor in the government health service, there were four doctors in private practice. Since these private practitioners were expensive, only the wealthy people of the village consulted them. Poor people used home remedies or resorted to folk medicine, including witchcraft.

Planning for rural health

As part of our coursework, Mabelle and I prepared a plan for work in backward areas of rural Maharashtra, India. Our goal was to provide basic health care to the poorest of the poor who were not reached by the government health system or private doctors, and to develop an effective health programme relevant to the needs and suited to resources of the rural communities.

We decided that instead of haphazardly developing a health programme we would take a specific area and concentrate on definite technical objectives that we identified as important. We studied the statistics available for that part of India, the various national programmes and health programmes of the Government of India and also our own experience at Vadala. We identified several health problems that we considered most prevalent, naming those that were serious enough to need intervention and from these chose those that we felt could be addressed easily.

The area was known to have an infant mortality rate of over 150 per 1000 births. At that time many developed countries had infant mortality rates as low as 13 per 1000 births. Over 80 per cent of the mortality was preventable, and so we hoped to reduce infant deaths by concentrating on preventive programmes. Maternal mortality was mainly due to lack of proper prenatal care and untrained birth attendants. Tackling this problem did not require high technology.[7]

We arrived at five basic objectives which we hoped to achieve in five years. These included:

- Reducing infant mortality rate by 50 per cent
- Reducing the maternal morbidity and mortality
- Reducing the crude birth rate by at least 10 points
- Bringing under control chronic diseases such as leprosy and tuberculosis
- Providing basic curative care

43

Our strategy

Some important strategies that made our plan different from the regular hospitals were:

Choosing a specific area

The population to be served would be identified according to our objectives and they would be served by the programme. In the hospital model, only those who happen to come to the clinic or hospital are seen. We planned to offer access to those who needed the care most, namely the marginalised, and go to them rather than wait for them to come to us.

Phasing of the programme

The population would be reached in a phased manner. A larger central village would be chosen as the headquarters. We would reach surrounding villages in an 8 kilometre radius in the first phase and then extend it to a 15 kilometre radius until a population of 70 000 was reached.

The epidemiological approach

We would survey communities and approach root causes of illness rather than focusing on individual sick patients. Although individual treatment would be provided, the emphasis would be on community diagnosis and introducing interventions to solve the health problems of a large number of people. For example, we would deal with the need for sanitation in the community as a whole rather than cater for a few individuals who have fallen sick as a result of bad sanitation and happened to come to us.

Integration of all services

Curative and preventive services would be totally integrated. Under five clinics, maternal and child health services, nutrition programmes for mothers and children and family planning would all be included along with basic curative care. All personnel would be involved in these services; none would confine themselves to only curative care. We had seen in other hospitals that the lack of such integration tended to disparage those involved in public health activities.

Community participation

Community participation was considered most essential in order for people to make maximum use of the health services and later to sustain the health service. At that time community participation in health care was a new concept and there was little information on how communities could be involved in health care. We hoped that the leaders of the community, the opinion-makers and others would help facilitate the programmes designed and planned by us, the health professionals. They would accept our suggestions and provide infrastructure, such as buildings and finances, to carry out the health programmes. We were naive and not sure how the community participation could be elicited. We expected the community to be involved in the planning, therefore we left the plan open ended and flexible.

Delegation of responsibilities

We would multiply our hands by training auxiliaries to take on most responsibilities of routine diagnosis and treatment of minor illnesses. Thus the doctor did not have to see every patient but would be freed to take on other responsibilities. This implied that the roles of most health personnel would need to change.

The health team approach

Health teams would go to the villages and undertake multiple activities such as health education, maternal and child health programmes and curative care. The ANM would hold under five clinics, provide prenatal care and basic curative care. Trained paramedical workers would be involved in tuberculosis and leprosy control programmes. Team members would complement one another and the doctor would be captain of the team.

Subcentres

For every 5000 population, there would be an ANM who would provide the primary health services. Unlike her government counterpart, this ANM would be well trained to take care of common health problems in the village. She would also be trained in all the priority areas. She would be helped by the health team and have a continuous in-service training.

The Health Centre

At the central village, would be a twenty-bed hospital for referral of more complicated health problems. We considered this hospital important because it was to support the preventive activities in the village and not emphasise tertiary care. Unlike most hospitals, it would be planned from the grass roots and not from the top down. Its function was related to the health priorities established earlier. Thus it would be designed to deal with surgical emergencies related to

45

childbirth, trauma surgery and family planning surgery. Diagnostic laboratory tests and X-rays would also be related to the priorities; to tests for sputum for tuberculosis, blood smears for malaria, blood for emergency transfusion, and skin smears for leprosy. This referral centre was not designed to deal with every illness. Patients with tertiary problems like cancer and cardiovascular disease would need further referral to hospitals in the cities.

Appropriate technology
Every attempt would be made to use materials and personnel/labour appropriate to the local situation. Hospital equipment that is readily available and can be maintained easily would be used.

Collaborate with other development agencies
We recognised that overall development was necessary and hoped that others interested in development would join us or that we could find an ongoing development agency for collaboration.

Our plan was discussed in detail with fellow students and faculty. Many doctors criticised the programme for delegating primary curative care to personnel other than doctors. Many felt the venture was too ambitious since we planned to carry it out in a remote part of the country and not as part of a university or large organisation.

Academic research or service? A dilemma

Our advisors at Johns Hopkins felt that such a programme should be located within a medical college as a research project. The college would ensure financial support and continuous professional guidance. If we went to a remote area, there would be no institutional backing and no guidance from the experts. We had many discussions with our advisors regarding the location of the project and spent many sleepless nights trying to arrive at a decision. Everyone advised us against going to a remote area away from an academic setting and even encouraged us to do this as a research project in a well known medical institution in India. We considered the advantages of working in an academic institution as against plunging ourselves into the villages. Some advantages were job security, career advancement, peer recognition, availability of experts, children's education, easy access to knowledge and literature, and financial security for the programme itself.

On the other hand, we were interested in the real situation of village communities where no help is available. We felt that medical college backing was not necessary; every rural area does not have experts to guide doctors, and neither do villages have institutions of

46

Map of India showing the position of Maharashtra State

higher learning. Also, few doctors were interested in our goals, to find practical solutions to improve the health of the poor in the rural areas. There is an abundance of doctors who would like to do research in an university setting but very few want to actually live in the villages. We wanted to learn and offer solutions in real life situations.

Ultimately we were committed to serving the village people.

We also saw practical advantages in starting a service project in remote villages. We would not be under pressure to complete the project in a set time or to follow instructions from the medical institutional hierarchy. Community participation would be difficult in the bureaucratic environs of the medical college. By depending on villagers for everything, including finances we would be forced to find ways of achieving self support.

Having made the decision to start the project outside a university, we now had to find a place to begin. We felt that the area should be a needy and backward one, where no other agency, apart from government, was working. We also decided on Maharashtra because at least I (Raj) was fluent in Marathi and familiar with the Maharashtra villages. Several districts in Maharashtra State fitted these criteria, including the districts of Bhid, Osmanabad, Solapur and the southern part of Ahmednagar district.

We had kept in contact with friends like Dr Telfer Mook. When we informed him of our decision to work in Maharashtra, he was delighted and promised to help us once we got started. We also had kept in touch with Marathi Mission. They had started a water development programme in Osmanabad district and had done some preliminary surveys. They suggested we join them to add the health component to their development activities.

True to his promise, Mr Bansilalji Kothari kept up his correspondence with us. He sent us details of the health situation in Jamkhed and an invitation to start work there. We also received a letter from a Member of the Legislative Assembly, Mr Abasaheb Nimbalkar, requesting us to start work at Jamkhed because that was his constituency.

Because we considered community participation so essential, we decided to go back to India and contact people personally in the four districts before making our final decision about location.

1   Mayfield, James. *Go to the People.* West Hartford, Kumarian Press, 1986.

2   Stampar, Andrija. *Serving the Cause of Public Health.* Selected papers of Andrija Stampar, Ed. M.D. Grmek, Zagreb, 1966.

3   Fendall N R E. *Auxiliaries in Health Care.* The Johns Hopkins University, Baltimore and London, 1972, reprinted 1979.

4   Taylor, Carl E. and Associates. *Child and Maternal Services in Rural India* Volumes 1 and 2. The Johns Hopkins University Press, Baltimore and London, 1983.

5   Morley, David. *Paediatric Priorities in Developing Countries.* Butterworth, London, 1973.

6   Halstead S B, Walsh J A and Warren K D (eds). *Good Health at Low Cost.* Proceedings of a conference sponsored by the Rockefeller Foundation, 29th April–3rd May, 1985, at Bellagio, Italy.

7   King, Maurice. *Medical Care in Developing Countries.* Oxford University Press, Nairobi, 1966.

8   Government of India, 1946, *Report of the Health Survey and Development Committee*; Chairman, Sir J. Bhore, Volumes 1–4, New Delhi, Suptd of Government printing.

CHAPTER 4

Health, bureaucracy and elusive politics

RAJ

July 1970

Mabelle and I and our two children, Shobha and Ravi, came back to India in July. We lost no time in contacting the Marathi Mission and setting up our headquarters at Solapur, a town near Osmanabad.

As assets we had our willingness to work, the goodwill of the Marathi Mission, and promises of help from our church friends in the USA although we did not know how soon that help would materialise. Friends and villagers pointed out our liabilities to us: 'You have spent over four years in the United States. Let us see how you fare in the villages without modern conveniences.' They did not think we would last, but we were eager to get started.

Firstly, we had to find a suitable area. Because our plan depended on the community participating in the health programmes, our choice depended on which community would be interested enough to be actively involved. Mabelle and I felt that finding a suitable place would not be difficult. Surely communities would be interested in health and would welcome us in a place where there was no satisfactory health care available. We were proved to be wrong. It was not going to be easy. Osmanabad, one of the four possible districts we had identified was the first to be visited.

We soon realised that we would have to define what we meant by a community. In practical terms, who were the decision makers in that community? Although ideally the village people themselves, particularly the weak and marginalised, ought to be consulted, we knew we could not get them together as a group without proper entry into the community. It was decided to approach the community through

50

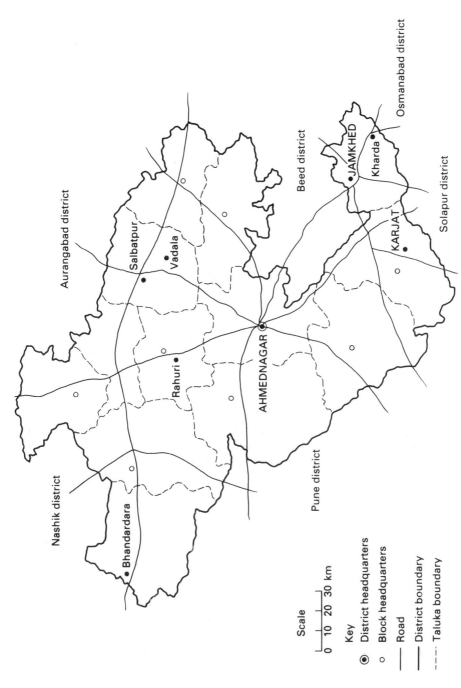

Sketch map of Ahmednagar district

Key

⊙ District headquarters
○ Block headquarters
—— Road
—— District boundary
----- Taluka boundary

Scale

0 10 20 30 km

Aurangabad district

Nashik district

Beed district

Osmanabad district

Solapur district

Pune district

JAMKHED

Kharda

KARJAT

Salbatpur

Vadala

Rahuri

Bhandardara

AHMEDNAGAR

their leaders, but we had to go through several levels of leadership and much protocol to get to the village level. The villages in themselves are like little kingdoms, brought together politically to form block level and district level leadership. We decided to meet first with the district level and later with the block level leaders.

Meeting the officials

In addition to the elected leaders, we also had to meet with the government officials in the districts as we wanted to work closely with the government. The government administrative structure at the district level is divided by function into an executive branch with the Collector at the head of the district, and the welfare and development activities administered by the Zillah Parishad with the Chief Executive Officer (CEO) in charge of the district activities. The development activities; health education, agriculture, irrigation and forestry are handled in smaller units called Community Development Blocks with approximately 100 000 population. The Block and Taluk do not necessarily overlap geographically. All functional units have officials that may have to be dealt with.

My friends introduced me to the Collector of Osmanabad District, Mr Gibbs, who showed interest in the welfare of the poor and was actually quite knowledgeable about the health of the poor in his district. Guinea worm infestation, the high incidence of leprosy and many other epidemics in the area were of particular concern to him. He perceived the gap in the government health system and recognised the need for additional health inputs. I discussed in detail with him the rural area health plan we had prepared. He showed keen interest and promised cooperation from the government.

Mr Gibbs went out of his way to take me with him on his tour of the district, introducing me to officials and leaders in different blocks of the district and pointing out areas where people were poor and did not have adequate health facilities.

Most of the leaders were interested in the health of the people in their constituencies and promised to meet us again for further discussions. Later we realised that their interest was mostly polite; only a few actually came forward for further discussions. As I travelled around Osmanabad district, I met many kinds of leaders and saw more of the caste system and the feudal structure at work.

We met one leader who was enthusiastic and promised to arrange a meeting with a few important people in his block. He took me to the block headquarter, a village of 5000 people. As soon as we arrived, my host despatched messengers to get the people together.

It was market day and people from outlying villages had come to buy and sell their produce. The leader ordered forty village heads to come for the meeting. It was an order not an invitation. About an hour later we were able to start. Although forty people were present, none of them spoke. They looked apathetic and disinterested and just nodded their assent to whatever suggestions were made by the leader who had complete control of the meeting. I wanted to have a dialogue to find out what the people there thought of our plans and what their expectations were. But my host told me that his people agreed to his suggestions and there was no need for further discussion. After the meeting we walked through the village to the leader's house.

Signs of poverty were everywhere, the village looking like the ruins of an old fort. Our host was quite enthusiastic about starting a hospital in his village and proudly showed us his palatial house and property of lush green fields with sugar cane and cotton. A score of bullocks and Jersey cows were grazing in a nearby field. He invited us for lunch into his palatial stone house. As we went up the steps we noticed clusters of thatched huts all around. Women and children peeped from behind mud walls. I wanted to meet with more people and talk to them. I tried to explain that I was interested in the community understanding what we were proposing and wanted the people to be involved in the health programmes. But my host said that whatever

The leader just had to give the order and people would follow

he did was acceptable to everyone. If we wanted the community to be involved there was no problem, he just had to give the order and people would follow. He would see to it that the people followed my health teachings. I needed land? Of course, he would be able to donate land to the project.

This was not the kind of community participation that we had envisaged. Neither our own plans or the real wishes of the people would be considered in such a set-up. At the same time he was also strengthening his hold on the people, many of whom worked on his farm as virtual slaves. We began to realise that it was not easy to get past the class and caste structures to mobilise true involvement of the people. We would have to look for other areas where we could start our work in a more democratic fashion.

Continuing our search for leaders, we encountered many different types. Some were interested in selling their dilapidated property at a high cost to us and others simply saw us as a threat. One local leader's brother was a medical practitioner. Seeing us as a threat to his brother's thriving medical practice, the leader prevented us from having meaningful discussions with the village people.

Are government health officials interested in working with NGOs?

The Collector had introduced me to the Osmanabad District Health Officer. A physician, with a diploma in Public Health, he was responsible for the health of the whole district. I explained that we were interested in starting health work in Osmanabad district. We talked about leprosy and vitamin A deficiency and the fact that Osmanabad had one of the highest infant mortality rates in the country. After our discussion I thought he would be pleased to work along with us. Imagine my surprise when he drew my attention to a large map of the district hanging on the wall. It had coloured pins stuck in it, indicating the locations of all of the primary health centres and subcentres. Pointing to the map, he said assuredly, 'The government is providing full coverage to this area. There is no need for another agency to work here.'

His response made me feel sorry for him. Osmanabad was one of the most backward districts in Maharashtra! Its infant mortality rate was over 139 per 1000 births as compared to Japan's 10 or the USA's 18 at that time. We realised that, because of his attitude we could not locate our project in Osmanabad. Although we had tried to establish rapport with different leaders and other health professionals, we could not site our project in that area. Our hopes of starting in Osmanabad were dashed to the ground. We also had learned our lesson that we should approach the government bureaucrats cautiously and only from a position of strength.

In the course of twenty years we have come across many health officials. Some are committed and willing to work with non-governmental agencies (NGOs), and more often prefer not to encourage NGO involvement and work in the very narrow confines of the system. Therefore, cooperation between the government and NGOs depends greatly on individuals and officials working in the system. In general the members of the of Indian Administrative service seem to have a better understanding of the health problems in rural areas than do doctors who are trained in the narrow tradition of curative medicine with emphasis on biomedical technology.

We had to leave Osmanabad and look elsewhere. We were discouraged by our attempts to reach the villages through the various levels of leadership in Osmanabad. Was our plan even possible? What should we do now?

We considered Rahuri, my home town. Rahuri had by now become prosperous because a dam had been built across the river. Some of my friends had become rich farmers and some had gained political power. On our arrival they congratulated us and asked why we wanted to practise medicine in a poor area. 'Stay here in Rahuri,' they said. 'We will give you money and put up a modern hospital and bring in all the modern technology. We have wanted to start a modern hospital on a cooperative basis, and now money is no problem.' I knew my Rahuri friends had other interests. They were not interested in reaching out to the poor people in the villages. We could not accept their invitation.

One option was to go back to Vadala and try out our new ideas in that medical institution. But we knew that Vadala hospital is a curative facility with communities adapted to the routine of the hospital. We were not sure how much we could change attitudes. The months were going by and we were anxious to find a location where people were willing to have us. Had we made a mistake in trying to start in a remote area? What could we do? We did not realise that our plans needed the intervention of an old friend.

CHAPTER 5

Community enthusiasm

MABELLE

August, 1970

On the outskirts of Ahmednagar, Mr Bansilalji Kothari stood on the highway, peering into passing vehicles. He had heard that Mabelle was going to Vadala and was sure to pass on this road. It was important that he meet her. He soon spotted her and frantically waved his arms to stop the jeep. Finally he jumped on his motorcycle and caught up with the jeep about 10 kilometres from Ahmednagar.

'I've been waiting for you since morning! Why do you want to go to Osmanabad District? Jamkhed is just as backward as Osmanabad. After all, it is only 20 kilometres from the Osmanabad District border. You can still take care of Osmanabad people from Jamkhed. We'll give you all the help you need. Please come,' he pleaded. 'The people of Jamkhed are waiting for you to come and they have sent me to contact you.' He reminded Mabelle that the invitation to come to Jamkhed had been made five years ago, just before the Aroles had left for the USA and had been repeated in his letters.

Mabelle got out of the jeep and talked with Mr Kothari. She reminisced about how she and Raj had helped the family planning programme in Ahmednagar district.

'Let's work together again,' he said. As they stood and talked, it started raining. Quite oblivious of the rain, Mr Bansilalji Kothari continued to entreat Mabelle to come to Jamkhed.

'At least both of you should come and see Jamkhed before you decide. I won't let you go until you tell me that you are definitely coming.' By this time, it was raining quite hard. At last, Mabelle agreed to go to Jamkhed as soon as possible.

Elated, Mr Kothari exclaimed, 'See, you have brought rain here.

This rain is a good omen. We have not had rain in Jamkhed for months – I'm sure you will bring rain to Jamkhed too!'

Jamkhed

Jamkhed is strategetically located at the boundary of four districts, all of them drought-prone and underdeveloped. Jamkhed connected these backward districts to the prosperous region of western Maharashtra, which included Bombay. Hundreds of labourers from these areas migrated seasonally to work in sugar factories in the northern part of Ahmednagar District passing through Jamkhed on the way to the factories. As they travelled through, these workers stocked themselves with grains and groceries and purchased bullocks for their carts. On their return, they bought cloth, agricultural implements and other household goods for use in the villages. As a result, Jamkhed had developed a good network of roads; bullock cart tracks and dirt roads ran out of Jamkhed like the spokes of a wheel. There was also a large cattle market. The local merchants traded in grains and other household necessities and the weekly market brought villagers from the surrounding districts to sell or buy grains, vegetables and other necessities. From Friday evening until Sunday noon, thousands of people came to this weekly market. Since it was customary for these people to bring their sick along to the market for treatment, Jamkhed seemed to be a natural catchment area for our work. During these three days, the four local doctors were also busy treating patients brought from the surrounding villages.

A few days later

The ride from Osmanabad to Jamkhed was long and dusty for the monsoon still had not come to that region. As we approached Jamkhed, the poverty was apparent. No crops grew in the fields. There were no trees and no grass. The hills were bare, studded with rocks and boulders. Herdsmen were following emaciated cows. Raj and I wondered what they were scrounging around for.

It was noon by the time we reached Jamkhed. No truck or jeep was in sight, only a roadside bus station with a couple of tea stalls made of burlap bags and tin sheets. Everything was dry and dusty and there were no trees or shade. At the bus station we stopped to drink water, but it was muddy and turbid. The man told us that he had brought this water from a well about a mile away, but that the well was drying up. 'It is the only source of water for Jamkhed,' he told us. We settled for a cup of hot tea instead.

57

A warm welcome awaits us

Mr Kothari and the village leaders were waiting for us. They took us to the village guest house – the best accommodation in the whole block. It had one room with an iron bed, a rickety wooden chair and a small table. There was no running water or electricity. We were told that we could live there until other accommodation was available.

Mr Kothari led us to the meeting hall, where leaders from different political parties and sarpanchas from neighbouring villages, government officials, shopkeepers, a few teachers, lawyers, and a couple of doctors were waiting for us. The small, cramped hall was overflowing with more than one hundred people from all walks of life.

After a formal welcome and the ceremonial exchange of garlands, serious discussion on our proposed health project began.

Mr Kothari told the gathered crowd how he had worked with us in the past and about his own concerns for health. 'These doctors were well trained in America. They could have easily continued in America or set up practice in one of the cities. Instead they want to work in the villages. The past couple of years, I have been corresponding with them and kept them informed of the health conditions in this area. As you know, I'm very much interested in the health of our people. In 1958 I was the Sarpanch of Jamkhed. You all helped me to arrange a vasectomy camp. As a result, 350 men underwent sterilisation operations. Your present Muslim Sarpanch was the first person in his community in Jamkhed to have the operation.

'In Jamkhed, we have an unusually high incidence of tetanus. I requested a research institute in Bombay to solve this problem. As a chairman of the health committee for the whole district, I have done a lot of work in preventing epidemics. I have been very active in family planning. Some of the leaders who are here have made fun of me for my enthusiasm. But the Aroles will tell you how serious this problem is. On your behalf, I want to promise them all the help possible. They want to work in the nearby Bhoom area in Osmanabad District. Our minister, the Honourable Shri Abasaheb Nimbalkar, and some of my colleagues are requesting them to reconsider their plan and we hope that they will work here.'

Local leaders and shopkeepers also spoke. They primarily talked about setting up a hospital with X-ray, laboratory and operating facilities. One of them said, 'The nearest medical facility is fifty miles away. Only the other day, a woman with obstructed labour died on her way to the hospital.'

One of the local doctors talked about the high cost of hospital care. He complained that many charitable hospitals had become expensive and excluded the poor. He hoped that we would be aware of this pitfall. The Dalit leaders vividly described the plight of their people, whose poverty often prevented them from getting medical care. They pleaded with us to provide free care to their people.

Raj addressed the crowd. 'We both have come to you with knowledge in our heads, skill in our hands, and concern for the neglected people in the village. We have not brought funds for buildings or equipment with us. Some of you have asked for a hospital. We can do that only if you support us. I ask that you provide financial support for the buildings and equipment. We especially need your support for our day to day operations. Our main concern is for those who are scattered in the villages. We want to reach them in their huts. We believe that many of their illnesses can be eliminated with proper education and simple preventive measures. But we need everyone to pitch in with us. We mainly want to train people to take care of their own health, and so need the cooperation of leaders and enlightened people like you in promoting preventive health programmes and family planning programmes.'

The local businessmen and traders were quick to assure us of financial support for the hospital services. 'After all, don't we pay for our X-rays and operations in the cities? We also have to pay for transportation and accommodation and we lose our day's business. If you provide these medical services, we shall save quite a lot and we do not mind paying a little extra to take care of the poor.'

Mr Kothari added, 'As chairman of the Health Committee for the district for five years, I have overseen one hundred doctors working in the Zillah Parishad. I have been trying to persuade them to visit these neglected people in the villages and promote preventive programmes, but these doctors prefer to stay at the primary health centres and set up their own private practice. They haven't taken any interest in the village work. I've only had seven years of schooling, and they probably think I don't understand anything. I'm frustrated. I really want to work with the Aroles and help them in making village people healthy.'

At this point, the Sabhapaty of the Panchayat Samiti (president of the block council) stood up and announced, 'Whenever we politicians gather together we fight among ourselves. Today we have come together for a good cause. We all agree that we need you to start your work as soon as possible. We have a veterinary dispensary in the cattle market. It has three rooms you can use for your medical work. As a chief of this block I offer cooperation for your work.'

The Jamkhed mayor then said, 'We have a Dharmashala (public rest house) next to the veterinary dispensary in the same marketplace.

59

I want to donate five acres of land

You can use it to keep patients till you build a proper hospital.'

While he was still speaking, Mr Mishrilalji Kothari, the ex-mayor of Jamkhed who was sitting in the audience, demanded attention. He announced, 'I want to donate five acres of land for the hospital. I am impressed with your concern for the poor. According to my religion, serving the poor is like serving god. I want to be a part of this noble work. I want to give you a gift of five acres of land to build your hospital.' We gratefully acknowledged this offer and said to him that we would go through the legal process of transferring the land later.

The mood in the hall had changed. The Sabhapaty said, 'As you can see, Jamkhed is adopting you. Now, we want to talk about the immediate problem of accommodation.'

He asked how many people we expected would be on the health team. 'There may be around twenty,' I replied. The Sarpanch (Chairman of the village council) then asked the local people, 'Can you

60

find a place where these twenty people can live?'

'I will empty the warehouse on top of my shop,' said Shri Madanlal Bora.

'We have some rooms,' said Shri Gulabseth Surana, another merchant.

Many others came forward with offers of facilities for the staff and rooms for the patients. We went with the leaders and saw the veterinary dispensary. The largest of the three simple rooms was 3 metres by 3.5 metres with a verandah. The Dharmashala, which they had suggested as a ward was about three square metres in area, It had only three walls; the front was open. Some houses were two-room dwelling places in the heart of town. None had toilets or running water, but they were the best that people could offer us.

The 2-hectare plot of land was at the edge of Jamkhed. While we were walking towards that land, it suddenly started raining and we took shelter in a nearby shop. The monsoon rain soon flooded the streets. We couldn't go out to see the land, since the stream separating it from Jamkhed had swelled with flood waters. The people were overjoyed! They felt that the decision to have us in Jamkhed was indeed being blessed.

That night, camped in the small room in the government guest house, we reflected on the day's events. We were touched at the warm welcome and our spirits were lifted. There was an obvious need in the area, the leaders were enthusiastic and the offer of facilities far exceeded our expectations. Here was the beginning of the community participation we were looking for. The Dalit leaders had been present and there was general agreement that there should be subsidised services for those who could not afford to pay. Jamkhed seemed to be the place where people were prepared to participate in the programmes. We decided to accept the offer of buildings and start the programme at Jamkhed.

Community participation requires mutual trust

In our altruism and enthusiasm we did not take into account that individuals unknown to an area would have difficulty in eliciting community participation. We quickly learned that one has to be known to the leaders or decision makers, or be part of a power group or an organisation that local people trust. Newcomers, no matter how well meaning their intentions, cannot expect people to respond immediately. In Osmanabad, we had not been known at all, but at Jamkhed some of the leaders at least had heard of us because we had worked in the same district at Vadala. And we had worked with

Mr Bansilalji Kothari. These few contacts were sufficient for the community leaders to accept us and take the risk of providing buildings for our use.

We stayed in Jamkhed for a few days and continued to talk to the leaders and other officials. The leaders wanted us to start a hospital for emergency surgery and obstetrics immediately in the simple buildings they had promised to provide. If we were really serious about 'community participation' in our programme, we would have to yield to this request. Setting aside our plan for an integrated preventive and curative service, we firstly responded to this need expressed by the leaders. We took it as a challenge to convert these simple dwellings into a 'hospital', thus responding to the immediate needs of the people. The Sarpanch and Mr Bansilalji Kothari personally directed the clean-up of the area around the veterinary dispensary. Heaps of cow dung and rubbish littered the region. The village council auctioned the cow dung as manure. Scores of bullock carts transported it to the fields, a difficult operation directed personally by the Sarpanch. The task was not easy; no sooner did they get the place clean, than the weekly Saturday market brought in hundreds of cattle and the place was once again covered with cow dung. The process of cleaning had to start all over again. Finally the village people got it as clean as possible and arranged for a regular weekly cleaning brigade, who would be paid from proceeds of the sale of cow dung.

With everyone pitching in, the Dharmashala, which was nothing but an open shed with a rough stone floor, was converted into a ten-bed ward. The three-room veterinary dispensary became our out-patient clinic. One room became the doctor's consultation room and another was used to dispense medicines. The third room was used to give injections and perform minor medical or surgical procedures. We used the veranda as the reception area.

At the other end of the cattle market, a farmer from a nearby village had built a house for his family. Since he was not in a hurry to occupy it, he allowed us to use it for a few months. This house was converted into laboratory, X-ray and operating rooms. The Panchayat had an empty warehouse a few yards away from the clinic, which was given to us to treat tetanus patients, who need a dark quiet room. The disease was quite common in this area, and we always had one or two tetanus patients under treatment in this building.

We needed housing for about fifteen people. Different landlords rented small houses for the young men and a couple of married workers. A local shopkeeper offered his warehouse as a residence for us and the eight unmarried nurses. This warehouse was on top of his shop

1970–1; the CRHP at the veterinary dispensary

and it measured 9 by 18 metres. Its three walls, missing fourth wall, tin roof and mud floor allowed plenty of sun, wind and rain into the rooms.

Suddenly a problem arose. We wanted to build a toilet and the owner of the warehouse would not agree to it, not wanting any filth near his house. Would we have to abandon our choice of Jamkhed because of his refusal to build a toilet? It took much persuasion before we were allowed our request, but soon afterwards the owner himself built a toilet in his house.

We divided the house into three sections. The eight nurses could live in one section, and we with our two young children in the second. The third was the common kitchen, bathroom, and the prized toilet. The bathroom door was so small that even I with my short stature almost had to crawl into it. There was no electricity and water was in short supply. Every day water was hauled in from a nearby well and stored in a drum.

Minister endorses community effort

By the middle of September we were ready to start the medical work and so on September 27, 1970, the Comprehensive Rural Health Project, Jamkhed (CRHP), was formally inaugurated. The leaders from Jamkhed asked the Minister for Rural Development, The Honourable Shri

63

Abasaheb Nimbalkar, the District Collector and other dignitaries to be the chief guests. They had sent appropriate invitations and had personally contacted the guests. A huge shamiana (canopy) was erected in the cattle market and the clinic building was gaily decorated. Over two thousand people from surrounding villages attended the function, including Sarpanchas, village council members, local leaders, doctors and other dignitaries. The Jamkhed people formally welcomed us. The minister and officials publicly announced their support for the health work and promised to help the project in whatever way they could.

Both dignitaries and people were pleased at the transformation of the place and the progress the village Panchayat (council) had made in a couple of months. The Minister for Rural Development, Shri Abasaheb Nimbalkar, praised the people of Jamkhed for setting up the health programme. He said, 'We leaders sanction a hospital. The experts take their time for a survey. The bureaucratic red tape takes years before the buildings are in place. There is another delay before the staff are recruited and they start working. Here at Jamkhed you have set up a working hospital in three months!'

In the meantime, we were being called upon to prove our clinical skills. One week after we established the clinic, a woman was brought with a ruptured uterus. She was in shock and could not make it to Ahmednagar. She needed blood, but relatives refused to donate any blood. We were able to persuade a village beggar to donate some. The surgery was performed under kerosene lamp and flashlight. The patient recovered and went home. Many other surgical and other obstetrical emergencies were managed successfully. These simple facilities were sufficient to treat many emergencies for which the patients otherwise would have had to go to Ahmednagar.

We did not wait for an ideal hospital building or air-conditioned operating theatre to provide services. We accepted what people had and made these places safe enough for surgical care. We kept a balance between the safety of the patient, proper use of diagnostic equipment and the meagre resources of poor communities. It is possible to practise clinical medicine in the context of the poverty of the community, without compromising the scientific principles of medicine. It is necessary to separate the essential standards from the non-essentials related to a wasteful, affluent life-style. Sterile techniques are essential, for example, but the village patient is sometimes more comfortable on the floor to which he is accustomed, than on a high, electrically operated bed.

CHAPTER 6

From leaders to people

RAJ

Translation of a song on village leaders composed by village women.
'The leaders want to sit in the palaces,
How can they know the agony of the poor,
Their time is spent in parties and they move about in fancy cars,
How can they know the agony of the poor'

A helpful contact

As we were establishing the clinic at Jamkhed, we continued to make contacts with the leaders. Like any other area in the state, Jamkhed had leaders at several levels of communities, with widely differing levels of awareness and concern for the needs of the people. The Honourable Shri Abasaheb Nimbalkar belonged to a village 24 kilometres from Jamkhed. He represented the Jamkhed constituency in the state legislature. A respected senior leader and vice president of the ruling political party in Maharashtra, he held an important position as the State Minister for Rural Development. Having experienced the hardships of rural life himself, he was quite concerned about the poor. A gentle and soft spoken person, he was always available to us for help and advice. Unlike most leaders we met, he remained in the background and solved our problems with quiet efficiency.

Not only did Shri Nimbalkar welcome us to the area, he also helped us set up the health programme. As a minister, he instructed the officials at all levels to cut through the red tape and fully cooperate with us. He helped us overcome the multitude of bureaucratic bottle-necks that plague health care in India. At our request, he was even able to get a paved road built between Ahmednagar and Jamkhed. When we first came, it took over four hours on a dusty dirt road to reach Jamkhed from Ahmednagar; the new road cut the travel time to one hour and a half. Later, Shri Nimbalkar helped solve the water problem at Jamkhed by having a dam constructed. This water supply has made relative prosperity possible in Jamkhed.

Enlisting the support of leaders of Jamkhed block

During this start up time, we also had to keep making contacts with the numerous leaders in the area. Through them we hoped to reach the individual villages. From the beginning, Mr Kothari took special interest in our work. Unlike most of the other politicians, he did not belong to the dominant caste but had earned recognition by means of his many unusual qualities. A born social worker, he was genuinely concerned about people. Wherever there was an emergency, calamity or sickness, Mr Kothari was the first to arrive on the scene and provide assistance. Holding his position through sheer dedication, hard work and usefulness to the people he had served Jamkhed, initially as a Sarpanch, then as Sabhapathy. Shortly before we came he had been elected Chairman of the Health Committee of the district. As chairman, Mr Bansilalji Kothari had first-hand knowledge of how the government health centres functioned. He knew how little the government spent on the rural poor and had many ideas about improving rural health services. However he hadn't been able to change the health system and was extremely frustrated, complaining that doctors spent most of their time in private practice and rarely showed interest in public health activities in the villages. Our ideas about community participation and mass health education appealed to him tremendously.

Mr Kothari continued to help us enthusiastically in every way he could, becoming our guide to the villages around Jamkhed, even acting as driver and mechanic on those trips.

Besides these two persons, there were about a dozen other important leaders in the area. Each of them nurtured his constituency and jealously guarded his territory. So it was crucial for us to remain neutral in our political affiliations. We accepted all invitations to go to the villages and talk to the leaders. We needed to establish relationships with all of them, independent of Mr Kothari's help.

We used our curative skills to win over many of these leaders. Some were shrewd enough to realise that bringing curative services to their constituencies would enhance their prestige. Others found their own reasons to work with us, but most were indifferent. A few were suspicious, feeling that we would later compete with them for political power; sometimes doctors practising in villages who acquired respect and money would indulge in politics. Some leaders were hostile to anyone entering their territory. In spite of our repeated assurances we could not convince one leader who saw us as a threat to his control that we had no political ambitions. While he was polite and never disagreed with us, he tried to discredit our medical treatment and raise misunderstanding between us and the community. Ironically, while harming the health programme, he continued to receive health services for his family from us. Most opposition from hostile leaders came in this subtle form.

We could not discern any particular pattern to the leaders' attitudes. They had different interests and each leader had his own set of values. All were struggling to stay in power. They felt very insecure if any one person became too popular, so Mabelle and I decided to keep a low profile in public. From time to time we publicly assured them that we had no interest in competing with them for leadership or political power. On the other hand, we gave them credit for any progress that was made in the village.

Despite all our contacts, we were still at the periphery of the village communities. We had to penetrate deeper into the village hierarchy before we could reach the common people, particularly those who had no access to health care. All the people we met during this initial stage could afford the health services provided in the cities. All they wanted from us was to bring such services closer to where they lived.

The village community

In those first few months at Jamkhed we learned more about the complex structure of the village community. Much has been written about the social structure of India with its caste hierarchy and its many local variations. Village communities may be seen as small kingdoms that completely encapsulate the majority of the people.

In a typical Jamkhed area village of 200 households, a couple of households were Brahmins, 50–60 per cent belonged to the dominant caste group, 25 per cent belonged to other castes including the Muslims, and the remaining 15 per cent were Dalits.

For centuries Indian society has been divided into scores of different castes and subcastes. Broadly speaking, there are four categories: the Brahmins, the Kshatriyas, the Vaishyas and the Shudras.

The Brahmins were the priest class. They had access to knowledge and were in charge of religious rites. The Kshatriyas were the kings, rulers and warriors. The Vaishyas were the businessmen, traders and landowners. These three groups today consider themselves high caste. The Shudras were the farm labourers and artisans, such as blacksmiths, carpenters, potters, weavers and washermen. Generally they served the dominant caste groups and were dependent on them for their livelihoods.

Each of these broad categories was further divided into castes and subcastes, which were constantly engaged in determining a higher position for themselves in this hierarchical system. Among these caste groups those who had money, land, property and numerical strength in the village became a dominant caste.[1]

Outside these four broad categories were the 'untouchables'. They were regarded as scavengers and their work related to cleaning up, disposing of waste and dealing with dead animals. For centuries they were denied access to property, arms and education. Mahatma Gandhi called them Harijans - a word he coined to denote that they are the Children of God, based on the concept that God cares for the poor and oppressed. That is how they are addressed by the majority of people. Many Harijans, however, prefer to be called Dalits, which means oppressed.

Officially, the Government has passed a law against the practice of treating certain groups as untouchable. In most Indian villages, however, discrimination against the Dalits continues in various forms.[1] There is little or no socialisation among different caste groups. Leaders often resort to using caste structures to gain political power.

In the villages the Dalits, like other caste groups, were further divided into subcastes and also observed a hierarchy among themselves. These divisions, along with their poverty, kept the dominant caste from considering the Dalits a major force to be taken into account. One Dalit man was in charge of a hostel for Dalit boys supported by the Government Department of Welfare. He formally represented the Dalits on various government committees and gave us insights into the problems of Dalits and caste discrimination, which was quite severe in this area. The Dalits were not allowed to draw water from the public well, but were required to ask a high caste person to draw water and give it to them. They could not stay in the main village but lived in a special section quite a distance away. Dalit workers, such as school teachers and clerks, who were transferred to the area often had to stay in the office or school building because no one would rent a house to them.

Members of the dominant caste were not necessarily wealthy. In a village a handful of families possess over 60 per cent of the land. The others depend on these wealthy farmers for their livelihood.

No signs of self-reliance

As I went round the villages, I found that the people looked up to their leaders for all decisions. Even personal matters such as buying and selling land or arranging a marriage had to be approved by the leaders. The elite earned this loyalty by acting as benefactors of the people in times of difficulty; lending money in times of need, acting as agents for legal advice and taking sick people to a hospital in the city. In this way we frequently met these village leaders. They accompanied patients to the health clinic and showed interest in the diagnosis and treatment. The patient usually deferred to the village leader for whatever decision had to be made. Anyone needing surgery first consulted the leader.

Those who did not belong to the village were looked upon with suspicion. Thus ordinary village people depended on the leaders to judge whether we were acceptable or not. Years of subordination had made the people dependent, fearful and wary of strangers. Under these circumstances it was an important first step to win the support of the village leaders and through them reach the people who had no access to health care.

At this stage, we decided, attempting to bypass the existing village power structure would be detrimental to the programme. We observed the experience of another well-meaning group that initiated a development programme, about the same time as ours, 32 kilometres away in the adjoining district. This group consisted of people highly educated in the fields of engineering, water development and social services. They wanted to empower the poor for their own development but they bypassed the traditional leaders and went directly to the village poor to organise them. They talked to the people about how they were not getting the benefits of development and how corrupt leaders and politicians were exploiting them. The village people, used to being approached by outsiders through their leaders, became suspicious of the newcomers. The leaders felt threatened and spread rumours about the motivation of this group. The result was that this highly motivated NGO group had to retreat from the area because they did not win the confidence of the leaders.

This incident taught us that we needed to establish credibility with the poor people through service. In our eagerness to serve the village people, we should not antagonise the leadership but in the initial stages take the existing leader into our confidence and gradually work with the villagers until true leadership emerged among these village people. The process had to be slower than we wished, with emphasis on sharing information and gradually empowering those at the lower end of this hierarchical ladder.

In addition to our contacts at the clinics in Jamkhed and the villages, we used every occasion we could to establish good relations with the leaders. We attended social events such as weddings, death

69

feasts and religious festivals, and these informal contacts resulted in invitations to visit the individual villages of the leaders.

It was evident that the leaders had already put us in a medical slot and expected us, as doctors, to provide such services as maternity care, X-ray and laboratory services, surgery and other curative care. This was the leaders' felt need. Did the poor village people also feel the same way? We wanted to talk to the them and find out, to have village meetings to explain our idea of the people's own involvement in the health care and preventive programmes. But the leaders were not so enthusiastic about involving the people. They started talking among themselves. 'Why do these doctors want to have village meetings and talk to everyone? Instead of just treating illness, they are asking too many questions about what people eat, and their income and other practices. They are interested in family planning and are talking about immunisation.' So the leaders would invite us in the daytime when most people were out working in the fields. They would assure us that the village people would not oppose any decisions made by their leaders.

Mabelle and I responded to all invitations to the villages. On one typical visit, when we left the main road we bumped along a dirt track with deep furrows. Soon the village came into sight. From a distance it looked like a mound of mud and stone ruins. As we came closer we saw that the ruins were actually houses of poor people. The houses in the centre were made of solid stone and the door posts had ornate carvings. We went into one of the larger houses. Its walls were over a metre thick and there were no windows facing the outside. Entering through a single massive door, we came to an open courtyard with rooms all around it. The front two rooms were for the men and visitors. The rest were occupied by the women and children. We were led into a room where the landlord was reclining on a mattress and pillow, playing with his grandson. He graciously welcomed us.

We talked for some time and he showed us the new tractor that he had recently acquired. Talking about his farm and his recent good harvest, he pointed to sacks of grain stacked in the corner, explaining that most of the grain was stored underground in houses like his. He spoke about his social activities in the village and proudly told us that he had just renovated the community hall for the village and now he was now thinking of building a temple.

I observed, 'Patil, (title for a landlord), you are a progressive farmer. How are the rest of the farmers in the village? I would like to know more about your village. Could you show me around?'

'Oh certainly. Come, I will show you around.'

The landlord's house

The patil put on his turban and we went into the street. He quickly passed another big house which I later came to know was the house of his rival. As we walked away from his house, we noticed that the streets had become filthy with the waste water draining into the streets. In fact, there was filth everywhere. We went into a house of a small farmer. The room was sparsely furnished. I noted to Mabelle the amount of food that was in the house. The woman was making the sorghum bread on a wood stove. There was a single, 100 kilogramme sack of grain in the corner.

At the edge of the village was the village community hall. We went in and saw that it was newly painted. 'You can use it for your clinic. There is plenty of space to examine patients here,' said the patil. He was just about to turn back to his house.

'Is this all your village?' I asked

'Yes,' replied the patil.

I knew that behind the wall and stream was the Dalit section 'But what about those huts there? Don't they belong to your village?' I asked.

'Oh, those belong to the Dalits,' was the reply.

'But I want to go there and see how they live,' I said.

We had to walk around the wall and cross the stream to the Dalit section of the village. The line of demarcation was distinct. An area the village people used as a dump was rife with pigs' dirt and stagnant waste water from the high caste house drains. The Dalit section turned out to be a cluster of mud huts with thatched roofs. There were plenty of children. Some were emaciated and had running noses. Flies clung around the sores that covered their legs. They looked miserable. In one corner a young man was lying. Thin and wasted, he was coughing and spitting all over the place.

Most of the women looked pale and tired. As we walked into the area the women quickly covered their heads with a fold of sari as sign of respect and went into their huts. The men bowed in obedience to the patil.

The Dalits' house

I went into a hut. It was threadbare, with only a few mud pots and some rags. There were no bags of grain and most of the pots were empty. In one pot were a couple of stale sorghum breads stored for emergency. A potful of carrots was boiling on a fire made with a handful of sticks and dried cow dung cakes. I pointed these differences out to Mabelle within the patil's hearing. I questioned the woman who was cooking. 'What do you have to eat today?'

'Carrots. Yes, they are cheap these days. This will be our supper for the seven of us. We cannot afford to buy grain unless we get some work.'

'Patil,' I said, 'Look at these children. That child is so thin. That young man is coughing. So many children have sore eyes and scabies. There seems to be more sickness in this area than in yours.'

The patil replied, 'Doctor saheb, no matter what you do for these

72

people they remain the same. Their dirty habits make them sick. See what filth we had to come through.'

'Yes, don't you think we should work for them? They seem to be very needy. They need to be taught many things about health. In addition to teaching them, immunisation will certainly will make a difference to their health. We also should think of doing something about this lack of food.'

The patil answered, 'Doctor, I agree with you that they need your services more than I do. But they are not people who can pay for your services.'

'As long as people like you pay my fees, I don't mind treating them free,' I replied. 'You know, if we can wipe out some of the diseases such as polio, there is less chance of your children being exposed to them.' The patil agreed.

By then quite a few people had gathered around us and started talking about their illnesses and other problems. The poor people felt honoured that they were being counted. We continued this practice of deliberately taking the village leaders to the poor communities to make them acknowledge that the poor deserved help. After all, treating the poor was in their self-interest.

The Dalit leaders started coming forward. They introduced us to the poor communities in the villages and encouraged the people to attend the meetings and voice their opinions. These poor people were available for discussion or medical service after sunset, late in the evening after they returned from work in the fields. Indeed, whatever activity we planned for the poor, whether it was a village meeting or a clinic, it had to be after their work in the fields was over.

Blueprint does not work

According to our original plan, we were to cover villages in a systematic manner, – spreading out in concentric circles in an 8 kilometre radius. In practice, the villages closer to Jamkhed did not show as much interest in participating in our health activities. They were satisfied with the symptomatic relief that the doctors in Jamkhed were providing. But the villages away from Jamkhed, without access to medical aid, were keen on our services. They also agreed to work with us in improving the general health of the village. They were willing to provide a place for the health clinic and volunteers to help. We started weekly clinics in such villages. After seeing patients, we would invite the villagers for a meeting. We explained our plans for preventive health programmes and we talked about prenatal care, immunisation, sanitation and nutrition. Such attempts at reaching the poor did not go unnoticed. Reactions from leaders varied from suspicion to concern.

Medical practitioners generally saw their patients in the clinic and also took house calls to attend sick patients. Usually they did not show any interest in the general condition of the people. Unlike these doctors, we were visiting the villages, having meetings and discussing people's general condition. Our ventures outside the realm of medical care made some politicians suspicious. They wondered if we would seek popularity with the villagers and later compete for political power. Therefore we had to go out of our way to explain to them that we were not competing with them but trying to find a relationship between poverty, isolation and health.

We feel sorry for you!

Our enthusiasm for preventive health activities was misunderstood. Although we were known to leaders of the district, the local village leaders had not heard about us. Rumours reached us that these leaders whispered among themselves that we had come to Jamkhed because we were not good enough to practise in the USA and that we could not make a living in Bombay or Ahmednagar. No wonder we had come to a remote place like Jamkhed! They felt sorry for us.

It became obvious that we could not undertake prevention and promotive work unless we proved to the leaders that we were competent physicians. Their criticism only confirmed that we needed to integrate curative and public health medicine in the villages; indeed, there was so much illness that both were necessary. We soon recognised that we could use our curative services as a springboard for establishing the preventive health activities.

Establishing credibility

We stepped up our curative activities in the villages. The village leaders usually gave us the village community hall or the Panchayat office or a temple to hold regular weekly clinics and they arranged for volunteers to help at the clinic. These volunteers also helped in the village surveys. By concentrating on sick patients and providing them with appropriate treatment, both in the villages and at Jamkhed, we deliberately kept the public health activities low key. Soon the village leaders began to appreciate our work and accepted us.

Survival takes precedence over health

As we gained the confidence of the people it became more and more evident that health was not a priority for the poor at all. It was only the leaders and well off farmers who felt the need for better health care. The majority of people were preoccupied with their very survival. Regular employment and the availability of food and water were their main concerns. They sought medical help for life-threatening illnesses and injuries. Sore eyes, scabies, episodes of diarrhea and aches and pains were considered part of life, not worth spending money on for a doctor's visit. The majority were not interested in our village clinics or in having a hospital in the area. If they were not interested in health, how could we involve them in health programmes? We realised that not only would we have to integrate preventive and curative services, but we would also have to respond in some way to their serious needs for food and water. We would have to address the issue of overall development.

Getting caught in the cross fire of power politics

Sometimes we inadvertently got caught up in village feuds. Ashta village was 13 kilometres from Jamkhed. The leaders invited us to work there. Teachers from a local high school helped us a great deal in our work. We had started good programmes for leprosy patients and mother and child health. We had talked with the leaders about screening patients for eye diseases like glaucoma and cataracts. One night, accompanied by an ophthalmologist, and a couple of nurses and paramedical workers we reached the village after sunset. Many patients gathered in the school building and under the light of kerosene lamps we began examining them. About an hour later, a mob of twenty-five people with sticks and crowbars charged at us, shouting and demanding that we leave the village immediately. They ordered the patients to go to their houses. These people did not seem to be in a mood to discuss anything reasonably so we complied and left the village. As we returned home we felt frightened and angry. Is that the way people were repaying our kindness? Was it right to expose our children and colleagues to dangers like this? The most upsetting thing was we could not understand why people came to attack us. We did not have to wait long to find out.

The next morning a delegation of poor people came to us. Mr Rokade, a patient with tuberculosis, pleaded, 'These intoxicated bulls are fighting among themselves and we poor are crushed in between. Please do not stop your clinic.'

They explained that a village council election had been held the previous month. The defeated party wanted to take revenge on their rivals by discrediting them. While the elected leaders had gone away for a wedding, they took the opportunity to embarrass them. A couple of days later the ruling party returned from the wedding and immediately came and apologised for the incident. They invited us back to the village. We told them that we would hold the clinic in the poor section of the village. The poor people held a reception and found a place for the clinic in their own area.

Episodes like this occurred in many villages. The opposing faction would deliberately misplace the keys for the clinic room or sometimes get drunk and use obscene language. In these cases people were not basically against us or our health programmes. Sometimes they were afraid of our activities. In such circumstances we temporarily discontinued our services, but usually were able to start the work again.

Listening, looking and understanding village politics without being involved, and lying low while leaders and people sorted out their differences was an important strategy we learned. It was slow and often tried our patience. But life in the village is slow and we had to be in tune with it.

A few villages proved difficult, although most cooperated with us. Sakat was one such village, situated in the hills and connected to Jamkhed by a bullock track. The village people invited us to Sakat and Mr Kothari accompanied us. A few kilometres from Jamkhed the road ended in the hills. The path was steep and narrow with hairpin turns, a combination of boulders and deep ruts. The village people met us with a bullock cart, but Mr Kothari decided to drive the jeep up. As it slowly inched up the road, the people walked in front, removing boulders and levelling the path. At last we arrived. The first item on the meeting that day was building an approach road for the jeep.

The village had a health subcentre building with housing for an auxiliary nurse midwife, but because of its isolated location they were unable to get a nurse to stay there. They wanted us to do something about this problem.

We agreed to visit the village once a week at first, but we wanted the road to be made drivable. The villagers readily agreed. Over one hundred people worked for three months, clearing the path, removing huge boulders and rocks, levelling ruts and hewing a road out of the hillside. It was a massive showing of cooperation and goodwill.

In time, all around Jamkhed, people understood that we were interested in the poor. We had entered these villages through their leaders and had established credibility in the villages as good doctors. We befriended the leaders by providing the type of health care only available in the city. By the end of 1971 we ran regular weekly clinics in twenty-five villages.

It had taken almost eighteen months just to learn from people what their needs were. We had entered the area through the political leaders and gone to each village through its leaders. We had discovered that the needs of the leaders are not identical with those of the poor and marginalised people. It became increasingly clear to us that curative services and preventive services needed to be integrated along with other development strategies. We had started looking for community participation in the villages but had found that no truly representative community exists there. The lines drawn by caste, economics, and the need for power have kept such a community from forming. We would have to find ways to help people to step across those lines and begin to dissolve those lines before true participation could be achieved.

1 Rao, Sangeetha R. *Caste System in India: Myth and Reality*. India Publishers and Distributers, New Delhi 1989.

CHAPTER 7

Team building

MABELLE

Finding workers

While the community was getting the clinic building ready, Raj and I recruited a core staff of nurses and paramedical workers. Because Jamkhed area was poor and backward, we faced serious constraints in getting a team together. Firstly, we discovered that hardly any girls in Jamkhed had finished high school, so local women health professionals could not be found. We turned to Ahmednagar and Aurangabad, the adjoining districts, to look for workers.

However there was little about our project to attract outsiders to work in it. As a new venture, we could not offer job security, nor had we the kind of regular hospital that most nurses and other medical personnel are used to working in. Many were concerned that as a new project it did not have financial stability. Jamkhed villages were known to be hostile to change and intolerant of outsiders. Its poverty and remoteness did not attract educated persons. Young nurses saw no chance of finding a husband in such an area, and older persons with families were put off by the lack of adequate amenities and did not want to come to a place with few educational facilities for their children. Even government officials regarded a transfer to Jamkhed as a punishment. Under such circumstances it was difficult to find workers.

We contacted friends, hospitals and nursing schools. We knew some parents whose daughters had completed nurses' training as ANMs (Auxiliary Nurse Midwives). We approached these parents and six families responded by allowing their daughters to join us.

78

Two pillars of the health team

One day Miss Helenbai (Akka) Ghodke from Vadala came to see us. She was fifty-five years old at that time and wanted to join us. Akka was not just seeking a job. She had a commitment to serve the poor village people. We had worked with her long enough at Vadala to know that she had blended the discipline acquired from her years in the army with the deep values of humane service from her mission hospital experience. In addition, her clinical experience and practical medical knowledge would be a real asset to us as we started delegating responsibilities to nurses. We welcomed her enthusiastically and knew that now we could leave the details of setting up the clinic to her.

Akka brought with her a young nurse Jerus (Jeribai) Shrisunder. Jeribai, tall and strong, was very fond of Akka, whom she had adopted as her aunt. Akka was her role model, inculcating values of service and hard work.

'My parents wanted me to join the government service,' she told us. 'There is money, security and prestige in working for the Government. One does not have to work hard. My sisters and brother are working for the Government. They pressurised me to get a government job. But Akka convinced me to work at Jamkhed. Although the salary would be low, there would be a sense of satisfaction in being useful and of service to the community.'

Many young men in Ahmednagar and Aurangabad were searching for jobs. Financial difficulties kept them from completing their schooling. We selected five of them. They did not have any skills in particular, but they were ready to learn and do any work. We also found a social worker, a leprosy worker, an accountant and a retired army driver to complete the team.

By September we had put the team together and it was time for us to start work. We decided to meet at Ahmednagar and go together to Jamkhed. Akka often recounts what happened that first day.

'It was the middle of September 1970. All the team members assembled at Ahmednagar. We were told that Jamkhed was 80 kilometres away and that it would take four hours to get there. We set out after breakfast and hoped to reach it in time for lunch. The sky was blue and there was no sign of rain. We crowded into two jeeps, the women into one and the men into the other. Everyone was in a festive mood. The men were singing. I was telling wartime stories to the nurses.

'About halfway, two hours later, we encountered torrential monsoon rain. The canvas top of the jeep did not keep the rain out. We assured ourselves that soon we would reach Jamkhed and everything would be fine. Further down the road we noticed that the streams were rapidly filling up. Very soon we were forced to stop, as one of the streams was not crossable. Neither could we go back. We waited for the water to recede. The hours went by as we sat huddled in the jeep getting wetter and wetter and with darkness falling quickly upon us. I was scared since these areas were known to be infested with dacoits.

'At last a bus large enough to cross the stream came by. The women were sent ahead to Jamkhed and the men stayed behind with our belongings packed in a trailer. We reached Jamkhed about eight o'clock at night. Tired and cold, we longed for a warm bed. Mr Bansilalji Kothari was waiting at the bus station. He gave us a hot cup of tea and escorted us to our new home. I wondered what was in store for me.

'We were led up a narrow flight of stairs. The staircase was so narrow that I had to walk sideways. The third floor consisted of a big hall with only three walls. The mud floor was ankle deep in water and the roof was leaking like a sieve. To make matters worse, in the dim light of the kerosene lamp I saw a bat hanging from the roof. So much for a warm bed! "What have I got myself into?" I thought. "Why did I leave my secure job at Vadala?" I burst into tears.

'Soon the men arrived with our soaking wet belongings. Thankfully, the village people had prepared a hot meal for all of us and provided us with dry warm bedding. Their warmth and friendliness soon wiped away my tears. I realised that I had come with a purpose to help those in need. I had been warned of the hardships and the fact that we would have to start with practically nothing. As the senior person, I should be supporting the doctors and giving courage to all these young women who had come with me.

'We all set to work. We bailed out the water, made our beds and went to sleep.'

Breaking the hierarchy

The next day Akka was up bright and early. She had found a stove and had cooked breakfast.

The team was a mixed group. Akka and Jeribai were trained and experienced nurses. Usha, Shanta, Greta, Leela and Margaret were young ANMs with a couple of years' hospital experience. Mr Vasant Jadhav was a leprosy technician. Then there was Mr Murlidhar Gaikwad, Mr Uttam Thorat and a few others. We noticed that first morning that Akka had already established hierarchy and intended to practise it at work or at home. She had already decided the breakfast seating arrangements. Everyone sat on the floor. Separate chairs and a table were reserved for Raj and me.

There they sat in strict hierarchical order. Akka in her starched white uniform was at the head of the team with Jeribai by her side ready to obey her commands. Then came the ANMs, also in their uniforms, sitting with their eyes glued to the floor. The men and women sat apart. The book-keeper and the young men, the laboratory technician, the aide and the driver were all there. All ready to take orders!

Raj and I walked in and sat at the lower end of the line near the driver. The group looked a little uneasy. Akka pointed to the chairs. Raj shook his head and said, 'No! It's time we changed this ranking. We are all here together with a purpose. We are going to work as a team. That means sharing responsibilities and working together and using our skills, using our intelligence and not being driven like a bullock.'

I suggested that we sit in a circle and so the line was broken. This circular seating arrangement has remained the standard since that first morning, regardless of the occasion; from meeting with the elders in the village to teaching village health workers at the centre.

Team spirit means respecting each other and helping each other. In traditional Indian society, women were expected to do the household chores in addition to their regular work. We noticed that the men on the staff also expected the nurses to do all the work of cooking and cleaning. Respect for women and the dignity of all work had to be inculcated among the team members. The entire staff shared meals together in the common kitchen. We took turns to clear the table, wash the dishes, clean the bathroom and fetch the water. Men found it rather difficult to do these chores since they had never entered the kitchen and helped their mothers or wives with such work. Raj set an example by being the first to wash the dishes and clean the bathroom. Jadhav recalls that the men would come in late because they were shy and felt awkward about eating and doing the chores together. The women too had difficulty in accepting their new role. I often saw a look of embarrassment on a nurse's face if she saw Raj or some other male member of the team doing a household chore. But these were important lessons in team building.

Understanding poverty

We had regular team discussions on how we could make our health education more appropriate to local conditions. One evening we were discussing nutrition and the fact that most people could not afford nutritious food. We wondered how people could live on Rs 1:50 (20 US cents) a day, for that was the daily wage of a farm labourer. A heated discussion ensued about how our health education was useless because we could not understand what it meant to live on such a low income. One of the team members suggested that we should try to do it ourselves; then we would understand the limitations of a low income. All agreed to try living on Rs 1:50 a day for a couple of months.

That meagre allowance did not permit us many of the foods we liked. Meals were simple, entailing mainly sorghum bread with onions, chillies and a vegetable. Occasionally we could afford to have lentils and yoghurt. Milk, coffee, tea, or meat were too expensive. I had a problem because I had never eaten the dry sorghum bread. It was quite a change after having lived in the USA.

Living on that tiny allowance revealed to us the plight of the villagers. Water was expensive. It cost one-third of our daily allowance to buy water to flush the toilet. We could not do laundry at home as it would require too much expensive water. Even the soap was expensive. The nurses had long hair and they could not wash it at home. So every Sunday we all piled into the jeep and went to a stream to do all the laundry and bathing. We continued this experience of living in poverty for a few months. We learned our lessons and decided to continue the common kitchen, but spend about 75 cents a day on food and water.

Health education – how relevant?

Could we ask the villagers to feed their children with milk, eggs and lentils when they did not have money even to buy enough sorghum? Sorghum bread was the staple food of the area. Could we ask them to build toilets when there was not enough drinking water all year round? It cost us Rs 0:25 to buy kerosene and boil enough water to drink. How realistic could it be to insist on drinking boiled water? Soap was expensive, almost a day's wages, so should we insist on washing hands with soap? How then could we talk to villagers about nutrition, bathing, washing hands? Poor people spent most of their earnings on food and very little was left to buy other necessities like fuel, soap and medicines. So we needed to find appropriate methods to provide health education relevant to their poverty. We began to look at inexpensive ways of maintaining health. And we needed to give relevent health education. Given the villagers' limited amount of money, we could not talk about many interventions. Is buying soap to wash hands as important as buying food to stay alive? We had to learn to make these observations and give appropriate messages. We had to learn to distinguish between scientific fact and imposing our middle-class culture and life-style on village people. We had to look for inexpensive alternatives – foods, safe water. Soap is not the only form of detergent. The poor people used soap nut, the fruit of a tree, which gave a good lather for washing. It worked just as well as soap. Many different types of greens and lentils available in the village were highly nutritious.

Our experience of living in poverty helped us to appreciate villagers' day-to-day difficulties. It was almost impossible to maintain good health with such a meagre income and so we began to think that alleviation of poverty must be part of any health programme.

As a team we also had fun together. Every Sunday when we went for the weekly wash to the stream, we packed our lunch and had a picnic. We sang and played games and had fun together. Our children were staying in Ahmednagar with their grandparents at that time, so some Sundays they came to Jamkhed to join us. It was fun for them to play in the stream. Sometimes we visited our children in Ahmednagar and had a good meal there. We enjoyed the shower, and did our weekly laundry.

Coping with village discomforts

Settling into living and working together as a team called for other adjustments, too. There was no privacy. Safe drinking water was a precious commodity. Dust and filth surrounded our house situated at the edge of the marketplace. When we looked down from the room we saw pigs wallowing in the dirt. There were rubbish heaps all over the place. Every now and then a strong gust of wind would whirl dust up into the room. And in the evening after a long day of work we wished for a shower, only to find hardly half a pail of water to wash off the dust and sweat. We were determined to get used to village conditions. We also realised that a little discomfort on our part could give so much benefit to this neglected community.

Akka and Jeribai had their own problems. They had to share a room with six other young ANMs and had no life of their own. They had to look after the needs of the other staff. Both by example and informal teaching, they helped nurses to become efficient, honest and caring professionals. This sharing of life and responsibilities certainly helped to build a strong core team.

Team training and sharing of responsibilities

Our work began at seven in the morning. After breakfast every morning, we met together with all the team members for a time of meditation and to discuss the previous day's experiences and plan the day's activities. Everyone was given an opportunity to voice problems and difficulties. This time of sharing has helped to keep up team spirit. For the past twenty-two years, we have continued to spend twenty minutes together every morning.

From the beginning our days were full of activities. We started visiting the villages both morning and evening. Raj or I took a team of ANMs and paramedical workers to hold village clinics to treat sick patients, to provide health education and immunisation, and also to do surveys to ascertain the health status of the people. Those who stayed back at Jamkhed were also kept busy. From seven in the morning till seven in the evening, patients from the surrounding villages and from Jamkhed itself came to the outpatient clinic.

Some patients were admitted for more serious illnesses and for surgery. These patients were scattered in different buildings: medical patients were in the dharmashala, while the tetanus patients were in the warehouse and the surgical patients in the rented house.

Patient's family as partners in healing

There was no central nursing station so the nurses had to visit different buildings to look after the patients. I saw that the nurses were tiring themselves out doing jobs that did not require much skill. For example, one nurse was occupied all day long just running around giving medicines to patients. One day Jeribai had to go to tube feed a patient several times. Since relatives stayed with the patients, I suggested to her that she teach the patient's relatives how to feed the patient. She was sceptical because the relatives were illiterate, but she agreed to try. The next day at the team meeting, she reported that the relatives were doing a great job of tube feeding. I said to the nurses, 'You have acquired precious knowledge and skills, but you spend precious time making beds, cleaning and bathing patients and distributing tablets. Now you have seen that the relatives can be taught to perform these services for the patients and leave you free to do other important tasks. In fact, we are already using this principle in our outpatient clinic. We give a week's medicine for children and trust the mother to administer the medicine properly. Then why can't you entrust them with a day's medicine under your supervision?'

This idea was new to the nurses and they were rather reluctant to accept these relatives as partners in healing. However, they started allowing the relatives to help them. Soon they appreciated the results and willingly taught the relatives other skilled procedures like feeding through a stomach tube or releasing a catheter. To do so meant demystifying nursing procedures. Although illiterate, the relatives were quick to learn.

The involvement of relatives in patient care kept patient morale high. The relatives were so pleased to be working with the nurses that they were eager to get more health education and soon became invaluable members of the health team.

Delegation of responsibilities to nurses

I needed an interpreter in the outpatient clinic. With my poor knowledge of the Marathi language, I could not communicate with the patients. The nurses took turns interpreting for me. This was a good opportunity to teach them to manage simple illnesses. Soon the nurses were examining patients on their own and treating them with me looking over their shoulder.

My difficulty with the language was actually an asset. There were so few educated women in Jamkhed that most patients could not imagine that I was a doctor. To them I was a doctor's wife who had picked up some medical information from my husband. 'She is so dumb she cannot even speak our language,' they would say. On the other hand, they accepted the nurses because they were familiar with women as nurses. A sense of humour is needed to overcome these prejudices. Patients often went to Akka or Jeribai to check if the prescription I had written was right. The nurses used to be amused by this and of course it improved their own self-image. They would chuckle at these incidents and repeat them to others.

Training for delegation

We taught the nurses new skills. They learned to incise abscesses, extract teeth, suture wounds and set fractures. Akka became skilled in removing foreign bodies from the nose, ears and eyes. Akka and Jeribai in turn taught the ANMs and others to take on more responsibilities. The nurses took turns at accompanying a doctor at the village clinics. In the villages too, they took on more and more responsibility so that after some time they were able to conduct these clinics on their own.

This delegation of responsibility in curative care gave them job satisfaction and enthusiasm to work under these difficult conditions

Akka setting a fracture

and broke the monotony of going out day after day to the villages. They used to come home in the evening full of stories about how bad the road was and how many times the jeep broke down. Jeribai recalls one incident in particular.

'One night we were returning to Jamkhed after a clinic 40 kilometres away. The road back to Jamkhed was through winding hills with steep ravines on either side. Suddenly the lights of the jeep went off. It was a dark night, well past midnight. There was no moon and the driver could not see the road. The jeep rolled to a stop just inches from the edge of the ravine.

'The only light available was a small flashlight. All of us got scared. We could not see anything in front of us. One of the men got down and walked in front of the jeep showing the way. The light of the flashlight was so small that we could hardly see a few inches in front of us. It was a lonely spot. Usually no vehicle used the road after dark. Suddenly, a truck appeared around the bend and by the light of the truck we saw that we were just inches from the edge of the road. A few more inches and we would have plunged down the steep ravine! We returned home in the light of the truck.'

Another night the team came home all excited. They had been to a clinic 36 kilometres away. 'That night there were more patients than usual and it got late. The village people were concerned. They told us that it was dangerous to travel after dark because the hills were infested with robbers. They agreed to accompany us part of the way. As we entered the winding hill road, we saw boulders lying across the road. Our village friends started talking loudly to each other as if to let the thieves know that we were protected. Then we saw three men wearing nothing but loin cloths, their oiled dark skin shimmering in the moonlight, quietly slipping away from behind one of the rocks. They had spears in their hands. They disappeared into the night. Our village friends got out of the jeep, and removed the boulders that blocked the road. They assured us that we had nothing to fear and that we could go on.'

Although frightening, such incidents assured us that the village people were concerned for our safety. We continued visiting the villages mornings and evenings, often returning home late at night. The nurses had an exciting time caring for sick patients in the villages and their increased responsibility in patient care kept their morale up.

Nurses face clinical challenges

The nurses often proved their capabilities in handling difficult situations. One day Jeribai and a couple of ANMs and paramedical workers had gone to Telengshi to conduct a village clinic. A woman with severe B-complex deficiency came to the clinic. Jeribai administered B-complex injection. Within a few seconds the woman complained of nausea, started sweating and went into shock. She became pulseless. Jeribai quickly gave her an adrenaline injection, started intravenous fluids and with other emergency measures revived the woman. While she and her team-mates were struggling with the patient, a huge crowd gathered around them. As the patient regained consciousness, the people burst into applause and congratulated her. Jeribai was too shaken up to respond. 'What could this crowd have done to me if the patient had died?' It was too frightening even to think about.

Another evening, Akka was at the Jamkhed clinic. A middle-aged man was brought in. A priest from a nearby village, he was in shock with profuse bleeding. Some young boys in the village had teased him about his affairs with women. Angered by this accusation, the priest took a knife and cut off his own penis. When he was brought to the hospital, Akka deftly caught the bleeding points, stopped the bleeding and sutured the wound. In the meantime, the laboratory technician got the young men to donate blood and the timely intervention saved his life. These incidents gave the nurses confidence in dealing with emergencies they would encounter in the villages when they were on their own.

Once these curative clinics were well established it was time to move into the community and start the health surveys and health education.

Re-orienting health professionals

Jeribai had always worked in the hospital and had no interest in survey and preventive work. She recalls, 'I was trained as a nurse. To me health meant patient, doctor, and nurse. The nurse faithfully carried out doctor's orders and made the patient comfortable. I enjoyed the hospital work and did not mind this new adventure, long hours of work, the poor salary and poor living conditions. What I dreaded most was going to the village and visiting individual's houses. I had heard that villagers insulted nurses and sometimes physically molested them. Every morning I would get up and begin to cry at the thought of going to the village. Dr Mabelle heard about my fears and so personally took me to Patoda, a village 10 kilometres away. Together we did a house-to-house survey. She came with me for a whole week and showed me how to greet people and explain what we were doing, how to ask questions and observe and document information faithfully. Sometimes we were mistaken for government family planning workers and village people were rude to us. But when they realised that we were from CRHP and interested in their mothers and children and not just family planning their attitude changed and they were cordial and cooperative.'

As Jeribai continued to be involved in preventive health activities their importance began to dawn on her. She says, 'One day, as I went around trying to persuade women to have prenatal care, I saw a woman in her eighth month of pregnancy with swelling of the feet, and complaining of severe headache. I told her that I would examine her and take her blood pressure and examine her urine. The woman refused. She only wanted a pill for her headache. I told the woman to come to the hospital immediately because there was the possibility of her getting convulsions and going into coma. The woman refused and shut the door on me. The village women laughed at me, saying that many women get swelling of the legs during pregnancy and there was no need to worry about it.'

Jeribai was worried about the woman as she returned from the village. The next day the same woman who refused advice was brought to the hospital with convulsions, Jeribai felt she had failed to prevent this woman from going into eclampsia. Fortunately, the woman recovered in the hospital but at the cost of losing her baby and at grave risk to her own life. After this incident, when Jeribai visited the village every pregnant woman wanted to be examined and was ready to take advice from her. Jeribai became enthusiastic about going to the villages for health education and preventive programmes. She became convinced of the importance of changing people's attitudes towards better health. Jeribai went on to take charge of the field activities. She continues to train ANMs and village health workers.

Continuous team training

Tuesday afternoon was set aside for staff training. In the beginning Raj or I conducted these classes. Gradually the team members took turns leading the sessions. Everyone, even the cashier and driver, was expected to participate in this training. From Akka to the watchman, everyone learned to give simple health messages to the people. Most village people do feel culturally closer to the watchman or the driver. They consult people who are more on their own cultural level. As they leave the clinic they ask the advice of the aide or the watchman at the gate and eventually follow the guidance given.

Apart from the nurses, ANMs and paramedical workers like Mr Vasant Jadhav, most workers did not have formal training and sometimes had little or no education. Many were school drop-outs. Those who were willing to learn and work hard joined us and stayed on. We tried to bring out their talents and impart new skills.

Mr Sitaram Wade enlivens the team

Soon more members were added to the team. Mr Sitaram Wade, who had been a prosperous cloth merchant, had plunged wholeheartedly into the freedom movement when he was young. As an active member of an underground patriotic organisation he had harassed the British Government.

One day, Mr Sitaram Wade came to us and said, 'I suffered in the freedom struggle, I lost my business. After independence, the leadership has ignored me since I belong to a minority caste. The values I had are no longer respected by the new leadership. I am quite disillusioned with them. For the past six months I have been watching you and your team. Your team members are equally dedicated. I would like to work with you. My children are all grown up and I am not interested in making money. I want to join you. I do not know how to give injections, but I can use my oratory and communication skill to spread the message of child care and family planning. I know all these villages and I can be your liaison.'

We had known about Mr Wade and his exploits during the freedom struggle. He was a gifted orator with a booming voice, often described as a cannon. With his treasury of poetry, humorous stories and quotations for every occasion, and fine singing, we thought he would be a good person for health education in the villages. Mr Wade was enthusiastic and full of life. He brought joy and laughter to the overworked team.

Attending the Tuesday training sessions, Mr Wade understood the messages and helped prepare the songs and dialogues. Under his tuition, the nurses and other workers learned how to speak in public and teach village people. He translated the health messages into songs and taught nurses and other workers to communicate. While accompanying the team to different villages he taught mothers about nutrition, child care and family planning.

As an underground political worker during the British Raj, Mr Wade had been to all the villages in the area. People knew and respected him. He was very helpful in identifying honest leaders, genuinely interested in the poor.

He especially taught the nurses and other field staff how to conduct themselves in the villages. As he participated in the training classes and discussions, he saw the connection between social issues and health. Child marriage, dowry, status of women, untouchability and corruption were some of the topics that he discussed with the village health workers.

Mr Wade often came to our home and narrated his past experiences. He always left us laughing as he told about his escapades. One evening he came in looking worried and depressed. He had noticed a light patch on his arm. His rudimentary knowledge of leprosy made him suspect that he had the disease. Not only was he worried about the disease, but more importantly, he did not know whether the team members would accept him. In his experience, leprosy patients were always driven out of the home. We examined him carefully and confirmed the diagnosis. We had snacks together and Raj held him and reassured him that he would have treatment. He would remain in the team and that there would be absolutely no change in his status.

Mr Wade was afraid to tell his wife and children about the disease. The health team, on the other hand, accepted him in spite of the disease. This made him feel closer to the team members. He started taking special interest in leprosy patients, eagerly learning about the disease from Mr Jadhav, the leprosy supervisor, and later devoting his time working as a leprosy supervisor.

The Story of Prakash Khandagale

One day a tall woman came to our house. Behind her stood a young man looking down, rather shy and uncommunicative. This is how Mr Prakash Khandagale was introduced to us.

The mother dominated the conversation. 'I want you to give my son any job,' she said. 'I lost my husband a few months ago and I am left with five growing children. Mr Khandagale has finished high school and he has done a typing course. Please give him a job. He will do anything you ask him to do.'

Prakash spoke very little. He had a slight lisp and was aware of it. Raj promised him a job. He started working in the office and we found he had many skills. Now he says, 'I was given a job as a typist and clerk. In the adjoining room the nurses used to give injections. During weekly classes I learned about health. We were encouraged to learn from each other. The nurses taught me to give injections. I was able to relieve the nurses.

'We were taught health education through flash cards and charts prepared at the project. Because my handwriting is good, I was given responsibility for making audio-visual material. I also had a talent for writing poems and articles. At Jamkhed everybody was encouraged to use his talent for the health service. Wade and Ganpat had similar interests. We sat together and composed many songs on health education.

'All around me team members were learning from each other. Surely I have acquired enormous knowledge. As time went by I began to go outdoors with the team. I learned to interview people and do surveys. While doing surveys in the villages, I saw the plight of leprosy patients and wanted to work for them. I was sent for the leprosy training. While I took care of leprosy patients in the villages I was introduced to farmers' clubs. In addition to caring for leprosy patients I worked in the villages in water and land development and afforestation programmes.

'My hidden talents have blossomed in this project and instead of just remaining as a clerk I have become one with the people. As a result of my work I see barren lands covered with lush forests. The fields that were full of weeds today produce nourishing grains and vegetables. In the early years people at Khandvi and at Kharda threw rocks at us. In the same villages good leadership has developed. Telangshi village was full of criminals. The people were rude. Yet from the same village came Muktabai who flew to America and told the world how she as an illiterate woman transformed Telangshi.'

Prakash Khandagale discussing an A-frame with farmers

Vasant Jadhav; development worker, leprosy supervisor, laboratory technician

Another member of the team was Mr Vasant Jadhav, a trained leprosy technician who had been working in another institution. He was not happy with his job of going around giving medicines to the leprosy patients in the villages. Since leprosy has a stigma, no one in the villages wanted to be identified with Mr Jadhav the leprosy worker. He had no respect from society and was therefore frustrated when he approached us for a job as leprosy technician. He learned about mother and child health, tuberculosis and eye care in the weekly training classes. At Jamkhed the leprosy control programme was integrated with other health programmes. As a member of the health team, he was accepted by the people. Local people had respect for the project and therefore he got cooperation from them. Later on, after the formation of farmers' clubs and the introduction of the village health workers, his job became easy. Over the years Mr Jadhav's vision has broadened from just distributing dapsone tablets to leprosy patients to providing holistic care to the people. His association with village organisations made him a development worker. He is interested in medical technology and shows an aptitude in the laboratory. Since learning to do many of the laboratory tests, he often helps out in the hospital as a laboratory technician. When asked what made him stay in Jamkhed for twenty years, he said, 'I am not alone, I have the support of the health team and the village community. I have job satisfaction because I contribute to the total life of people. I feel I am recognised and people value my service.'

Not all who joined us in the beginning stayed on. Two of the ANMs left after six months because they found they could not adjust to village life. Another nurse got married and left us to join her husband.

We had recruited a social worker from Bombay. He had no exposure to the villages during his training. Yet he did not feel it necessary to have any orientation to village work. He felt he was superior to other health team members because of his training in Bombay and could not relate to them. He was not willing to change his timetable to suit the village people. He did not stay long with us.

A retired government officer came as general administrator. He wore a starched uniform, believed in hierarchy and refused to sit on the floor with the rest of us. His condescending attitude to the villagers and rudeness to the daily labourers created unhappiness in the community. Local leaders requested us to make him leave and promised to find someone in his place.

The team has gradually expanded to about fifty people. Those who could not be comfortable as part of the team left after a few months. Most of the original team members still continue to work with the project. From the beginning, social, economic and political dimensions of health were well understood by the team which is now broad based, consisting not only of doctors and nurses, but also of social workers, agriculture experts, politicians, construction workers, mechanics and village people.

None of these people is in any way exceptional. The majority of the team members came from Jamkhed block and from the nearby districts of Ahmednagar and Aurangabad. Many did not even have the qualifications necessary to get a job. Yet every person has talents and the potential to grow. There are people like Wade and Prakash Khandagale in every community. We have to identify them and use their talents in health and development work.

The educational level of these non-professional team members ranges from illiteracy to junior college level education. Monetary gain has not been a motivating force. In fact, most technical people receive far less than they would earn in government service.

Job satisfaction is what attracts them. From driver to doctor, every one finds fulfilment in his or her job. There is scope to develop individual talents and improve existing skills. Career advancement is dependent on practical innovation rather than degrees and seniority. Therefore a spirit of enquiry pervades the team.

Many workers describe the Jamkhed project as a 'river flowing with knowledge freely available to all.' All are encouraged to share information and experience and learn from each other. Over the years many of the team members have acquired multiple skills. This prevents boredom and also reduces the number of personnel required.

Workers with qualifications for jobs in the cities do not want to go to the villages, and there is no point in sending them where they are not interested. On the other hand, local village people can be trained to provide necessary services in the villages. The principles of teamwork rather than strict hierarchy, continuous training and improvement of skills results in a free flow of communication between different members of the group. Sharing of responsibilities and involvement in the planning have contributed to the smooth working of the team.

This realistic approach has helped us to keep the team members together for the last twenty-two years.

CHAPTER 8

The health centre:
discovering village talent

RAJ

One day in March 1971, Shri Mishrilalji came to us. He said: 'I am a 75-year-old man. Anything can happen to me. Please accept my gift of five acres of land to build the hospital.' An auspicious time on Monday at twelve noon was selected for signing the legal document. A large crowd of his clan, neighbours and friends gathered to witness the occasion. The local government officials and the lawyers prepared the deed. Flowers and sweets were brought to celebrate the occasion. Fifteen minutes before the appointed time, Shri Mishrilalji had a massive heart attack and died. A sudden silence fell on the crowd and the family members were grief-stricken.

We were dismayed. What was in store for us? How would the superstitious villagers react to this incident? Would they blame us for the tragedy?

After thirteen days, the official period of mourning was over. Shri Mishrilalji's two sons invited us to their home. They announced that they were going to keep their father's promise. Not only would they donate five acres as promised by their father, but they would donate two more acres of land. They were glad that he was in the act of doing a good deed as he left this world!

An advisory board for CRHP

We had established clinics in Jamkhed and twenty-five surrounding villages. As we met with leaders from these villages to discuss how we could be effective in our health work, leaders from different villages made various suggestions. Soon the leaders decided to form a Central Advisory Committee so that they could channel their suggestions

95

through one body. We discussed the composition of this advisory body, ensuring that the ordinary village men, women, Dalits and other marginalised groups participated in it.

Shri Abasaheb Nimbalkar was chosen as chairman and Mr Bansilalji Kothari as secretary. The committee met informally once every two months or so. We freely shared with them all information on our financial resources, our professional abilities and limitations. This transparent sincerity motivated them to help us genuinely in whatever way they could. The members of the committee helped in gaining the cooperation of the village communities. They introduced us to more village leaders. Mr Kothari often went round with us in the evenings and introduced us to the various leaders and villages. The committee members were especially helpful when we established 'fee for service' guidelines, explaining to the people how important it was that those who afford should pay the prescribed fees for health care. With their intimate knowledge of the economics of the people, they were able to tell us how much people could afford. They advised us to keep Jamkhed clinic open throughout the day to make it more convenient for patients travelling long distances.

The committee also found people like Ramling Varade and Ganpat Waibhat and Khansaheb to help us in our work. Their contributions to the project are described later.

Building a health centre

Indeed, the Advisory Committee played a crucial role in the development of the health centre in Jamkhed. They pointed out that the health programme had extended to many villages but the existing makeshift facilities were not adequate. A proper operating room to deal with obstetrical and surgical emergencies to support our village clinics was a pressing need. They suggested that we build sufficient facilities in Jamkhed to take care of the increasing work, and offered to provide volunteers for building and supervision and to supply stones, bricks and sand for building.

First, we need water

We took up the plan to establish a more permanent health centre at Jamkhed, accepting the 2 hectares of land given by the sons of Shri Mishrilalji. One question loomed large. During the three summer months water was just not available in Jamkhed. Was there underground water in the land that Shri Mishrilalji had given us? The people feared that if we did not get enough water for the health centre, we would abandon the project.

The tube well

We too felt that a good water supply was important, both for construction of the centre, and later for patients and staff. The wells in the vicinity had dried up. The geologists we consulted were rather pessimistic about striking water in that locality, since the whole area had very little subsoil water, but we decided to drill a tube well.

The necessary drilling rig was hired and we started. Water is precious to people, so not surprisingly, a huge crowd turned out to watch. There was much chanting and fervent prayers by priests of different religions. A real solidarity filled the air. Soon the people started cheering as the water gushed out of the ground. As the drilling continued, more water continued to flow. There was much singing and dancing that day. Now that water was available we could go ahead with our building plans.

We did not want the health centre to be a stereotypical hospital, and it did not necessarily have to meet standards set by the urban elite. Because it was supporting the health activities in the villages, it should be a place where ordinary villagers felt comfortable. In order to reduce patient costs, we hoped to encourage relatives to participate in the care of the patients, and so we wanted to provide enough facilities and space for relatives to stay and cook.

Exploring building plans: time and money are the essence

Initially we consulted an architect to draw plans for the health centre. He showed us several designs of conventional city hospitals and was not interested in our ideas of simplicity and relevance to village conditions. He was out to sell his modern hospital plan, telling us that the health centre alone would cost us at least Rs:700 000 ($100 000). We did not plan to spend so much on the building as there was also the equipment and other furnishings to buy. We gave up on him.

After a discussion of our difficulties with the Advisory Committee, Mr Kothari introduced us to Mr Ramling Varade. 'Mr Varade is just the man for you as he is a storekeeper and foreman working in the government building and construction department. He has only seven years of formal schooling but we consider him to be an expert in building work. Most of the recent buildings in Jamkhed have been built under his guidance. He is known for his integrity.'

Mr Varade was both frugal and practical. After listening to our ideas, he made initial drawings for the health centre. He explained some of the problems facing us: wood was expensive and not readily available; cement had to be procured through government permits. Using these materials, it would take two or three years to build the health centre. How could we wait that long? We saw that the local doctor was building his house and that even after two years of work, it was not complete.

Mr Bansilalji Kothari told us that he had seen a building being constructed in Ahmednagar with prefabricated steel and aluminum sheets. The team of workers came from Spicer College in Pune. Under an 'earn and learn' scheme, students put up these prefabricated structures. We requested that they build our health centre and the college agreed. Within six months they finished the building, which has a built-up area of 10 000 square feet. There are facilities for outpatient and inpatient care, X–rays, a clinical laboratory and operating room. The total cost of the health centre building came to Rs:250 000 ($32 500).

Not only did we save time, but we gained a structure that could be dismantled easily! We could move without too much trouble if we did not succeed in Jamkhed. Then residences for the staff had to be built. Again the village community deputed Mr Ramling Varade to help us with the plan, which he did willingly. He understood that we wanted buildings in keeping with the life style of the people. After making many valuable suggestions, he finally drew up the blueprints.

Even after the completion of the health centre and residences and other buildings, Mr Varade continued to be associated with us. A well-read, self-taught man, he had attained the highest scholarship in the national language, Hindi. He was quite a character, with an ideology and ideas about the Indian social structure that were totally opposite to our own. He was therefore one of the few persons in Jamkhed with whom we could have stimulating discussions. Mr Varade firmly believed that the Indian social structure is not oppressive to the poor, but that the poor themselves are responsible for their poverty. He did not agree with our idea of empowering the women and the poor. His strong beliefs helped us to understand another point of view. However, he respected us for our concern for the people. Out of that respect he eventually helped us construct over two hundred dams and an equal number of wells. He taught a large number of people simple techniques of conserving water by building check dams. He has consistently refused remuneration for his services.

People's involvement reduced building cost

The farmers donated stones, lime and sand from their fields for the buildings. Mr Chandulalji, son of Mr Mishrilalji, who donated the land, procured building materials at no profit from shopkeepers. As a professional contractor, he helped us keep costs down. This cooperative effort resulted in the buildings costing only half of the market rate.

In the meantime we applied for funds to EZE (The Central Agency), a non-governmental donor agency from Bonn, Germany, which was prepared to pay the capital costs of the health centre and other buildings. The agency could not believe that good building work could be done at such a low cost, so they sent an architect to investigate. He was impressed with the work, and appreciated the people's participation in reducing the construction costs. He said, 'Most of our recipients exceed their building budgets and ask for building grants. You have constructed good buildings at half the expected cost!' The money thus saved was used for other buildings.

From the EZE grants, we equipped the health centre. We kept in mind the principle that the more expensive and complicated the equipment, the higher the maintenance costs. So, wherever possible we tried to make use of local materials and designed appropriate equipment. Ordinary table lamps mounted on stands proved good operating room lights at almost one-tenth of the cost of regular operating room lamps. An X-ray machine was needed to help in the diagnosis of tuberculosis or for long bone fractures. A simple X-ray machine powered by ordinary domestic current is sufficient for the purpose. This choice of appropriate equipment and technology considerably reduced the cost for the poor villagers.

From constructing buildings to artificial limbs

As the work expanded, new members were added to the team. One was Ganpat. Our first impression of Mr Ganpat Waibhat was that of a man in tattered clothes counting bricks and stones for health centre construction. He had been recommended for this task by Mr Varade and local leaders. Ganpat's father had died while he was young and his mother walked out on him leaving him to the care of his grandmother, who imparted values of integrity and hard work. After seven years of schooling, he joined his grandmother in selling snacks at the weekly market. They did not make enough money to support his wife and four children and so remained poor.

Mr Ganpat describes his journey that began with this simple job. 'When I heard about the Comprehensive Rural Health Project, I wished to get a job there. I was poor, the village people had no respect for me and I was unable to get a job. I had no education and I thought to myself that it is not possible. Then Mr Varade offered me a job on the construction site. I was overjoyed; as I sat on the rubble counting bricks I would imagine myself doing many things around the health centre.

'As I helped Mr Varade, he trained me in different aspects of building construction. I worked very hard and spent all my time observing and soon I was given more and more responsibility in building supervision.

'I found that working in the project was different. Here there was no hierarchy. There was no master–servant relationship. All not only worked together, but shared their knowledge with others. I thought to myself that here knowledge flows like a stream, sustaining life as it flows on. Dada (Raj) and Bai (Mabelle) have come with a lot of knowledge. Regardless of their educational status, those who come

Mr Ganpat Waibhat counting stones

100

in contact with them not only acquire that knowledge but they in turn learn to share it with others. **There are so many educated people in the world who have knowledge, but they are like stagnant cesspools because their knowledge does not flow.**

'I was determined to take any new challenge and work hard to prove myself. The more I worked, the more responsibilities I was given. I learned about conservation of water and soil and later supervised well digging and land levelling under the Food for Work programmes.

'The project had bought puppets for health education but the man in charge of these had gone on leave. I approached the doctors and asked if I could show these puppets in the villages. I was afraid that they might not like the idea. The doctors made me to sit down on a chair and gave me a cup of tea. Then they asked me how I was going to do it. I recited a few dialogues and demonstrated how I would show the puppets. These expensive puppets were given to me for practice. I was overwhelmed with the confidence that Dada and Bai had in me. Since I was a poor man, the villagers had not entrusted me even with one rupee credit. I went home and practised the hand movements and dialogues the whole night.

'We had a get-together with the staff, and a friend of mine and I presented a humorous skit. We both acted well and kept the audience

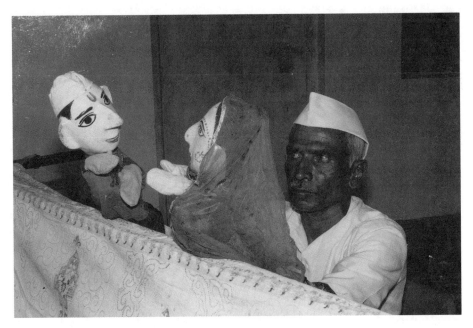

Ganpat and his puppets

101

roaring with laughter. Dada asked me to form a drama group in the villages. It would be good for our health education. We formed drama groups in the villages and in Jamkhed. We all worked very hard. Our club was awarded a prize at the state level and I too got an award for my acting.

'As I look back at my experiences in this project, it looks as if I am galloping on a horse and, like kings of the past, I am conquering different fields. I learned to make puppets and helped in making decorative articles. The project had started artificial limb manufacture under the leadership of Moses Guram. In my spare time I would sit with Moses and learn about limb making. I was selected to go to Jaipur with Moses and learn about the Jaipur foot (artificial lower limb for amputees) from a world-famous orthopedic surgeon, Dr Sethi. For three weeks I absorbed what Dr Sethi personally taught me about limb making and we returned to Jamkhed. We went to see Dada (Raj). After talking about our experiences at Jaipur, Dada said, "I have admitted four amputees. You have learned a new skill, so provide them with the prosthesis – the Jaipur foot."

'That night I went home and wept. What confidence is placed in me. Even without seeing my work four patients were ready to be fitted with prostheses! I had never been out of Jamkhed in my life, and yet was sent over 1000 kilometres away to Jaipur, to learn from a world famous doctor, who did not have time to teach other doctors. I pinched myself to see if I was dreaming. Here was Ganpat to whom the villagers did not care to return greetings. I had no self-value. Today I am called doctor. People respect me. The project has given me dignity. I have learned that anyone can do what I have done. It only takes the innate intelligence that most people have, hard work and proper guidance to succeed. I am continuing to work and take up new challenges as they come.

'I am so grateful for opportunities to learn, that I am determined to work even harder for the project. Some people ask what is there in the project and I say discipline, love and cooperation are some of the qualities of our team.'

Mr Ganpat's creative talents have been particularly useful in the area of appropriate technology. Whether it is decorating the hall for a function, landscaping, staging a health exhibition, designing toilets or making artificial limbs, Ganpat is ready to put his mind to it. He comes up with ideas that are practical and relevant to the local situation.

Today Ganpat is a confident man, respected in the community. He has improved his farm and does not need to have a regular job at the centre. But he continues to work with us because of the many opportunities to use his talents and skills.

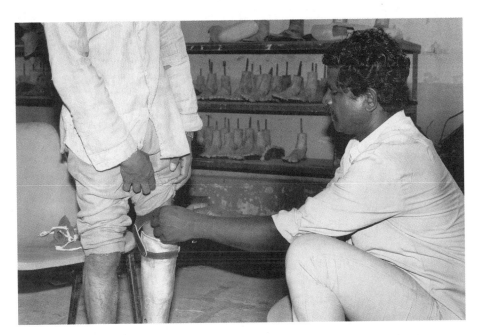

Moses fitting a limb

The story of Moses the construction helper

Another person who joined the team was Mr Moses Guram, who comes from the east coast of India. His family was poor and there was not enough to eat. As a young boy, he left home in search of a job, and he landed in Pune, 1300 kilometres away. There he found a job as a helper at Spicer College. He came to Jamkhed with the college team to build the health centre.

After the building was finished, Mr Moses wanted to stay. He had fallen in love with our young cook. He had only three years of schooling, but had a strong physique, so we gave him the job of night watchman. An industrious fellow, Mr Moses helped the motor mechanics and also spent his time watching Mr Ravikant Bhanushali, the X–ray technician and electrician. Every worker is expected to share his knowledge and skill with those who show interest. Soon Moses learned from Mr Bhanushali who also taught him all about electrical circuits and how to operate the generator. As Moses showed aptitude and interest, he acquired new skills. He went to Jaipur to learn to make the Jaipur foot from the orthopedic surgeon, Dr P. K. Sethi, who had developed a prosthesis appropriate for the Indian life-style. Today Moses is in charge of a workshop that manufactures artificial limbs, calipers and other equipment for physically handicapped persons. Moses reflects: 'I was trusted and knowledge was freely available at Jamkhed. Others shared their knowledge and skill with me. I was nobody. Today people call me doctor. Many doctors and professionals take my advice. I have been associated with manufacture of four thousand artificial limbs and calipers that were provided to needy people in the state of Maharashtra. The Lions clubs and Rotary Clubs organise camps. They invite me with the team to manufacture limbs. I see my picture appear in the newspapers.

'You cannot imagine the joy I get. Twenty-four hours a day I keep thinking of how to improve the prosthesis. How can I make the caliper simple and light enough that a small child can use it? I have a dozen young men working with me. I share all the knowledge I have with them and encourage them to be like me. My brothers and sisters are working in the Middle East and call me to join them. I tell them, "**Money cannot buy the joy that I have in my work!**"'

It was difficult in the beginning for professionals like ourselves to entrust semi-literate people with planning and implementing major programmes. We learned not to underestimate local talents. Over the years we have learned that trust leads to increased self-confidence bringing out many hidden and dormant talents in people.

CHAPTER 9

Community participation: farmers' clubs

RAJ

'*Community participation is not inherent, it has to be developed.*'[1]

The community leaders had invited us to work in the Jamkhed area. They introduced us to the village communities, provided accommodation for the staff and the health centre, and helped recruit workers. We considered participation by the leaders alone insufficient and endeavoured to involve ordinary villagers in all health activities, from planning to implementation to evaluation. We felt that unless poor people were involved in the planning and implementation, their needs would be overshadowed by those of the elite. The constraints of limited resources would make it mandatory for the village people to take part of the responsibility for their health, and their participation would ensure more universal acceptance and utilisation of health programmes. We needed to know more about their perceptions of health and their expectations from health professionals.

Many aspects of health need total community participation. For example, the physical environment of a village needs to be protected by the whole community rather than by only a few individuals. To eradicate many harmful traditions and superstitions requires community action. Much of the under-nutrition among women and children is chronic starvation and is directly related to poverty and to the low status of women. The solution is not to build a medical clinic, but to change the people's attitude towards women, children and the poor. Non-medical interventions such as better agriculture and proper distribution of food could alleviate the medical problem of malnutrition. Similarly, access to safe drinking water for the whole community

105

could control water-borne infections. Community collaboration in all sectors of development is essential for the health of the people.

Organising communities

The village leadership came from members of the dominant caste who had ruled the villages for centuries. The village council consisted of members of the upper castes and did not follow principles of democracy. Local Panchayat members had syphoned off the fruit of development for themselves and their relatives. So despite government and NGO projects and aid, most of the poor people remained poor or became even more destitute. The ruling caste group could not truly represent poor people. We therefore decided to bring together poor people to represent themselves. To do so meant changing attitudes in order to change conditions. Oppression continued for centuries had left the poor, low caste groups diffident and fatalistic. They were both apathetic and cynical about their own improvement as well as being suspicious of outsiders like us. Since the dominant groups never listened to them, they remained closed and fearful of expressing their opinions freely. CRHP tried to instill confidence in the poor people by making a point of visiting them and organising them. They were given priority in health care.

The village is not a homogenous structure

In the villages, people are separated by caste; the dominant caste groups keep away from the low caste groups. A more representative group of people from all strata of society had to be formed. Since different caste groups did not freely socialise, we devised some excuses to bring them together. One such attempt was a game of volleyball. In several villages, including Ghodegaon and Pimpalgaon, we initiated a game of volleyball and invited young men from different caste groups to play. Since women had no place in the village society and did not participate in any activity outside the home and work place, we decided firstly to involve the men. One of the CRHP social workers stayed in the village and ensured that the poor and low caste villagers participated in the game.

The volleyball game was an innocuous pastime and met with no objection. Every evening, many men gathered to play or watch the game. After the game was over, they continued to sit around and chat. The discussions often centred around their problems with agriculture, poverty, credit from the banks and migration to the city in search of jobs.

106

Volleyball was open to all. As both rich and poor came to play, they were drawn together in discussions. Some were genuinely interested in improving their agricultural livelihood but did not know how to proceed. They needed support and a forum to express themselves. Others talked about the need for cooperation among themselves to deal with their problems. Soon these informal meetings after the volleyball game became more organised. They decided to call these groups farmers' clubs, (FC) since many participants were involved in agriculture-related occupations.

We also found some other strategies to bring village communities together. In Bavi, young people were organised around a project of building a community hall for the whole village. CRHP encouraged people of different castes to work together. Out of this group effort a farmers' club was formed. In Zikree and Ashta, the young people were interested in acting in dramas. Mr Ganpat Waibhat of CRHP helped them with acting and different caste groups were drawn together to form farmers' clubs. In Halgaon young people gathered to form singing groups. CRHP helped them to get musical instruments.

The farmers' clubs were not rigid organisations with a hierarchy of office bearers, but loose, informal groups. From time to time they collected membership fees, each club deciding the amount and frequency

Farmers' club meeting

107

of payments according to the ability of the individual villagers. Those who could not pay in cash contributed in kind or labour.

Well-to-do farmers quickly recognised the benefits of such an organisation. The poor, on the other hand, were suspicious because they never benefitted from any new programme aimed at improving their lot. But CRHP had demonstrated to the poor through curative services, water development and community kitchens that we cared for them. We had to be diplomatic in discouraging the better off farmers from dominating the groups and in helping the poor to take leadership. In some villages where the dominant castes made it difficult to organise the poor, we had to abandon the idea of forming farmers' clubs temporarily. Later on, successful farmers' clubs themselves went to such villages and helped with the organisation of new clubs. In four or five villages, the political leaders felt so threatened that they foiled every attempt to form a farmers' club.

Farming interests lead to seminars

The farmers' clubs needed information on various methods of farming, credit through banks, and access to seeds and fertilisers from reliable sources. CRHP agreed to help the members by holding three-day seminars every three months at Jamkhed.

Experts from the nearby agricultural university were invited to talk to the village people about appropriate methods of agriculture. They taught new methods of dry land farming especially suited to the needs of the poor farmer. New varieties of seeds were introduced. Landless villagers learned about poultry and other farm animals such as goats and cows.

Government officials explained various agriculture and animal husbandry programmes meant for marginalised groups and made credit available to them.

In addition to the experts, successful local farmers shared their experiences. These sessions were much appreciated by the members, because the experienced farmers gave practical hints and ideas not covered by the experts.

The participants spent the evenings discussing issues relevant to their villages. They exchanged ideas with one another in small groups. These seminars became very popular; some seminars were attended by as many as four hundred farmers.

The seminar setting was the first opportunity that poor village people from different caste and social backgrounds had to come together and live together. So these seminars broke down social barriers. Initially, the high caste men did not share food with others, but when

Farmers' club three-monthly seminar

they saw the hospital staff freely socialising with the poor, they changed their behaviour. They also discussed social issues such as drunkenness, child marriage, the dowry system and unnecessary expenditure on weddings and death feasts. They discussed their own village problems and compared the progress they had made with that of other villages.

These seminars extended far beyond agriculture. They became the platform for discussing various issues related to health and development. As they became more popular, they covered a wide variety of subjects. Farmers' club members shared what they learned in the seminars with people from their own and neighbouring villages.

For four or five years the quarterly seminars were held in Jamkhed, attended by approximately three to four hundred farmers from sixty villages. As the numbers grew, these gatherings took place for a group of ten to fifteen villages in one village. The host village usually took care of the boarding and lodging of the participants. In their own villages the farmers' club members met once every couple of months, depending on village size and programmes the club undertook. The health team visited each farmers' club once a fortnight or once a month. Thus a continuous exchange of information went on among the farmers themselves and also with the health team.

Farmers' club – catalysts for village development

The primary purpose in developing the farmers' clubs was to form a local working group for health activities. Village people were organised around their self-interest in agriculture and related occupations. Many poor farmers did not have farm implements and often rented them from richer farmers at exorbitant costs. Several clubs bought farm implements, such as ploughs, seeders, spray pumps and winnowing machines for use by their members. CRHP helped them to procure the implements by providing 50 per cent of the capital in the form of loans. These implements were rented to farmers at a price they could afford. Similarly, farmers' club members procured good seeds and fertilisers and distributed them to their members. Local merchants and banks extended credit to them for this purpose.

Participating in activities such as these provided the villagers with opportunities to cooperate with one another and help the needy. The caste barriers among the poor people gradually disappeared. Farmers' clubs provided proper information on good agriculture and even worked with poor farmers in cultivating their lands. The Ghodegaon farmers' club helped develop 60 hectares of land belonging to Dalit farmers. Farmers' clubs in Halgaon, Rajuri and Khandvi helped improve the lands of poor people.

One major cause of rural indebtedness was food bought on credit. From July to September poor people often had to borrow grains from well-to-do farmers until their crop was ready to harvest in March. For a quintal (100 kilogrammes) of grain borrowed in August, they had to pay back two quintals in February; 100 per cent interest every six months. Often poor farmers did not have grain for repayment and had to sell off their land or their animals to settle the loan. The farmers' clubs developed grain banks. They collected food grains at harvest time and loaned them out to the poor farmers without interest. Food for Work coupled with these grain banks, abolished indebtedness for food in the area.

The farmers' club members put into practice what they learned at the seminars. Improved farming techniques helped them to increase farm income. Bavi and Ghodegaon farmers compared themselves with a couple of villages without farmers' clubs. They demonstrated that the village with active farmers' clubs had twice as much as food production as villages with no clubs.

Bavi had a farmers' cooperative that included almost every family in the village. The 150 hectare plot belonging to this cooperative remained fallow. The farmers' club members organised the cooperative to level the land, construct check dams and dig wells. Badam of

Bavi says, 'Bavi village was very poor and many village people stole the crops from surrounding villages to survive. Many of us used to migrate out to stave off starvation. But today we produce enough food to meet our needs and no one has to leave the village in search of food.'

We were aware that cooperatives among small farmers in India had often been tried and many had failed. Yet some cooperatives, such as the sugar factories, were successful. The strategy for success required maintaining a delicate balance between encouraging private enterprise while at the same time supporting cooperative efforts by which people could help others at the same time as they helped themselves.

Our experience with a cooperative society in Durgaon illustrates the difficulty of finding and keeping this balance. Forty Dalit families had been given by the Government about 150 hectares of land for a farming cooperative. They were also given loans to develop the land. An artesian well at the centre of the land produced abundant water, resulting in the added benefit of a stream. The Dalits did not use the water themselves because they had not been able to work well together. Instead, their wealthy neighbours used the water to grow sugar cane and effectively prevented the Dalits from using it. These people had previously used this land for grazing their cattle. They did not want these Dalits to prosper, so they kept them divided. If the Dalits tried to cultivate their land, the wealthy farmers sent in their cattle to destroy the crops.

The Dalit farmers wanted to form a club to get out of their indebtedness and to improve themselves. The CRHP social worker worked with them, introducing them to the proper officials for the many government programmes for the Dalits. They felt that they would be in a better position to guard their crops if they lived in the centre of their land. In the process, their ties with one another would also improve. The Government became interested and other NGOs also developed an interest because the land was fertile and the water was plentiful. But the people were not really ready to work together. We usually started with small programmes and as the people learned to work together and developed skills of decision making and self-determination, they increased their activities. But in Durgaon, the plans were made for them without waiting for them to develop themselves. The involvement of the Government and NGOs attracted too much attention. The neighbours with vested interests were powerful enough to divide the Dalits, thus ensuring that the cooperative was liquidated. The Dalit families were left only with a few goats. From the failure of this enterprise we learned how important it is for people to have enough time to develop their own self-confidence and to organise.

111

Only when people are clear about their own goals, can they face opposition and succeed. Time bound programmes often do not allow sufficient time for personal development. Ultimately, the people themselves have to decide what they want to do. Others cannot plan for them.

Concern for health begins: the veterinary worker

During the seminars and other informal gatherings, farmers' club members discussed aspects of health programmes. But villagers, we found, had more interest in their farm animals and the health of those animals than in the health of their families. Mr Madhukar Sastare, a prominent member of the Khandvi Farmers' Club, admits, 'If a woman or a child died there was not as much sorrow as when a cow or bullock died. Death of an animal meant economic hardship for the family. We villagers believed that women and children were expendable but our animals were not, because our livelihood depended on them.'

The farmers' clubs requested that we teach basic veterinary care to at least one member in each village. Veterinary courses were arranged. The young men selected by the farmers' clubs learned to give immunisations, treat simple common illnesses and improve the breed of animals, and were taught about different varieties of fodder. These veterinary workers became popular and they continue to improve their skills through refresher courses that are conducted from time to time. They have succeeded in preventing deaths of farm animals from epidemics and have helped improve the village economy. Increased milk supply and better incomes coupled with proper health education have improved the nutrition of mothers and children.

Child nutrition

Initial surveys in the area showed that 30 per cent of the children under five were severely malnourished. Vitamin A deficiency and anemia were common among mothers and children. Since most of the malnutrition was related to chronic starvation, the farmers' clubs were organised to improve food production and distribution in the area. In the early stages, club members helped establish community kitchens to feed the women and children. Initially CRHP contacted relief agencies like OXFAM, UK, and later the Churches Auxiliary for Social Action (CASA) to provide some food for these programmes. The farmers' clubs also collected food grains and other ingredients such as vegetables, oilseeds and coarse sugar. They cooked a nutritious porridge and distributed it every morning. The club members then identified

The morning feeding programme

lands in the village that they began to cultivate to provide food material. As they became better organised, they improved the land and added water resources. Gradually, over a period of eight to ten years, the community kitchens were phased out as nutritious food became available and village health workers provided nutrition education. The farmers' club members continued to weigh the children regularly and plot their weights on a 'Road to Health' card.

Health surveys

Once the farmers' clubs were well established and functioning, they became active in health concerns, beginning with health surveys of their own villages. Initially, the health team, consisting of the ANM and the paramedical workers collected health information by visiting village people and interviewing them. However the village people did not trust the strangers and often withheld information, giving only information that they thought would please the team. They also had reservations about exposing their own private affairs and would not readily divulge information related to abortions, economic status and certain diseases such as leprosy. There was a tendency not to talk about health conditions that they thought were a curse from a goddess or about treatment received from a local healer.

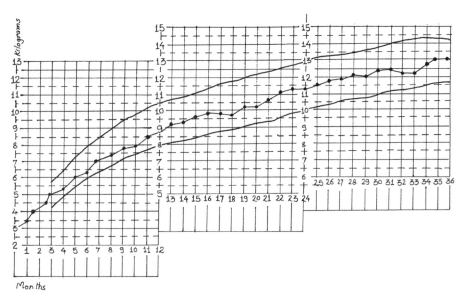

The Road to Health programme

Farmers' club members were a great help in collecting health information. They began by introducing the health team to the village people and assisted in collecting information. They were especially helpful in eliciting such sensitive information as attitudes to family

114

planning, incidence of abortion, feeding practices, and attitudes to chronic diseases such as leprosy and tuberculosis. The health team helped the club members understand medical terms. Soon, with the help of one or two paramedical workers, club members surveyed their own villages and learned to analyse the survey results. In this way they gained understanding of the health status of the village and we could involve them in formulating health programmes.

At first the health team was not enthusiastic about involving the village people in the health survey. But soon the teams were impressed at the way the farmers' club members were able to help them with the surveys. The village people felt proud that they were involved with professional workers and that they were able to contribute something useful. Close ties grew up between club members and the mobile health team. Members supported the team when it visited the village every week, usually deputing a couple of people to help in the clinic. They volunteered to register patients and kept the premises clean. In the clinic itself they helped with the patients. Club members drew up lists of children requiring immunisation, calling from house to house, convincing mothers to have their children immunised. They also helped in transporting patients to the health centre in emergencies. Most poor patients did not have a bullock cart, so club members would find one and take the patient. Whenever they could they sent a motorcycle ahead to get the centre jeep to meet the bullock cart on the way. In many villages they had their blood groups checked and lists of possible donors were kept handy. In case there was need for blood, the club members would bring some donors along.

The village epidemiologist

The discussions on health at the club gatherings focused on common illnesses and the high infant mortality rate. Soon club members began to understand relationships between the environment, sanitation, water pollution and insects, and the prevalence of disease.

No one had ever told these people that there were many things they could do to prevent disease. They had always felt that diseases were beyond their control. Now they found that even in their state of poverty they could take actions which would make a difference in their own health and in the health of their children.

Waste water

The farmers' clubs in Ghodegaon, Bavi and Khandvi decided to clean up their villages. The house drains opened into the streets. The waste water mixed with the rubbish heaps forming dirty puddles and fostering the breeding of flies and mosquitoes. The construction of simple soak pits in front of each house to drain the waste water underground was feasible. The members first constructed soak pits in front of their own houses. In the villages, houses are built right up to the road, so the soak pits had to be constructed in the street itself, but this was not difficult because the streets were not paved. A pit 1 m × 1 m × 1 m was dug in front of the drain opening, then filled with porous material such as sand and broken bricks and covered with planks. The efficiency of pits like these was demonstrated to the rest of the village people and farmers' clubs encouraged them to build more. Villages like Bavi and Khandvi successfully kept the waste water off the streets by this method.

Farmers' clubs and health education

The farmers' clubs often participated in health education activities. They wrote skits, songs and plays on various health and social issues. Clubs from Bavi, Khandvi, Ashta, Pimparkhed and other villages prepared dramas dealing with superstitions related to leprosy, tuberculosis and other common diseases and performed these plays in different villages. The club members also identified charlatans who were trying to mislead sick villagers and exposed their tricks. A farmers' club member explains, 'I saw a crowd gathered in my village. A man was pretending to be a divine healer having extraordinary powers. Village people had brought their sick relatives to him for healing. Among the many things placed before him was an egg that was jiggling about. He was moving a flame around the egg and chanting meaningless words. I picked up the egg and the shell broke and a beetle came out. The trickster had placed the beetle and carefully glued the egg shell back together. With the heat of the flame the beetle moved inside, causing the egg to move! The man was exposed and we asked him to leave the village. We identified many tricks like this and showed them to people, not only in our own village but in others as well.'

Shri Gulabrao Mandlik, another such 'healer,' worked not only in Bavi and surrounding villages, but spent the summer every year working among the slum dwellers in Bombay. The farmers' club members talked him out of cheating people. In the meantime his father, who had leprosy, was cured at CRHP. Gulabrao himself was impressed by the changes taking place in his village. He decided to give up his tricks and become an active member in the farmers' club. Remembering the many tricks by which he had hoodwinked his customers, he made up skits depicting healers like himself cheating people.

116

Later he went around the villages identifying healers like himself and exposing their tricks. He became effective as a health educator.

Participation in mass health activities

The members of different clubs get together and plan and implement mass programmes. For example they plan eye camps. In the first few years there were many blind people in the area needing cataract surgery. Club members were involved in the camp arrangements from registration of patients to holding the flash light during surgery and carrying the patients on the stretchers after operation. They also helped to keep the premises clean. In each camp over three hundred patients would undergo an operation. It was heartening to see centuries old traditions breaking down as people, old and young, rich and poor, high caste and Dalit all working together, sweeping the floor and doing chores which are normally considered degrading and so left to Dalit women.

Social change

Farmers' club members improved agriculture and nutrition for children, and the health of the people in the villages. The seminars at Jamkhed helped them to look at social issues in their own villages. One such issue was rural indebtedness. For example, a clever money lender came to live in one of the Jamkhed villages and gradually became a leader of the village. To gain popularity, he provided loans, often forcing the villagers to accept the loans. His practices set people against one another and in the meantime he bought up their lands and properties. Soon he controlled the village and perpetuated injustice there. After the farmers' club was formed in the village the members recognised the mischief that this individual had played. Club members arranged a series of meetings with the village people and explained to them how this individual had divided the community for his own benefit. The whole village recognised the harm he had done and asked the money lender to leave peacefully.

Empowerment

Traditionally the poor do not question the actions of the landlords. As people became empowered they expected the full cooperation from the landlords in the activities that affected the whole village. In one village, the farmers' club decided to construct a community hall. At a village meeting they decided that every family should participate in one way or other in building the hall. All able-bodied people provided

117

their labour. Some donated money or use of their bullock carts or building materials. One rich and powerful family refused to contribute. All the villagers decided not to work on their farm. The family realised that they had to cooperate with the village people. The club members then accepted them, but imposed a fine. Incidents like these demonstrated to the poor that they had power to improve cooperation for constructive work.

Drunkenness was a problem in many villages. The farmers' club members removed illegal distilleries from the villages and provided alternative jobs for those involved in bootlegging the cheap, often dangerous alcohol. They also persuaded alcoholics to stop drinking and imposed fines and other punishments on those who made a public nuisance of themselves. In Ghodegaon for example the farmers' club had a committee to punish those who made a nuisance of themselves after drinking. They had another committee to ensure that the justice meted out was not too harsh, for example, a severe beating. Once a man was caught and he was fined. The committee decided to install an electric street light with the fine money, in front of his house, as a constant reminder to him of his behaviour.

In Sakat and Telengshi some groups had formed robber gangs and were established dacoits. The farmers' club members helped them to improve their farms and give up stealing. In one village the farmers' club members could not persuade the gang leader to give up his business and had to expel him from the village by legal means.

Social norms forced poor people to spend exorbitant amounts of money on weddings. The wedding party had to provide a feast for the whole village. Poor people often went into debt in this way. The bride's parents were made to give an unreasonable amount of dowry. This custom not only put a family deep into debt but also led to ill treatment of young married girls by their in-laws and sometimes even to 'dowry deaths'. Child marriage, though illegal was common in villages. The club members encouraged parents not to get their daughters married before the age of eighteen, the legal age of marriage in India. The farmers' clubs arranged group weddings where brides were not made to give dowry and the wedding feast was shared by ten or twelve couples getting married on the same day. This practice of having group weddings has also helped to prevent illegal child marriage. These community weddings have become popular. Donations are collected to provide the household articles for the newly weds. The village people contribute expenses towards the wedding feast, canopy, flowers, music and procession. Sometimes wealthier members of the wedding party help defray the expenses. In a village it is common to see ten to fifteen couples getting married in one place. It also has helped to breakdown caste barriers. Traditionally, even if a Dalit has a wedding, he is expected to provide the raw materials to the high caste people in the village so that they can have a feast cooked separately for them in a different section of the village. In such community weddings the whole village participates. Couples belonging to different caste groups get married and have a single wedding feast. The food is cooked by volunteers who are people from different castes. There is total integration of the different communities.

As they became involved in village concerns, the farmers' club members began to understand the problems of women. They realised the importance of involving women in village improvement and allowed their own women to form women's organisations (Chapter 14).

This participation did not happen overnight. The interest of the people in their own health had to be cultivated. Each farmers' club had its own interests and own priorities in regard to agriculture water resources and afforestation. In Bavi they have been interested in watershed development. In Khandvi the farmers' club took an active part in an afforestation programme. The Bavi farmers' club was also interested in eradicating leprosy from their village. The only programmes common to all the villages are related to health.

Problems encountered

Organising these farmers' clubs was not easy. No village is homogeneous. Various factions and caste groups had to be brought together. This process was long and often frustrating requiring a lot of patience. We at CRHP had to be careful to keep a low profile. Vested interests were always a threat to the delicate bonds that were being formed. In villages where the leadership was well established, the power groups prevented people from coming together.

In some villages, the farmers' clubs tried to formalise their organisations by electing a president, secretary and treasurer. Soon we realised, members were spending their time campaigning for the posts and fighting among themselves, rather than doing constructive work. It was decided to keep these groups informal to ensure more active participation. We encouraged the groups to be more dynamic 'Movements' rather than static institutions.

The farmers' clubs also tended to enter into village power politics, with its numerous factions detrimental to genuine development. During and even after Panchayat election, factions often spent so much time fighting among themselves that active development work was abandoned. Defeated parties might sabotage programmes planned by the ruling party. We persuaded the clubs to avoid these kinds of futile exercises. Farmers' clubs worked hard to bring unanimous elections in the village and focus the Panchayat's attention on improving the village. This did not mean sweeping problems under the carpet and producing a false sense that everything was okay. However in some villages we felt that unanimous results would help in carrying out more community activities and in addressing social and justice issues such as caste discrimination.

The farmers' clubs also tended toward 'tidal' involvements as the men's interests ebbed and flowed. Their work in the fields was seasonal and they did not work every day as the women did. They brought this behaviour to their clubs also. The social worker had to constantly work with them to stimulate their interests. We had to continuously introduce new ideas. The people needed to be challenged from time to time. Sometimes they began to take the health teams and the village health worker for granted and expected the village health worker to do all the work by herself. Constant dialogue helped keep their interest in health alive.

By 1975 there were thirty farmers' clubs in Jamkhed block. Gradually this movement has spread to more than 110 villages. The clubs became the local executive group for all CRHP village activities.

People have lived for centuries as encapsulated groups. To break these barriers and bring them together needs patience. They lived together in master–servant relationships, and so needed to change their attitudes towards each other. They were also used to rivalry. The seminars at Jamkhed proved invaluable in breaking down some of these attitudes. Removing them from their own environment and providing opportunities to look at each other in a different light made a difference. Men of different caste groups and economic status attended these seminars. While at Jamkhed they had to socialise with their own fellow villagers. When they returned to their own village the bond created at Jamkhed could not be ignored. A platform was also provided for open and frank discussion on issues pertaining to exploitation and injustices in the villages and their own role in it. The process was slow. Social workers like Mr Arun Londhe spent time in the villages identifying men who were socially minded and anxious for change. Bringing together like-minded people and providing a platform to voice their hopes and aspirations proved useful in the formation of these clubs.

1 Madan T N. Community involvement in health policy. Socio-structural and dynamic aspects of health belief. Society, Science and Medicine 1987; 25(6): 615–620.

CHAPTER 10

Times of crisis: stepping stones for progress

MABELLE

Drought and famine

Perhaps the greatest factor in improving the conditions of the poor was the involvement of the people themselves. Opportunities to enable this involvement presented themselves particularly at times of crisis. We were able to put forward alternative means of coping with drought and famine and their repercussions, especially on the very poor. Indeed, a crisis of drought and famine in the early 1970s led to vast improvements in the water supply, in child health care and in employment generally. Times of crisis became the platform on which our objectives as health workers met the felt needs of the people. This dynamic meeting of interests was where change took place. We were able to facilitate the poor people to organise and help themselves and to challenge such age old traditions as caste discrimination and virtual slave labour.

No water: what does it mean?

During our second year of work at Jamkhed, there was no rain at all. Day after day farmers looked anxiously at blue skies where no clouds were to be seen. All day long the howling wind scattered the dust across the parched brown fields. The monsoon season came and went with still no sign of rain. This cycle of drought, which occurs about once every ten years, made conditions very difficult for us. Even when it did rain, this area never had enough food grains. Oil and fresh vegetables were always imported from other regions.

The drought meant that people had neither food nor jobs, for almost the entire population depended directly or indirectly on agriculture. As we went from village to village, we saw scores of women and children with empty vessels on their heads, searching desperately for water. Here and there they found water holes or a well in one of the fields that had not yet dried up. The scene was a very disturbing.

One morning in Zikree, a village near Jamkhed, I saw several women at a well. Some had climbed down into the well and were scraping the bottom with a coconut shell. As the water trickled out they scooped it into their pots. Each woman took from fifteen to twenty minutes to fill up her pot, but still the water was quite muddy. The Dalits, of course, did not have access even to these sources. In some places a farmer who did have water was willing to sell some to them, but on the whole they just had to suffer the drought.

We had to respond to this crisis. The problem was complex: it was necessary not only to find water, but to ensure its fair distribution. We also saw our chance to develop better sources of drinking water and even perhaps put a stop to the traditional practices that contaminated the water supply.

What could we do?

Our first step was to contact a state level, non-governmental organisation called Action for Agricultural Renewal in Maharashtra (AFARM). This agency specialised in drilling deep tube wells, using modern machinery, to provide water for drinking and irrigation. In Maharashtra they had to drill up to 100 metres to strike a source of water. In collaboration with UNICEF, they had made a greatly improved hand pump which could draw water from such a depth. We became members of AFARM and invited them to help us drill tube wells for drinking water. We also asked for experts in water development to advise us on the availability of ground water. Relief agencies, including OXFAM and Christian Aid, both from the UK, came forward to fund this programme.

Determining sites for the tube wells was critical. We held many village meetings to discuss possible sites, and we ensured that all parts of a village community were represented at these meetings.

Please dig here

One night we met with the village people at Rajuri and found ourselves again facing caste division and discrimination as we asked them where to place the tube well. The Sarpanch suggested a site next to his office, which was in the centre of the village.

'Do you think that everyone will be allowed to take water from this well?' Raj asked.

'Yes, of course!' chorused all the high caste villagers. Raj looked at the Dalits. They also nodded affirmatively but did not appear convincing. When we started back to Jamkhed, a group of Dalits waited for us a couple of kilometres away from the village. They waved to us to stop.

'Doctor, is it possible to have another well for us Dalits?'

'But all of you agreed to have a well at the centre of the village,' replied Raj.

'Yes, we have to say all these things publicly. But we know that if even one high caste family objects to us touching the well, we cannot have water. These leaders are not going to support us. In spite of laws, they continue to discriminate against us. We could not say these things openly to you for fear of incurring their wrath.'

Raj assured them that something would be done and we continued home. What was true in Rajuri was also true in other villages, in Ghodegaon, Sakat, Patoda and Pimpalgaon. We had many discussions with the health team and other friends about how to deal with this problem of untouchability. There were not enough resources to install separate pumps. Nor did we wish to perpetuate this discrimination. How could all sections of the community have one source of water? What if the only source of water was located in the Dalit area? We knew by experience that caste discrimination was relaxed if it suited the high caste families. They did not touch a cobbler, but allowed him to measure their feet to make leather shoes. They did not touch a dead animal, but wore shoes made from the hide of the animal.

Water divining: a sixth sense solves the problem

We needed an excuse to put the tube well in the Dalit section of the village. The geologists had already declared that ground water was scarce. They warned that we would be fortunate if 50 per cent of the bores struck water. The village people had great faith in water diviners, who were highly regarded and respected in drought prone areas like Jamkhed. We knew of a geologist, an engineer who was not only a good scientist but who also had a sixth sense for finding water. We invited him to Jamkhed and asked him a special favour. Could he go around the whole village looking for water and ultimately find it where the Dalits lived?

Since he had worked in development in rural India, he understood what we were talking about. Indeed, he was really excited at the idea. He went around divining water spots and succeeded in identifying about forty sites in the Dalit areas of the villages. Wells were drilled and pumps fitted in. The Dalit women were happy. Water was now available at their doorsteps, a luxury they did not have even during normal times. The high caste women, on the other hand, found that they had to walk far from home in search of water. At times like this, when the caste observance did not serve their purpose, they quickly forgot tradition and conveniently began drawing water from these new pumps. As village after village started getting a pump in the Dalit area, the high caste people realised that they had been duped. But it was too late for them to react, because they too had the water they needed.

You can't trick the diviner

In a some places the dominant caste did not like the idea of the tube well being near the Dalit locality, so they changed the spot to suit their convenience. Normally the geologist would identify a spot and place a marker. The spot would be guarded by the village people. Later the drilling team came to drill at the marked spot. In Pimparkhed and Chinchpur, some high caste villagers moved the marker to a place away from the Dalits. When the hole was drilled, the well turned out to be a dry bore. The culprits were ashamed. In another village, the Dalits had a good water supply from an open well. The high caste people became jealous and threw rubbish in the well, making the water undrinkable.

At Jamkhed we too faced the same water shortage. The only water we could get was from a well 8 kilometres away. We had to have the barrels hauled by bullock cart and jeep. It cost Rs:70 a day to provide water for the health clinic, health workers and patients.

Water divining was very exhausting for the geologist and he could not divine more than a couple of places each day. He explained that he experienced a special sensation in the presence of underground water, and one day told us that his sleep was being disturbed in the guest room at Jamkhed, convincing him that there was plenty of water under the room. So we asked him to find a spot just outside the guest room, which he did, and a successful tube well was installed. Subsequently he showed us some other spots, and we have never again had any shortage of water for the health centre or the staff at Jamkhed.

After the geologist left, we continued to drill tube wells and so what started as a famine relief programme ended with 160 wells providing safe drinking water, one of the main pillars of good health, for 150 villages.

A joining of objectives: water supplied with health education

This provision of water for the village people when they needed it laid the foundation of primary health care in the villages. Here the need of the people coincided with CRHP's objective to provide safe water in order to reduce water-borne diseases.

The Dalits were now sure that we were not there to exploit them, but that we had their welfare at heart. We had gone out of our way to get water to them. This particular strategy was perhaps the most important of all in winning over the poor people of the villages.

Years later, some villages held meetings to celebrate and acknowledge our service to them. Seated on the podium, we would wonder what act of ours had most impressed the village. Was it a life we had saved? The number of emergency operations performed or blind people were cured with cataract operations? To our surprise, we found the people were most grateful for one thing: water. Villagers coming to the platform did not mention anything about operations or cures. Instead they thanked us for bringing water close to their homes and meeting their most important need at a crucial time.

A tube well is over 60 metres deep and has a diameter of 10 to 15 centimetres. A casing pipe would be inserted up to a depth of 7 metres to prevent surface contamination, and a hand pump was installed over the tube well. But simply installing a tube well was not enough to ensure a safe water supply. We also had to provide intensive health education.

Villagers are often suspicious of new ideas. They were suspicious of the newly introduced tube well water. Older people mentioned that the water tasted different and had a peculiar odour. They would rather walk a long distance to collect water from their usual, often contaminated source such as an open well, pond or stream. The young people of the villages were extremely helpful in educating the older folk so that they would not revert to using contaminated water from the streams and ponds once the drought was over.

When the village people had understood the importance of safe drinking water, they agreed to maintain the pumps. Some farmers' club members were trained to repair the pumps, and communities agreed to pay for spare parts and repair. The village people took the responsibility of keeping the premises clean.

At Mathkuli, the Sarpanch of the village appointed an elderly man to guard the pump to prevent children from playing with it. There was always a gap of about a week between drilling the well and installing a concrete platform and a pump. If the hole was not guarded, the children were sure to fill the tube well with pebbles and stones.

Thankfully, the use of hand pumps meant hard manual work, which deterred people from wasting water. Therefore no stagnant water stood near the pumps or on the village roads to form a breeding place for mosquitoes and flies.

We were the first to introduce tube wells on a large scale in that area. Often we initiated programmes that were later expanded by the Government. We could not usually provide more than one tube well in each village; there was always a need for more. As the villagers became more organised, they demanded these services from the Government and thus succeeded in acquiring two or three additional tube wells in each village.

What does it mean to be hungry?

Next to the lack of water, food shortage was the most serious consequence of the drought. The poor had no stocks of grain and jobs were scarce, since farming operations had shut down. Nearly all the village people depended on these activities for their livelihood. Farmers who had land but no water joined the farm labourers in search of work. Prices of food grains began to rise.

Once we were visiting a village where the Sarpanch owned over 20 hectares of land, but no water. The land lay barren and useless. It was late evening when we arrived and, as a courtesy, he invited us for supper. Not fully understanding the drought situation, we accepted his invitation.

His family did not have enough sorghum flour. They mixed what they had with wild grass and prepared a meal for us. Many poor people resorted to collecting wild grasses, of which 'Barbada' was one variety. This grass seed had a thick husk, so when people mixed it with the sorghum to provide increased bulk, it caused health problems. Its high fibre content caused impaction in the intestines.

Raosaheb, the Sarpanch of Bavi, lamented, 'I have been a good farmer and had six bullocks and two cows. When the rains failed there was no green fodder for the animals and dried fodder had to be imported. Throughout these couple of years, the fodder prices continued to rise rapidly and soon I realised I was spending more than one hundred rupees per day to keep the animals alive. I was hoping that the drought would be over soon, but my hopes were dashed. Soon my cash was spent and I gradually stripped my wife of her gold ornaments to keep the precious animals alive. Even after everything was gone, the animals needed food and they began to starve. I was ultimately forced to sell the animals at a give-away price. My wife joined as a labourer at the government relief work. It was very humiliating for us high caste people, since our women do not go out in public; they stay in purdah at home. However, because she is not used to hard manual labour, she earns very little compared to the Dalit women, who have done this kind of work before. I am really worried about my farm after the drought is over. Now I have no animals to till my farm.'

The drought was particularly severe on women and children. Many poor men left their women and children behind and migrated to the cities in search of work. These women and children had nowhere to go. Mothers boiled a little raw sugar in water as the only source of food. Whenever the children were hungry or cried, they were given a little of this syrup to appease their gnawing hunger.

As we went from house to house, we now saw severe malnutrition and vitamin A deficiency everywhere. It was certainly more than the 30 per cent we had originally found in our initial surveys.

Community kitchens stave off hunger

People were especially concerned about their starving children. Here again, the community's urgent need to combat hunger coincided with our concern for mother and child nutrition. The desperate need for food inspired us to begin a nutrition programme. It could be the starting point for child development programmes. Villages willing to participate actively in this programme were selected. The farmers' clubs were our partners in organising 'community kitchens'. This meant that all children, especially the poorest in the village, were guaranteed at least one nutritious meal a day. Food was chiefly supplied by OXFAM. The farmers' club organised these kitchens, keeping track of the food grain and cooking the meals. The village people provided the large vessels needed to cook the porridge, a mixture of broken wheat, legumes or pulses mixed with vegetables and raw sugar. Local shopkeepers donated raw sugar. Local people collected firewood. The children also helped, by gathering sticks for fuel and bringing water and seasoning for cooking.

Farmers' club members weighed the children regularly every month and maintained the 'Road to Health cards.' Indeed, these community kitchens became a starting point for many child health activities.

Food over caste

One good effect of the programme was that it broke down caste barriers. One morning I went to a village unannounced. The pre-school children were all seated on the ground. A few small children sat on their mothers' laps, but most were alone. Each had a brass plate for food. These children were clearly separated into two groups. The Dalit children were obviously sitting apart, although untouchability is outlawed. I acted as if I did not notice their neat segregation but went among the children and mixed them. I put all children with white caps on one side and girls with blue skirts another side, thus dismantling their neat arrangement.

Those who cooked and served were from the high caste group. I took a serving platter from one of the high caste men and served a few children. Identifying some Dalit men, I asked them to continue serving. They were hesitant. I offered my support to them and pressed them to serve the food to the children. The high caste elders standing around did not like the idea but could not publicly protest, since observing untouchability is a criminal offence.

Sometimes the conservative elders tried to take away their children from a common feeding programme. They spanked them and told them not to mix with low castes. However, the pangs of hunger brought these children back for a meal the next day. After some time, the high caste mothers gave up and allowed their children to attend the nutrition programmes. Later, the farmers' clubs devised another strategy to defuse the caste problem. Each child was asked to bring a glass of water and pour it into the cooking pot. Water touched by children of different castes went into the pot, thereby thoroughly 'polluting' the whole food. Once the children started eating together, the process of breaking caste barriers was initiated throughout the whole community. Our task to eliminate untouchability was made easier by the support of some young high caste men who were progressive.

Each child was asked to bring water and pour it into the cooking pot

Problems created by donors

Sometimes donors of food set rules for distribution without under-standing the local culture. Such rules often excluded the poor from the programme. For example, some international NGOs donated food for the nutrition programme on condition that only children under five accompanied by their mothers would receive the food. But most mothers could not accompany their children to the feeding programme; they had to work and earn money for the family; so the really poor children actually suffered more.

Older children also suffered from these exclusive rules. Most babies are cared for by their older sisters. Generally, girls leave school by the time they are ten years old. They either help their mothers in collecting water and firewood or they take care of the animals or babies. Nearly three-quarters of the children in the nutrition pro-gramme were brought by their older sisters. According to the donors' rule, the mother accompanying the baby shared the meal with the baby but the sibling did not.

These older children could not understand why they could not get food, they were hungry too. The result of such rules was that only those well off mothers who had time to take children to the programme would get food. We also sometimes saw the older sisters bring the younger and then stand at a distance making signs to the little ones not to eat, so that they could share the food afterwards.

The village people said the community kitchen should be open to all children because all were equally hungry. We agreed with the villagers. How could a hungry child care for her younger sibling? We found additional resources to open community kitchens for such children in need.

Beginning of child-to-child programme

There were over thirty community kitchens. Both under-fives and older children came regularly for the nutrition programme. Since the older siblings were practically acting as mothers to the small chil-dren, we organised them in a child-to-child programme. These older children learned how to feed the babies and take care of their health needs. Immunisation, oral rehydration, clean water and a safe environ-ment were some topics the children learned. Gradually, school drop-outs joined this programme. In addition to child health they learned to read and write and to sew and take care of animals. They also learned to grow kitchen gardens and the young girls learned more about motherhood. Though the community kitchens were temporary

129

and served children's nutritional needs for only a few years, out of that emergency situation a more permanent child-to-child programme was developed.

Employment in times of famine: Food for Work

During the famine able-bodied men started migrating to the cities and towns in search of work. Yet the area could not afford to lose these men; they were needed to develop the villages when the famine conditions subsided. Once the famine ended, new opportunities would open and new challenges would need to be met. It was essential to provide temporary employment for these men now.

We thought of initiating Food for Work programmes, in which the villagers would do developmental work (developing land, constructing small dams, levelling the land, digging wells and improving roads), and be paid with food. Certain government and other organisations in India had started Food for Work programmes as relief measures. CASA, the Churches Auxiliary for Social Action, a nationwide Indian non-governmental association was one. Though CASA had started as a relief organisation, the leadership was open to new ideas on development, so we discussed with them the possibility of starting a food for work programme in the Jamkhed area. Our goal was not only to provide relief from the current hardships of the drought and famine but to create a self-sustaining system whereby the villagers themselves organised the programmes. It would be our responsibility to share with them alternative means of improving their living conditions, then leave them to adapt and carry them out. Since farmers' clubs were beginning to play an integral role in health-related activities, we decided to get them involved in Food for Work programmes.

The farmers' clubs decided that these programmes were not just to be relief projects such as the local government was undertaking at that time. Instead they should expand to include programmes for developing land and water resources. Experts from AFARM, AFPRO (Action for Food Production, a national NGO that promoted development activities throughout the country) and the government departments of irrigation and soil conservation were invited to the meetings. They taught simple techniques of conserving soil and water to club members.

With this knowledge the farmers' club members could make long-term plans for developing the land for agriculture. In consultation with team members, they developed guidelines for the Food for Work programmes. They employed fellow villagers to dig wells for irrigation, put in small check dams, level the land, build approach roads

130

The Food for Work programme; building a check dam

or make soak pits for sanitation. One person per family from the high caste groups and two persons per family from the lower castes could be employed in this programme. Each worker was assured of 3 kilogrammes of wheat per day, along with cooking oil.

The villagers usually worked in groups of ten, which included one person who was disabled by age, blindness or leprosy. Their inclusion in the group gave them some earning capability as baby-sitters or water-fetchers. The other group members also were encouraged to share and care for those with disabilities. Each day the group had to perform a reasonable amount of work, as defined by the farmers clubs. Since the pay in the Food for Work programmes was better than that in other forms of employment, most villagers were encouraged to work hard.

Jamkhed is a hilly area. Heavy rain erodes the hills and carries away the topsoil to the valleys. The rich farmers own the fertile land in the valleys and the poorer farmers own the more barren land on the slopes. When villages like Rajuri, Sakat and Bavi became interested in Food for Work programmes their farmers' clubs decided to take a long-term view of land and water conservation. The planned to build small check dams across streams in the hills, thus storing water and preventing soil erosion. Each check dam was approximately 255 metres long, 14 metres broad and 7 metres high. It took approximately thirty days for one hundred people to build such a structure without any machines.

The next step was to dig open wells to be fed by water percolated from these dams. Levelling the land and constructing proper embankments would increase food production. Growing trees in these areas would further retain water and conserve the soil.

Altogether, these Food for Work programmes turned out to be a tremendous success. Since they were organised by the villagers and directly benefitted the poor, enthusiasm was abundant. The poor farmers decided whose farm would be improved first and who would get employment. Therefore it was in their interest to make the scheme work. This kind of programme provided continuous employment for the poor, improved their land and so enabled them to produce a variety of food materials and improve the family's nutrition. It also prevented unnecessary migration to the cities. Over the course of ten years, more than 1200 hectares of land were levelled and brought under cultivation, 336 irrigation wells constructed and 326 old wells deepened and repaired. Over 200 small check dams were built across streams and gullies. The programme became so popular that, as time passed, the participants increased up to 2000 per day.

Even after the famine ended, this programme remained a major tool in the health and development programme. These poor, neglected farmers and labourers developed a pride in themselves and their work, which in turn boosted the strength of the programme.

FFW means higher wages for the poor

The Food for Work (FFW) plan was later used to equalise the balance of power between the rich farmers and their workers. Traditionally, the abundance of labour and the scarcity of work allowed rich farmers to pay very low wages. Moreover, women earned less than men. Only at harvest time were labourers paid good wages, since farmers were anxious to get the crops in quickly before they were stolen. Rich farmers demanded work from sunrise to sunset. However, the Food for Work programme provided an employment alternative for the poor and they could demand fair wages.

In the past, when large scale development programmes had been brought to the villages, village people had to bribe their supervisors. Their only role models for many programmes had been their own corrupt leaders. These problems were discussed in the farmers' club meetings. The best way to overcome them, the members decided, was to pay the people according to the work done. For the first time people understood that they would be rewarded for hard work. Years later, after Food for Work was discontinued, they continued to work hard on the fields; they had acquired a work ethic.

From breaking stones to health camps

During the drought, the Government had been organising road-building work camps all over the region. The work required breaking the stones needed to build roads. All over the countryside we saw people sitting in the hot sun with no shade, hammering large boulders into the gravel required for road building. The small stones required steadying with one hand in order to break them. This frequently caused injuries to the fingers, hand infections and especially, tetanus. We had to do something about these injuries. We regularly visited the work sites and set up clinics for treatment.

We taught the people how to prevent many injuries. More importantly, we decided to immunise hundreds of these workers against tetanus and contacted the District Health Officer, who provided the necessary vaccine.

These government famine relief work camps gave us an opportunity to introduce health education and preventive programmes. The farm labourers are accustomed to long breaks to eat their lunch. This was the only time of the day that they came together. Our health teams visited the work sites during the lunch break and held informal discussions on health issues. They also had a chance to talk to women about child care and nutrition and encourage pregnant women to have prenatal care.

Here was a good opportunity to involve the local medical practitioners, because there were a great many work sites to cover. Most were registered medical practitioners but had no formal medical qualifications. We invited all these practitioners in the area to join us in the mass tetanus immunisation campaign. In addition to vaccines we provided the practitioners with a few medicines to treat common illness and injuries so that simple medical problems could be treated on site. The response was good; most of the practitioners promised to give at least one or two afternoons per week to this programme.

Soon after, we organised a medical association of doctors in the area. This association later became active in undertaking frequent health promotion programmes which included eye camps for cataract surgery and camps to detect polio and operate on children with contracture. Under the association's auspices, we carried out family planning camps, as well as dental and hearing disability camps.

Political crisis solves a discrimination problem

Another crisis provided an opportunity to strengthen and consolidate primary health care in the area. In 1975–6, because of political unrest, the Government imposed a state of emergency throughout the country. Under its new twenty-point programme, it launched many projects to alleviate poverty and assist the less fortunate. The government bureaucracy was directed to help the poor and end many unjust practices in the villages. Many poor farmers lacked capital or farm implements to cultivate their land and it remained fallow. Sometimes the rural elite used the land illegally as grazing grounds for their animals. In Chincholi, for example, forty Dalit farmers were unable to cultivate their lands for such reasons. We took advantage of the prevailing situation. The CRHP social worker contacted the government official, who offered the Dalits protection and encouraged them to settle on their land. We helped them secure loans from the bank. Forty houses were built and thus a community was established. CRHP helped them bring over 40 hectares of land under cultivation. Under changed political circumstances the village leadership assured them of cooperation. One village leader even donated 1 hectare of land to establish a health centre to serve his and the surrounding villages. During this period the Government encouraged well-to-do farmers to help poor farmers cultivate their lands. With the governmental support, the newly organised farmers' clubs helped the poor and marginalised to secure farming land and helped cultivate it.

During this time, the Government established new housing colonies for the homeless in the villages. We ensured a safe drinking water supply in these settlements; that action in turn became an entry point to initiate health activities for these marginalised groups.

Calamities such as drought and political emergency were used to elicit community participation at the grass roots and establish a broad base for primary health care. We learned to look for opportunities in unusual situations to improve the health of the people.

CHAPTER 11

The auxiliary health worker

MABELLE

Recruitment of auxiliary nurse midwives

By the end of our first year at Jamkhed, we had started weekly clinics in twenty-five villages. Farmers' clubs were taking shape in many villages and starting to participate in health programmes. We were now in a position to move on to the next phase of the project, that of placing one Auxiliary Nurse Midwife (ANM) for every five thousand people in the villages. This arrangement, we hoped, would fulfil our objective of making health care available at the doorstep of the villagers. Our ANMs were to stay in large villages. There they were to run under five clinics for preschool age children, focusing on nutrition, immunisation and care of minor illnesses and providing prenatal and postnatal care for the mothers as well as the services of a midwife.

At Johns Hopkins, when we were planning the project, the role of the ANM was discussed extensively. Her training and job description made her a cornerstone of the health system. In India, ANMs were among several kinds of auxiliary health workers trained by the Government to work in rural areas. According to the government plan, there was to be one ANM for each ten thousand people in rural areas. We decided to recruit ANMs, give them further training and make them the key workers in the villages.

When we started the project and began to recruit ANMs, we found that most of them had been trained in district and city hospitals and had no experience of working in the villages. The ANMs were mostly girls with only eight years of schooling and two years of training as an auxiliary nurse midwife. Most were from lower socioeconomic backgrounds and all were part of a society that did not respect women. Inclined to be diffident, they had difficulty communicating with village people. In an attempt to demand respect, they often sounded rude and impolite. They had no practical experience of working in villages, collecting health information or teaching; skills essential to health educators. Although trained in midwifery, they had not learned to treat minor illnesses, taken individual responsibility or worked alone.

We had envisaged ANMs as the main providers of care in the villages, but found their training woefully inadequate. Akka took the newly recruited ANMs under her wing and began to train them rigorously. She taught them to work on their own and gave them better nursing skills. They learned how to sterilise needles and syringes and instruments under village circumstances and the correct method of giving injections. They were taught child development and growth monitoring, schedules for immunisations and guidelines for diagnosing and treating common illnesses. In addition they needed to learn how to suture wounds, open abscesses, give intravenous fluids and do episiotomies. They became much better prepared to take individual responsibility for patients and not merely to carry out doctors' orders.

Sitaram Wade helped them learn the proper use of polite language and how to approach village people. Later they learned how to use audio-visual aids that would help them in their work of educating village people about health.

Akka used her military discipline in her vigorous training. In addition to teaching technical subjects, she gave the ANM rules for their behaviour. I often talked with her about the way she taught the ANMs. Akka had studied in nursing school over forty years before. She treated these young ANMs the same way she had been treated then. I often heard her say to them, 'You must not walk alone, only in groups. You are not to speak, unless spoken to. You must cast your eyes down and do your work.'

It amused me to hear this and I often remonstrated with Akka. 'They must have liberty. They have as much right to walk with their heads up and voice their opinion as I have.'

'But you do not understand our position as women in the society,' cried Akka.

'Since then people have gone to the moon and you still want to stick to the bullock cart. It is time we women take our rightful place in society,' I replied. 'These girls will stay in the villages and be in charge of the health subcentres there. They will be the leaders in the health field. They must be bold and confident and must become good communicators. They should be able to speak with authority on health matters. Are you asking them to go into purdah?'

'Yes, I know that. Every day we learn new things over here. We have to change. After all, this is "the project," is it not?' was Akka's reply. It was her way of telling me that she did not approve of these new ideas, but she would comply.

Though the ANMs learned curative skills, it was difficult to orient them towards preventive health. Their orientation was hospital based nursing and their ambition to become operating room nurses. But at Jamkhed the ANMs were managing patients who attended the health centre and the weekly clinics, and enjoying the work, the upgraded skills and the greater responsibility.

Now it was time to move them to the villages. When these nurses and ANMs had been recruited, they had been told that this project was going to be different, with more interaction with the community. Their role would mean being involved in health promotional activities. They also knew that one day they would have to go to the villages around Jamkhed. In spite of our training, the nurses and ANMs hoped that they would not have to be involved in health education and in other preventive care activities. Hospital work and curative clinics were ever so much more exciting. 'I can train chimpanzees to carry out orders and mechanically hand over instruments in the operating room. But it takes a human being to go out into the villages and change their attitudes and behaviour,' said Raj to the nurses.

The ANMs' difficulties

In the meantime I was getting to know the ANMs in the government service. Since I was the only woman doctor in the area, these young women used to come to me with their medical problems and shared their difficulties with me. Most came from villages and their parents worked as labourers on farms or as village artisans. Their parents were so poor that they wanted their daughters to have a job and support the family rather than get married. These unmarried girls had to live alone but since they came from lower castes they had difficulty finding housing. To make matters worse, they were looked upon as girls of easy virtue in the villages. There were many instances where these girls were molested.[1]

Thus they lived in a state of physical insecurity. Their superiors did not provide any support. Some ANMs did not trust doctors either.[2] So they often made friends with a local Sarpanch family or some other influential person and sought protection from them. Because of these difficulties, many did not stay in the villages in which they were posted and did not accept posts in interior villages such as Sakat. These posts lay vacant.

The ANMs told me that their job included house-to-house surveys, immunisation, deliveries, and family planning activities. In practice, however, they said that they were forced to spend most of their time motivating couples for sterilisation operations. Their job security, promotion and future career depended on this single function.

The village women did not deem them competent even as midwives because they did not have children of their own. Since they did not have the support of their superiors, they did not want to take any risks. They had lost any self-confidence they once had. The traditional dais (birth attendants) and relatives continued to conduct deliveries without referring to them. They also complained that they did not have any medicines to treat simple illnesses. For minor health problems, they had to direct patients miles away to the primary health centre. Therefore the average villager did not perceive the ANM as a useful person. To cover the population of ten thousand, the ANMs had to work in several villages, walking from village to village because there was no means of transportation. In this area it was not culturally acceptable for women to bicycle between villages. The amount of time required for record keeping also kept the ANMs from visiting villages other than those in which they lived.

In spite of these problems, these ANMs preferred to work with the Government because they were highly paid compared with the average villager and they had job security.

These problems did not seem unsurmountable to us. After all, the ANMs were effective in Narangwal, so why could they not be effective as village health workers in Jamkhed? But our ANMs were also raising fears about staying alone in the villages and were not enthusiastic about leaving the safety of the health centre. We specifically addressed these problems. Unlike the ANMs who worked alone on the lowest rung of the government hierarchy, our ANMs were part of a health team. Each would have the support of other team members who would be regularly visiting her. I assured the ANMs that Raj or I would visit them once a week and they could come to Jamkhed every Sunday. In the villages the farmers' clubs not only supported the ANM, but also were actively involved in health activities. They were ready to help in house-to-house surveys or collecting children for immunisation.

We also ensured that, by giving them more skills, our ANMs had adequate training in dealing with the common health problems in the village and that they had enough medicines and equipment. We took legal responsibility for their actions and prepared 'standing orders' for their guidance. Transport would be provided to go to other villages.

As an experiment we started with three villages. For security each ANM took a companion with her. We visited them once a week and they came to Jamkhed every Sunday. They worked hard, but in spite of all our support they complained of loneliness and were afraid to stay alone, saying that if they had to stay in the villages they might as well work for the Government and get much higher salaries.

We become matchmakers!

One solution occurred to us. Why not get these young girls married to young men who could be trained as multipurpose workers? Then the couple could stay in the village together. Later we might even offer them incentives, such as a house of their own, if they would settle in the village.

The centre had many applications for jobs from young men. Potential as bridegrooms for the ANMs became a criteria for selection. Most applicants were school dropouts or men with no particular skills. We recruited a few men and trained them as paramedical workers. We then started matchmaking by encouraging the women to find husbands. This had to be done diplomatically. Rural Indian society is very conservative. Sexes do not mix. The parents of our prospective couples were rather displeased and did not like our match making attempts. They insisted that arranging marriages was their prerogative as parents. But we told them that the couples were adults, capable of making their own decisions, even if we were influencing those decisions.

Initially we were successful in getting eight ANMs married to men working as paramedical workers, technicians or drivers.

Failure!

In our village experiments, the ANMs stayed in three villages for a year. Then we studied their performance. We talked to the village people about their work. One of the villages studied was Sakat, where Miss Usha Nikam was an ANM. The leaders were happy with her work. She responded to the calls of the mothers any time, day or night, treating mothers with anemia, children with coughs and colds, and diarrheas and skin infections. Usha and her companion went from house to house conducting a health survey. They tried to get mothers interested in the benefits of prenatal care, safe delivery and immunisation. Usha spent hours trying to convince women about the need for family planning but despite all her efforts, she was not able to change the women of Sakat. Pregnant mothers did not come to her for prenatal care or call her for deliveries. Rather, their mothers or other relatives conducted the delivery. Twice they had called a dai

139

from a neighbouring village and not Usha, the ANM. Many pregnant women believed that a childless woman could cast an evil spell on the newborn baby, so unmarried or childless ANMs were not called to assist in childbirth. On the other hand, the placenta was considered unclean, and therefore they occasionally called Usha to deliver the placenta. Women did not really accept her advice about children either. 'What does this unmarried young girl know about women, pregnancy and deliveries?' they would say. 'We never had any injections or tablets when we were pregnant. Why should we take injections now?'

Our evaluation showed that Miss Usha's experience was not different from that of other ANMs. All three ANMs were doing well in treating patients. All were finding similar difficulties in being accepted as midwives and in educating for preventive health care.

The results of the evaluation disturbed us greatly. We were almost three years at Jamkhed and village people were not accepting the ANM. We had pinned all our hopes on the ANM as the major player in the health system. Now we were finding that neither she nor the people were interested in her performance. Raj and I had many discussions on the issue of ANMs. One day Raj said to me, 'I am beginning to have second thoughts about ANMs. We are spending so much to keep them in the village'

'Yes,' I said. 'I was just going through what Usha and the others have done in the past year. I am really disappointed that they have not been called to conduct deliveries. In the whole year Usha has been called only twice. There is not much change in acceptance of immunisation. Only 16 per cent of pregnant women in these three villages have accepted prenatal care. The ANMs are good in curative work and they certainly make good nurses in the hospital. But they are not good as health promotion workers.'

Raj replied, 'It's hardly worth spending so much money just to treat a few illnesses that can be prevented. The ANMs are costing us much more than we thought. They are not mobile and are not able to go to the surrounding villages. It means we need one ANM for a village. That is impossible.'

I agreed, 'The village people cannot afford to employ an ANM in each village. They are too poor. We have to rethink this whole issue of a worker in the village. We need someone who understands village women and can communicate with them. So many harmful practices need to be changed. The ANM is not the person to do it.'

We decided to talk to the village people about this problem.

Raj went to Sakat regularly on Friday evenings. After seeing the patients, he sat with the Sarpanch and other leaders and chatted with them. The Sarpanch often told Raj that they were pleased with Sister

Usha. They appreciated her work. She was prompt and readily saw patients regardless of the hour. Her treatment was effective.

During one of these sessions, Raj explained to the leaders that giving medicines after people fell ill was only part of the care. Most illnesses could be prevented. Raj explained, 'In the past six months one newborn baby died with tetanus, another died within a few days of birth from infection. If only their mothers had called Miss Usha Nikam for delivery, those children would probably still be alive. Today I have seen more than thirty patients. Many sick children were brought to me. Some had diarrhea. Scabies is common. Women are pale and suffering from anemia. Some children are sick because they do not have enough food. Others come for night blindness. Most of these illnesses can be prevented. They do not need expensive treatment. There are ways to prevent illness. Much illness can be prevented if there is clean water and children are fed properly. If only women listened to Usha, Sakat would be a good place. What can we do to reach the village women?'

'Dada, we understand what you are saying,' said the Sarpanch, 'but you know how women are. They have never been out of Sakat. They like to hold on to old ideas. Usha sister tries to teach the mothers. Our women think that Usha sister is too young and she has too many new-fangled ideas. What can she know about child care? She does not have her own child.'

The Sarpanch then went on to talk about Mrs Joshibai, a woman from a nearby village. She had four years of schooling and was trained as a family planning promotor. She accompanied the mobile team and talked to women on family planning. 'But look at Mrs Joshibai,' he said. 'I have seen her teaching women and they listen to her with such interest. She is one of us. Mrs Joshibai dresses and speaks like a village woman. Our women understand what she is saying. She comes to our house or meets the women in the field and makes herself at home. But nurses are different. They dress differently. Sometimes our women do not understand their language. They use big words and strange phrases that we have never heard before. They keep aloof, and do not like to meet our women in the field. They are not able to explain things to women and not sensitive to our beliefs.'

The more we thought about the problems of the ANMs the more convinced we became that the ANM is not suited to be the agent of change. She could be trained as a good technical person, but in the villages we needed someone who could readily communicate with the people, someone who could change people's attitude and harmful practices. We could not blame the ANM for the failure. Her very background, training and past experience and her own value system

141

made her unsuitable. She was aspiring to become urbanised, having entered the profession to get away from the village and the indignities that the poor girl is subjected to there. In the city she had enjoyed a certain amount of freedom and a better life. Now we were trying to make her go back to the village and to identify with village women – the very things she wanted to forget. She was being forced back.

In the 1930s, Dr C. C. Chen had experienced similar difficulties with city-trained midwives. In his work in Tsien he found Chinese villagers trusted their own traditional birth attendants and could not trust young, unmarried, city trained midwives.

Another important consideration for us was financial. An ANM could provide service only in one village because of her limited mobility. Village people may be able to pay for medicines. But they could not afford to pay the salary of the ANM. The ANM could be used more effectively if she visited the villages once a week as part of the mobile team.

A new role for the ANM

Akka had trained the ANMs well in dealing with health problems. They had learned good technical skills which could be used more effectively in the health centre. So we changed the ANM's role. They were brought back to the health centre and worked as nurses there, with increasing responsibilities. They continued to form part of the mobile team that supported the village activities. But we still needed a primary worker for the village. We decide to find those workers another way.

Years later I visited Narangwal in the Punjab, India, where pioneering work had been done using the ANM as the primary care worker in the village. I found that differences between Jamkhed and Narangwal were marked. The educational qualification of the family health worker was also much higher. They were at college level, whereas our ANMs had scarcely nine years of schooling. In the Punjab the green revolution had brought about socioeconomic development. The people had access to services. Their attitudes were progressive and more open to change. Good roads linked the villages. Bicycles and mechanised transportation was common. All this helped the family health worker (ANM) in her work.

The Jamkhed area was so poor that people did not know where the next meal would come from. Under these circumstances they clung to their own beliefs. Even in villages of fifteen hundred people, the only bicycle was often that belonging to a school teacher or government functionary!

Once we identified the role in which ANMs worked best and with the most satisfaction, they were effective. Over the years the ANMs have become the backbone of the health centre at Jamkhed, taking on major responsibility of patient care. They are continuously trained and their skills improved under the watchful eye of Akka and Jeribai.

Mrs Meena Nimgaonkar, an ANM who joined CRHP in 1974, shares her story: 'My father is a labourer in a sugar factory. I am the eldest in the family. In order to support the family I became an ANM. My father asked me to apply to Dr Arole for a job and I was called to Jamkhed for an interview. When I reached the health centre I was worried about my interview, and wondered how long I would have to wait. At the entrance to the health centre a woman was selling snacks and fruit. I asked her where Dr Arole's office was. She pointed to a simply dressed person standing under a tree talking to people and told me to just go and talk to him. I hesitated. From my experience in the training hospital, I had imagined the doctor to be dressed in a suit and tie, sitting in a modern office with attendants and peons guarding the door. How could I, an ANM, approach the doctor? As I walked towards him, he noticed me and came forward and asked me if I was Meena, the ANM who had been called for interview. I said 'Yes'. He asked me about my training and about my family. He then directed me to the guest house and told me to meet the other ANMs and see the health centre and the village work with them. If I liked the work, I could accept the job.

'As I met the nurses, I was surprised to see them wearing colourful saris and cheerfully conversing with one another. I was taken aback. I was told in nursing school to be always serious and always look down and wear white uniforms. On a visit to the health centre and the villages I saw ANMs like me independently examining and treating patients. One ANM was assisting a senior nurse setting a fracture. I met another ANM in the pharmacy. She knew different medicines and their use. I was so impressed with their knowledge and skills. They looked so confident. I decided to stay.

'I worked for a couple of years, but the salary at CRHP was low and I had to support a large family. My friends told me that if I worked for the Government I would have a secure job with plenty of salary and the prestige of being a government servant. I secured an appointment as ANM in the government service and was sent to work in a small village subcentre where I was alone. I had great difficulty finding accommodation. My mother had to come and stay with me, as ANMs were not safe in that village. There was no team and no medicines even to treat minor illnesses. The doctor from the primary

Mrs Meena Nimgaonkar in the ward

health centre visited me once in a while and scolded me for not bringing in enough women for sterilisation operations. I had to walk to surrounding villages. Most people did not welcome me as they knew that I would be talking about family planning and had nothing else to offer. If there were sick mothers or children I did not have medicines to give them. I thought of my time at Jamkhed and remembered how much trust I had enjoyed. There everything was available to take of sick people. I had learned to treat patients and had enjoyed working in the villages with the support of the doctors and other team members. There was the great satisfaction of serving people and I had been entrusted with so much responsibility. Within a few months I decided to leave the government job and begged Dr Arole to take me back.

'I joined Jamkhed again and decided to be worthy of the trust. I am now at the health centre, working harder than ever before. I enjoy the confidence and support of the other team members and nurses.'

With the withdrawal of the ANMs from the village, they became far more comfortable in the health centre setting. They readily joined the mobile team, and provided the maternal and child health services in the villages and started working at the health centre as ward nurses and in the outpatient clinics. Most ANMs who joined the CRHP in the early years continue to work in the project. **Flexibility in planning and constant evaluation of the programmes and performance enabled us to change the role of ANM.** The ANM thus became the cornerstone of the health centre and a member of the mobile team providing secondary health services and individual care at the health centre. Her performance has continued to improve as she gains job satisfaction and there is continued in service training to improve her skills. The ANM has an important role to play in the health system.

1 Jeffrey, Roger. *Politics of Health in India*. University of California Press Berkeley, 1988: Pages 271–273
2 Bang, Rani. Nurses: the cursed women in the medical system. In *Health Care which way to go?*. Bang, Abhay and Patel, Ashvin, J. (eds). Voluntary Health Association of India, New Delhi, 1982

CHAPTER 12

A worker for the village

MABELLE

May, 1971

One hot summer evening, Raj was seeing the long line of patients in a remote village tucked away in the hills. Suddenly, a scream rent the air. A ten-year-old boy ran across the street shouting to the women to get out of his way. He had been bitten by a cobra. The men took him to the temple and laid him there. Raj heard the cries and ran to see what had happened. He implored the people to allow him to give the anti-snake venom, but in vain. Nothing would convince them to allow the injection. Later, Raj heard that the boy had died.

Could this bondage of fear, superstition and lack of scientific knowledge ever be broken? Could we ever get through these barriers of harmful tradition?

A good idea

We needed a person to work in the village. Someone like Joshibai, who could contact the women and teach them. We talked to the village leaders and farmers' club members. One day the Sarpanch of Sakat said to Raj, 'You need a person to talk to our women? Why not train one of our village women? I am sure we can find someone who would be willing to come and learn.'

Raj and I discussed the suggestion. 'It sounds like an idea worth trying. The ANMs are so unhappy in the villages. We have tried to involve village schoolteachers in health education,' said Raj.

I replied, 'Remember the few schoolteachers we tried? They were more interested in using the syringe and selling multicoloured tablets than giving health education!' In fact, we have one of these in Sakat. He tells mothers not to feed sick children. He scares mothers about immunisation.'

146

'We don't have experience with illiterate women. Joshibai is certainly good at teaching village women. But she has only been to school for four years. How can we teach illiterate women?'

I wondered about this and replied, 'Are not women learning all the time? They take care of the home, they cook, they care for the animals, they raise vegetables. You think they do this without knowledge?'

'There is another important side to this idea; women's development!'

'Let's pursue this idea. Let's talk to people in other villages.'

We discussed the Sarpanch of Sakat's suggestion, of training a local village woman, with people at Ghodegaon, Pimpalgaon and Rajuri. They too agreed and the farmers' clubs in these four villages started looking for health workers.

It was not easy for the farmers' club to find women willing to be village health workers in a setting with so many constraints, both cultural and social. Women generally did not attend public meetings. They did not come to the village square and were not allowed in the area where the elders were sitting. They were confined to their homes or walked to the fields on the outskirts of the village. Serving others was considered a demeaning job; nurses and other hospital workers were looked down on by the people, especially the high caste. A health worker had to be willing to go from house to house to promote health. But women who walked freely in the streets and talked to strangers were looked upon with contempt.

Health workers would also have to stay overnight at the CRHP centre for training. Those with family responsibilities could not be away, and moreover, many families objected to women staying out of their homes overnight.

The honorarium we could offer was not attractive enough for affluent women. If there was any voluntary work to be done in the villages, they forced the poor to do it on their behalf.

We had to rely on the village leaders and the newly formed farmers' clubs to select the VHWs (village health workers.) It took several community meetings and weeks of searching before nine women were selected.

The first nine village health workers

Sakat was the first village to respond. They persuaded the village kotwal to depute his wife, Janabai Sanap for training. She was about twenty-five years old and had recently undergone a tubectomy at CRHP. She had three young children; her mother-in-law agreed to

147

take care of them in her absence. The Sakat farmers' club was active and they promised to support her.

Mrs Janabai was soon followed by Mrs Bayadabai Dalvi, a 23-year-old woman sent by the Sarpanch of Ashta village. Bayadabai was living with her widowed grandmother and her mother, who had left Bayadabai's father because he had leprosy. Bayadabai's mother sent her to school for four years and then married her off at the age of twelve. But four years later her husband's family sent her away, fearing that Bayadabai would give leprosy to the family. Bayadabai returned to her mother and grandmother. Her grandmother owned good land and they were prosperous. From childhood, she had experienced ostracism because of her father's disease and also because all three women did not have husbands. Her relatives shunned her family and they were not welcome at any family function.

When Bayadabai was asked to go to Jamkhed, she welcomed the idea. She was relatively free, she had plenty of time and she did not have to worry about her livelihood. She had always worried that one day she would get her father's disease, so she was keen to learn about leprosy. She thought the disease was extremely contagious and spread rapidly. Yet she noticed that the CRHP doctors and others treated the leprosy patients in her village with sympathy and compassion. They touched the patients and did not mind sharing food and sitting next to them. They did not seem to be afraid of contracting the disease. This impressed her a great deal.

In Rajuri the farmers' club chose Mrs Salubai Sadafule. She was thirty-five years old, was physically strong and had a pleasing personality. Her husband had left her because she had lost her first baby in childbirth. She lived with her widowed mother and younger brother. They all worked as daily labourers and were often unemployed. The family barely had a place to live or enough clothes to wear. Salubai was very happy to be associated with the hospital. She was positive that this association would ensure her daily bread.

Mrs Vatsalabai Sonawane was selected by Halgaon village. She and her husband earned a living by fishing and working in the fields of the landlords. The river usually dried up in the summer, forcing them to be farm labourers. They were poor and did not possess any land of their own. Vatsalabai added to the family income by roasting chickpeas and peanuts for local shopkeepers.

Vatsalabai had never been to school and was shy about coming to Jamkhed. Yet the village leaders believed that she would benefit from such training. When she saw their enthusiasm, she could not help but come for the training.

The Bavi farmers' club was interested in finding a woman to

work as village health worker, but Bavi was steeped in casteism. The high caste women did not leave their homes without a veil completely covering face and body. They did not allow free movement of Dalit women in their village. As a sign of respect, women had to remove their sandals when they walked past the elders in the village. In such a traditional village no woman came forward to be a health worker. The farmers' club solved the problem by selecting a woman from the adjoining village of Halgaon. Her farm was halfway between Bavi and Halgaon. Mrs Shantabai Hambirao had already seen Vatsalabai at work and was favourably inclined to follow her. Initially the farmers' club found a house for her in Bavi; later they built her a new one.

Shantabai and her husband made their living by supplying water to the village. They placed a leather water bag on a buffalo's back and went from house to house selling water from the nearby well.

Anjanabai came from Nahuli. Her family owned a few acres of land. Since the farm did not yield much, she used to work on the 'Food for Work' programmes of CRHP as a daily labourer. The village leaders selected her as village health worker, but she refused at first. She told them that even though the project people talked about training women as health workers, she felt that she would not be able to learn and would end up washing dirty, bloodstained linen at the hospital. How could an illiterate woman expect to be trained in health care? Her son was a witch doctor and she knew that such things required special skills. Finally, out of curiosity, she decided to give it a try.

Muktabai Pol of Telengshi was forsaken by her husband because she had tuberculosis. Her father brought Muktabai and her brother to CRHP for treatment of tuberculosis. Muktabai's brother had extensive disease and we could not promise a cure for him. On the other hand, Muktabai could be cured easily. The father was disappointed that his son could not get well. He was not interested in Muktabai because she was a girl. He took both of them away. Later Muktabai walked 32 kilometres to the centre, stayed there and got well. During her recovery she worked with the nurses in the wards and attended the training sessions with the other village health workers. The Telengshi farmers' club chose her as the village health worker. In addition to these women, Lalanbai and Yamunabai were in that first group of village health workers.

In the beginning these women were shy and rather reluctant to attend the classes. Yamunabai says, 'I used to come all the way from Ghodegaon to Jamkhed and reach the gate of CRHP, but did not get the courage to go inside. Instead, I sat all day under a tree and in the evening I returned home. Kisan Sole and other farmers' club members would ask me questions and they realised that I had not gone to the class. The next time they took me right to the classroom and I had no choice but to attend.'

Salubai says that she had to pay attention in the class, because when she got back, the Rajuri Sarpanch always asked her what she had learned.

Confronted by the problem of caste

All these women came from different caste backgrounds. Our first task was to integrate them as a team. Their prejudices were deep and they found it difficult even to eat together. When Vatsalabai came to the dining room for the first time, she found all the women sitting together on the floor and eating. The only place left for her was next to Salubai, who was Dalit. She could not tolerate a Dalit sitting next to her while eating, so she served herself and went and sat a little apart from the group. Janabai noticed this and called her to come and sit with the others. When Vatsalabai objected to sitting with Dalits, Janabai, who by this time had got over her own caste discrimination, drove the point home by taking her plate to Salubai and asking her to share the plate with her.

This was a good lesson for women like Anjanabai who did not like to socialise with low caste people and was thinking of leaving the training programme. But at the same time she was learning things she had never heard before and was enjoying the training. She finally decided that learning was far more important than worrying about caste.

Realising that we would have to deal first with the caste issues, I talked about the irrationality of caste prejudice. I took the women to the X-ray room and showed them the heart shadows of men and women from different castes on the X-ray screen. The shadows all had the same shapes. I told them that everyone had the same kind of blood cells and that everyone's blood was red. During one group project, I had them stitch several blankets together into a single long one and all slept under it on the floor. As the caste feelings within the group gradually began to fade and they had opportunities to share their problems with each other, they realised that as women they had much in common.

Are we inferior beings

No matter what caste they belonged to, the women discovered, they were treated as inferior in their own homes and communities. They

150

Women of all castes slept under one blanket

were made to feel that they were good for nothing. Their life was one of subservience and hard work on the farm and in the kitchen.

This poor perception of themselves became evident when I asked, 'Who do you think is the most intelligent creature?' One woman said, 'The rat, because it hides grain so effectively.' Another said, 'The cat is smart at catching the rat.' The bird and the cow were also mentioned, but no one talked about themselves as being intelligent. For them, intelligence was related to ability to survive!

Then I asked, 'What about you women? Don't you think that you are more intelligent than these animals? You help build houses, you grow food. You light a fire and cook a variety of food. Women like doctor-in-bai do operations, other women are teachers, women drive cars and women like Indira Gandhi rule the whole country. Why, women even fly aeroplanes. Can any animal do such things?' Their eyes started shining when I told them that women had as much intelligence as men. It was a matter of having equal opportunities for women. 'Society has denied these opportunities to you women, but you should regard yourselves as capable of doing anything.' I told them.

This aroused a lot of discussion. During the session, each woman was asked to look at herself in the mirror and boldly say her name. 'I am a woman and I am proud of my womanhood. I have a name. I am not just a woman belonging to a certain caste or someone's wife. I am a person in my own right. I have as much right and freedom as the Sarpanch or anyone else. I am intelligent. I am capable.'

When they first came, some of the women used to say, 'We are like the shoes on your feet.' These images had to be eliminated. The

151

trainers also tried to do away with hierarchy by sitting down in a circle with them and spending time listening to them. The women soon found that they were respected. Whatever they said was taken seriously and they were not slighted. They were encouraged to express themselves freely. They had never experienced this kind of freedom before.

These women had come reluctantly to the training, thinking that they would have to obey new masters, and were quite surprised that such was not the case. They had found something completely new. The staff interacted with them. They shared their meals with other members of the health team, including doctors, and were treated as equals.

Anjanabai recalls that after the first couple of sessions, her hesitation was replaced by a longing to attend the class every week. She started looking forward to coming to the class. At the training centre, they did not have to cook or do any cleaning. Every minute was free for them to attend classes and discuss matters among themselves or with the CRHP staff.

Gradually the women became open and communicative. I asked them about practices related to childbirth and child rearing. Their eyes lit up; all wanted to tell us about the village practices. Salubai told me that mothers did not breastfeed newborns for the first three days. Instead, a cotton or cloth wick was dipped in diluted goats' or cows' milk and given to the baby to suck. Sometimes, she said, the grandmother watching the baby would fall asleep, let go of the wick, and the baby would choke on it.

Bayadabai said that village women didn't give their infants solid food until they started eating of their own accord. Sometimes even infants of eighteen months did not get solids. Mothers continued breastfeeding until the next pregnancy. They believed that a pregnant mother's milk was harmful to the baby. Therefore if pregnancy occurred when a baby was only a few months old, the mother would abruptly stop the breast milk and feed the baby on diluted cows' or goats' milk. Usually this dilution was two parts water to one part milk.

Anjanabai explained that villagers believed that chicken pox and measles were caused by the wrath of a goddess and that the illness worsened if medicine was given. Therefore, mothers often hid such children whenever the health team came to the village. She shared even more delicate information about village practices such as abortion and the neglect of female children.

The harsh reality of village life and its impact on health were aptly described by Vatsalabai: 'You do not want children to die. But is there any use having too many girls or having a blind girl? There are times when such girl babies are not welcome. Mothers sometimes

152

do not feed babies they do not want. It is not common, but it does happen. We have our own methods of family planning. The other day, Usha sister was enquiring about abortions in the village. The women just shook their heads as if they did not know about abortion. But I know that there is a woman who performs abortions. It is our method of family planning. We have to protect that abortionist so we say there are no abortions. Village people are not going to tell outsiders the truth, but they will tell me. I am from the village.'

From these discussions we recognised that these women would make good health educators. They would be able to preserve traditions that promote good health and remove the superstitions and practices that are detrimental to health.

The trainers reinforced certain cultural practices beneficial to health. For example, a special celebration was held when the child's first tooth appeared. The child was given solid food prepared out of cream of wheat, milk and sugar. Family and friends fed the baby on that day. However, the feeding remained symbolic, for that day only. The VHWs were taught to revive this practice on a regular basis.

Poor communities had another practice for night blindness. A child with night blindness was taken to three different families outside of the community. He or she collected food from these three families. The food was mixed and alfalfa leaves were added to the mixture. With this practice, they had experienced beneficial effects on night blindness. We encouraged this practice and made sure that they added alfalfa leaves (a rich source of vitamin A) to the food.

The women came to the health centre for training at noon every Friday and left for their villages on Saturday afternoon. There were no regular buses and they often walked 10–16 kilometres to get to CRHP. At the centre they not only learned new things, they enjoyed the company of other health workers, with whom they shared their problems and successes in the villages. Years later I asked them, 'Why not come to the centre less frequently, say, once a month?'

Salubai answered, 'We don't come just for training. We come mainly to experience closeness with other workers. We are like live coals; together the fire keeps us burning. Alone we shall be extinguished.'

During the week they shared their newly acquired knowledge regarding pregnancy, child nutrition, family planning and other health concerns with the village people, travelling from house to house promoting health. Sometimes they came across sick children needing treatment, but had to wait till the team returned to the village to get medicine. Village people were impressed with their work and asked us to teach the women to treat minor illnesses. Their special request was to train them in conducting deliveries.

153

Muktabai with mother and child

We responded and taught the VHWs some simple home remedies: cold sponging for fever; an oral rehydration solution – salt, sugar, water and the lemon juice for diarrhea; and vapour inhalation for blocked sinuses. The women also shared their experiences with home remedies and their knowledge about certain medicinal plants and herbs. We identified the beneficial remedies and encouraged the women to use them. The leaves and fruit of the neem tree were effective against scabies and head lice, and the extract of tulsi leaves was good for coughs.

I wondered if the women were capable of dispensing some medications on their own, without a physician. We knew that all women have to store and handle different kinds of spices in routine cooking and that they correctly identify these spices and do not make mistakes about the ingredients. We decided to give each woman a few common medicines in tablet form. The tablets were easy to store and transport and could be simply identified by size, shape, colour, smell and taste. These tablets included aspirin, antacid, cough sedative, sulphadimidine, iron–folic acid, ergot, vitamin A capsules, chloroquine, and calcium lactate. We taught them to distinguish these tablets from one another. For example, chloroquine had a bitter taste, and vitamin A was in the form of pearls. In addition, they were given antibiotic eye

154

Muktabai with medicines

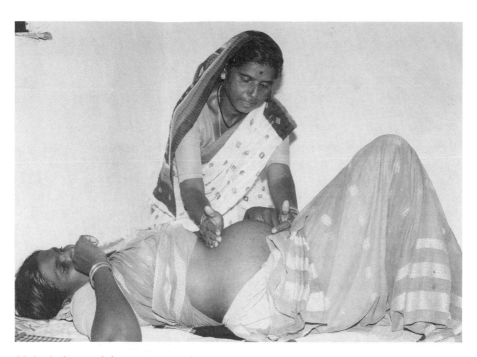

Muktabai examining a pregnant woman

155

ointments, oral contraceptive packets, dressing materials, antiseptic solutions and other supplies such as condoms. The women were then taught how to use these drugs correctly. It was emphasised, however, that their main work was health education and changing many attitudes of the village people.

The VHWs were not traditional birth attendants. But in response to the village people's request, they were taught to conduct safe deliveries. They also learned to recognise abnormal pregnancy and labour and to refer the patient to a nurse or the hospital when necessary.

Village health worker needs to be compensated

Most of these women were poor. They needed to be compensated for coming to the health centre and for their service in the villages. One alternative was to pay them from CRHP funds. This alternative could make them seem mere hirelings and it would minimise the voluntary nature of their work. It would also change our relationship from equal partners to masters and servants. The second alternative was to make the village Panchayat pay them a salary. But most village Panchayats were so poor that they did not even have a few rupees to pay for electricity. Even if money for salaries was available, the VHWs could end up being domestic servants of the Sarpanch and the Panchayat members.

We decided to cover their bus fare and their boarding while they were at the centre and to pay a symbolic honorarium of Rs:50 a month. Social workers like Mr Arun Londhe talked with them and found ways to help them improve their incomes. We arranged bank credits for them to improve their land, to set up small businesses such as marketing vegetables, having a grocery store or raising goats and chickens. They were encouraged to charge fees for service and recover the cost of drugs. Traditionally villagers paid for deliveries by giving grains, cloth for a blouse and money for bangles. The VHWs used their discretion in giving free service to the poor. The farmers' club members were vigilant to see that they did not overcharge and resolved any conflicts that arose. These village health workers became self-employed and often carried their vegetables and other wares as they made house calls. They could work without being slaves to anyone. This secure economic base helped them to have a good standing in the village. They could afford to be involved in the health work without being worried about where the next meal was coming from.

The health team visited their villages regularly. These village health workers became the interface between the health professionals and the community. Within a year, the backlog of immunisations was over. Pregnant mothers were coming in for prenatal care regularly. Whooping cough disappeared from these villages, the weights of children were increasing, and malnutrition in the under fives declined.

The patients who came to the weekly village clinic and the centre also changed. Formerly, the outpatient clinic at the centre saw a large number of children. Now all this was changed. We saw very few children with diarrhea or pneumonia at the hospital. Women with signs of toxemia or a history of difficult labour were brought to the centre by the VHWs, well ahead of their delivery time. More patients with suspected leprosy and tuberculosis came in for X-rays and laboratory confirmation.

We had begun with limited expectations. These nine women had started working reluctantly. They had begun as promoters of health. After training, they had become birth attendants and were gradually acquiring skills that would make them fully-fledged village health workers.

Their experience was certainly encouraging. In the meantime many villagers were impressed with their work. We were asked to train a village health worker for each village. Now we had the responsibility of training scores of women. It was time to streamline the training programme.

CHAPTER 13

The village health worker training

RAJ

'Come, women, come! Bring your pots with you, the river of knowledge is freely flowing. Fill your pots and share it with everyone you meet.'

Training more women

The farmers' club members and senior village health workers like Lalanbai and Yamunabai met with the CRHP health teams to formulate broad guidelines for selecting and training new village health workers.

Based on their own experiences, they felt that middle-aged women were most suited to the position. Not only are they closely concerned with the health of their families, but they can relate best to women and children, who constitute two-thirds of the population. These are the ones who need health care most and yet are the last to receive it.

Good nutrition, safe drinking water, a clean environment, and a rational attitude toward illness are the foundations of good health. In most cultures, and especially in developing countries, it is the women who are intimately involved with establishing these foundations. A village woman works on the farm and grows food or buys it from the market. She chooses the ingredients and cooks for the family. She preserves the leftovers. As the mother, she chooses the family water supply, be it a river, a pond, open well, or tap, collecting and carrying it home and storing it. She uses water for cooking and cleaning and disposes of the waste water. It is the woman who cleans her house and its surroundings. It is the woman who collects firewood, cow dung or crop residue to make a fire for cooking. It is also the woman who breathes in the polluted air from smoky stoves in dingy rooms.

But perhaps most importantly, women are the custodians of tradi-

158

tions and values. Women's illiteracy, superstitions, and forced isolation from the rest of the world result in poor health for everyone. Ultimately, poverty, especially among women, becomes the major cause of ill health. Yet it is the woman who has to care for the sick in the family.

In traditional societies around the world, only a woman can reach pregnant and lactating mothers and teach them about their own health and that of their infants. A sensitive subject such as contraception can only be discussed by women because most women do not talk about their body to strangers, especially not to men. Older women with children are accepted as worthy of giving advice. This factor had to be kept in mind when choosing health workers.

The village health worker is perceived as a bridge between the village community on one side and the professionals in the health system on the other. She represents families in the community, especially the poor with health needs. Therefore, she has to be a true representative of the poor. She must be a resident of the village in which she works, with real roots in the community. The wife of a government functionary, who does not represent the disenfranchised and is likely to be transferred, or a young unmarried girl who would leave the village after marriage are not suitable choices for the task.

Since practically all the poor women were illiterate, we could not expect an educated woman to be representative of such a community. From our experience with the health workers, illiteracy does not seem to be an obstacle to learning tasks necessary for a village health worker.

Selection of the village health worker

The farmers' club members took an active part in selecting the village health worker, usually organising a village meeting late in the evening, when all the village people returned home from the fields. They also invited us to participate, and we were accompanied by a senior village health worker from another village.

In a village of about two hundred households, about forty to fifty men and women would attend the meeting. The farmers' clubs ensured that all caste groups and factions were present. They could do so because of the apolitical nature of the club. By consensus, the people selected one woman as a village health worker.

Problems in selection

Occasionally there were problems in selection. Sometimes a local leader would try to get his mistress or a relative selected so as to control her. We would notice an expression of disapproval among the people, although they would not openly voice it. On such occasions, we had to diplomatically bring the meeting to a close and wait until the people came up with a suggestion at more informal meetings. We were greatly helped in this process by members of the farmers' clubs from other villages and other senior village health workers. Occasionally we could not shake off the nominees of the leaders. In one village for instance, the leader insisted that we have the woman of his choice. The village people obviously did not approve, because they knew that she would not be sensitive to the Dalit issues, but they were not strong enough or inclined to oppose the leader. The leader was also persistent that we work in his village. We accepted the woman as a village health worker on a temporary basis with the hope that an active independent woman would come forward eventually. Farmers' club members from neighbouring villages and other VHWs eventually helped to mobilise the people into action.

Sometimes there were factions in the village that could not agree on any one person. They then requested us to be a referee. We deferred the decision until tempers were cooled and left it to the farmers' club from another village to help in the selection process. In a couple of villages we did not work at all because of factionalism.

In Khandvi, the farmers' club selected a frail elderly woman. The village people explained that she would be more respected than a younger woman and they would help her. They were true to their word. A few years later they selected a younger woman to take the older woman's place. We considered selecting the right person important and sometimes it took several meetings before the farmers clubs came up with a suitable person. Since we had no targets to complete and no time limit, we took our time in the selection process.

The training programme

Initially, the women selected as new village health workers were given a week-long orientation course at the CRHP centre. The senior VHWs befriended the new women and acted as their guides. They explained the facilities and showed them around the premises. They helped them get acquainted with us, with Akka and Jeribai, with Arun Londhe, the social worker with the paramedical workers like Vasant Jadhav, and with the ANMs.

Firstly we made the women aware of themselves and their own place in society. We used the same process as for the original nine workers to improve their self-image and make them aware of the social injustices that existed in their own lives and in their villages.

160

Then, each one stood up and introduced herself to the others and demonstrated at least one talent she had. Some sang, some told simple stories, some played games, some balanced pots on their heads, some mimicked others. Some of the women surprised even themselves with the talents they had. The senior village health workers took the lead part in the first days of this orientation.

Vatsalabai said to them, 'We were nervous and scared like you when we first came to CRHP. Now we have become bold and confident. In my village, Halgaon, many children used to die. Now I go around the village to teach mothers how to feed the babies, and I weigh them regularly and get them immunised. Now children in my village are healthy. I am sure that when you receive training here, you too, will succeed as I have.'

Anjanabai talked about the importance of family planning. She said, 'When I was a child, about thirty years ago, there were only thirty to forty houses in my village. Now the number has almost doubled. Has the land doubled to feed so many more people? There used to be plenty of firewood to cook because the hills around Nahuli were covered with trees, but now they are barren and we have to spend hours looking for a few twigs to cook with. More people means more land to be cultivated, more food. Only now have I understood the importance of having fewer children.' The women nodded in agreement.

Bayadabai shared with them her own misery as a daughter of a leprosy patient. She told them how she found leprosy and tuberculosis patients in her village and helped them receive treatment.

Jeribai summarised what was being done in the villages. She explained that mother and child care, family planning, sanitation, and control of leprosy and tuberculosis were some of the areas that would involve them.

By now some of the new VHWs had overcome their shyness and they shared their perceptions of illness and deaths in the village. Many were impressed with the knowledge the senior village health workers had and the kind of things they were doing in their own villages, though some were frankly sceptical. The senior village health workers then invited them to their own villages to see for themselves. The women went in groups of three or four to stay with the senior health workers for a week. Usually this visit to the village became a turning point in their attitudes. Fear and cynicism were replaced by enthusiasm.

Girjabai Kapse recounts her week's experience when she stayed with Shantabai in Bavi. 'The first thing that struck me was the way in which we entered the village. We just walked past the village square, greeting the elders of the village. Shantabai did not stop to take her sandals off. I asked her about it and she replied, "We women have as

At the well, Shantabai gave out contraceptive pills

much right to walk in the village as men have. We must assert ourselves. Of course, we, too, must be worthy of the respect. I have gained this respect because I have helped so many families in their time of illness. I have helped deliver the children of so many women. Many children have had high fever or diarrhea and I have gone and helped them."

'The next morning we went to the well with Shantabai. She told us that many young women come to the well to draw water. This is the best time to get them alone, since the older women of the house do not come to the well. It is a good time to speak to them about family planning. Shantabai also gave out the contraceptive pills, which the women hid in the folds of their sari. She also came to know that a young girl was pregnant for the first time and was able to give her advice on what she should eat and also gave her iron–folic acid tablets.

'After this, we went to the village square. The farmers' club members had already prepared porridge for the children. Shantabai helped the men weigh the children and record the weights on the growth cards. She explained that it was important to get the correct age on the card. The usual way to figure out the birth date was the way we village people do it. First, find out which year the child was born by asking about an important event; a drought, an election or even the Sarpanch's daughter's wedding, anything that may have occurred during that particular year. Then the month is easy, because in almost every

162

month there is a religious festival, so we can find out at what phase of the moon the child was born. Finally, using a calendar, a fairly accurate date within one week of the birth date can be found.

'We went through the growth cards with Shantabai, noting the occasional child that had not gained enough weight during the month. Such a child needed special care and their mothers had to be contacted to find out if anything was wrong. Was it a minor illness? Was it a lack of food or was it necessary to refer the child to the health team when they came on their weekly visit?

'Shantabai noticed that one malnourished child had not come, so she requested one of the farmers' club members to collect her. This child was the fifth girl in the family and her mother was not concerned about her, so Shantabai was taking a special interest in her. She gave the child some extra food. A healthy child is an asset to the family and she was trying to convince the mother that her daughter needed to be cared for.

'By nine in the morning, Shantabai was through and we went with her to work on her farm and we helped her weed the fields. A group of women were also working in the neighbouring fields. During their lunch break, Shantabai went over and started talking to the women about what she had learned at the CRHP that week. It was interesting to see that Shantabai used every opportunity to share what she had learned with other women.

'In the evening, after our meal, we went to visit some houses. Shantabai had divided the village into five areas and every day we visited one area. We went into the courtyard of the first house. Women from the surrounding houses soon started gathering. Shantabai inquired about their families and children and how they were getting along. She took care of a couple of children with diarrhea. Then she took out her flash cards and talked to the mothers about introducing solid food to the babies, because that had been the chosen topic for the week.

'The mothers asked Shantabai a lot of questions about why they should take the trouble to feed the babies. "Wasn't breast milk enough?" they asked her. "Well, when do we fertilise our fields?" Shantabai would reply. "When the grain is ready to be harvested or when the plant is tender and growing?" Some would nod understandingly. Others, however, still had their doubts. After telling the mothers to send their young ones to the nutrition programme, we would leave.

'During that week, we went to see Shantabai conduct a delivery. She had been following the woman for the past three months. The woman had been given the TT (tetanus toxoid) injections. Firstly, Shantabai examined the woman to make sure that the baby was in

The delivery kit

razor blade

length of twine

cotton swab

gauze pieces

the correct position, explaining to us that if the shape of the abdomen looks like a watermelon seed, it was all right. However, if it was like a custard apple seed, it was abnormal and the mother would need to be sent to the centre immediately. We listened to the baby's heart by placing our ears on the mother's abdomen. Shantabai also showed us how to feel for the baby's head. It had gone down into the pelvis. This was going to be a normal delivery. We assured the woman that all was well and gave her plenty to drink. Soon, it was time for her to deliver. Shantabai had earlier taken two pieces of cloth (a torn old sari) from the mother and made a package with some gauze pieces, cotton swabs, a length of twine with which to tie the umbilical cord and a razor blade. This package had been sterilised at the centre and kept ready in the pregnant woman's house. Shantabai now took the package. She broke the glass bangles on her wrists and carefully washed her hands. In the meantime, burlap was spread on the cow dung floor. Shantabai opened the package carefully, without touching anything, and took out the cloth and laid it on the burlap. The mother lay on this sterile sheet which acted as barrier from the cow dung floor. Another piece of cloth was used to support the perineum to prevent tearing as the baby was delivered. As soon as the baby was born, Shantabai made sure that the it cried. She wiped the baby's mouth, then tied the cord to separate the baby. I was scared that the placenta would go and stick to the heart, but Shantabai reassured me. In our village we never tied the cord and separated the baby from the placenta till it was expelled. The baby was healthy and crying vigorously. After the placenta delivered and the mother and baby were cleaned up, Shantabai told the mother to put the baby to her breast. I was again surprised. Shantabai told me that not only was the colostrum good for the baby, but that the mother would also benefit because the uterus would contract and there would be less bleeding. "As a matter of fact," she told us, "the other day, in Halgaon, the placenta had not delivered for some time. Vatsalabai immediately made the baby suck at the mother's breast and the placenta was expelled immediately and there was no bleeding. We have been taught these things at the centre."

'The family was happy that a boy had been born. As was the custom, they gave Shantabai a few kilogrammes of grain, cloth enough for a blouse, and money to replace the bangles that she had broken.'

'The week was quickly over and we had a good picture of what our role was to be. We returned to our villages enthusiastic to begin work.'

The senior VHWs became attainable role models for the new VHWs who could identify with the senior women and ask them questions more freely than they could ask the health team. The senior VHWs on the other hand had gone through the same experiences as these new trainees and were able to understand their difficulties and guide them. Each senior VHW thus became a teacher and guide for a group of five or six new VHWs. When these new VHWs had sufficient experience, they in turn became role models for the next group to be trained.

The new VHWs continue to come to the centre every week on Friday noon and returned on Saturday afternoon. This training is continuous; some women, like Lalanbai, have been coming to the centre for training regularly since 1972.

Since these women are illiterate, it would serve no purpose to write training manuals. Nor can they take notes. In village society, oral tradition followed by hands-on experience is the most common way of learning. Village girls learn values and traditions from listening to their mothers and elders. The values are often communicated through folk tales, songs, dramas and dialogue. The day-to-day skills of cooking, child care, animal care and farm work are acquired with hands on experience. We followed these traditional methods for teaching the VHWs.

The training is participatory with much group discussion. It is built on what the women already know. They have a popular knowledge of diseases and they have nomenclature for different illnesses, syndromes and symptom complexes. They have different words to distinguish acute diarrhea from chronic diarrhea, dysentery or cholera. Similarly, they have different phrases for spasms of tetanus and convulsions of eclampsia. Both witch doctors and modern doctors use terminology that common people do not understand. Therefore, we make every attempt to demystify health and medicine. We use village women's words for different diseases and spend time learning to understand their vocabulary. Often the words are quite descriptive of the illness. For example, 'dhanurvat' (tetanus) means a person curved like a bow. As illiterate women, they have to depend upon observation and memory. As keen observers, they vividly describe different diseases. They have seen most common illnesses and are familiar with the signs and symptoms. They could distinguish whooping cough from bronchitis or a rash of measles from that of chicken pox and could mimic the malaria chill. They could describe a dehydrated child and were aware that a depressed fontanelle and sunken eyes were ominous signs for a baby with diarrhea.

We learned that these village women had concepts of the causes and effects of illness. They believed eating certain fruits resulted in coughs and colds, certain pulses caused stomach upset and peanuts harmed the livers of babies. Therefore they withheld these foods from children to prevent illness. Believing that a goddess or evil spirits caused diseases like chicken pox and cholera, they thought that the rational treatment was to appease the goddess with gifts or sacrifices.

Village people also have a concept of prevention of disease. They wore different charms and amulets to ward off evil and burnt chillies in the fire so that the irritating smoke would drive away evil spirits. To prevent illness they did not expose newly delivered mother and baby to the elements that are full of evil spirits.

We, as modern doctors, also believe in etiology, palliative care and prevention. Our concept of bacteria invading the body to cause infection is similar to their concept of invasion by a goddess or evil spirit. We therefore could put these concepts together and discuss them in the light of their own beliefs and experiences.

The women had first hand experience of surviving in an adverse sociocultural environment. They taught us how village people perceive disease in the context of their poverty and how they respond to various situations. Village women know that if a woman in labour is not progressing and the baby's hand came first, she had very little hope of surviving. The village community would then keep a vigil, often in the middle of the night. They would make a line from the village well to the mother's house. Water was drawn from the well and the water pot passed from hand to hand and poured in front of the mother's house. This was a demonstration that the community cared for her and was participating in the ordeal through which she was going. The women taught us many customs related to health practices in the village. We in turn tried to explain modern methods of diagnosing illness and treating it. The training was therefore a two-way process. Both teacher and taught gained in this sharing. We taught the trainers not to intimidate the women with high sounding medical terms and to make the village health workers comfortable so that this free exchange would be possible.

Cultural adaptation is necessary

Cultural adaptation was necessary at times. Most poor homes did not have spoons or other measuring containers. Lalanbai said to us, 'We are used to measuring with our hands and fingers. We have definite measurements with our hands which everyone understands. There is "moot bhar", which means a fistful, "pasa bhar" means a palm full, "onjal" is the cupping of two hands together as a measure. "Chimut bhar" is a three finger pinch. "Nakh bhar" means a minute quantity.' Almost every house has a water jug called a tambya, measuring approximately half a litre. The VHWs could easily teach mothers the oral rehydration solution using a moot bhar of sugar, a chimut bhar of salt in one tambya of water and add the juice of one lime. These measures were based on an average woman's hand. Women with larger or smaller hands compensated for the difference. Similarly, time and distance were measured in their own characteristic way. Half an hour was described as the time taken to have a leisurely lunch at noon after a morning of hard work. Distance was measured in the number of steps covered by an average person rather than the number of metres.

The VHWs had difficulty with abstract concepts. Every topic had to be explained in concrete terms using familiar examples as far as possible. We found ways to relate most health practices to agriculture and animals, with which they were more familiar. For example, farmers weeded out excess plants in the fields to allow the remaining plants to grow well. This example of spacing could be used to talk about family planning.

We did not follow a strict curriculum though eventually all the topics were covered. The training was designed to help the village health workers progressively increase their knowledge and skills, as they came week after week. Each week they went back to the village and observed, discussed and practised what they had learned during the week. With each visit their knowledge increased.

Anjanabai describes this on-going training, 'I keep on coming to

CRHP, because every week we learn something new. **Knowledge was sunk in a deep well, inaccessible to poor people like us. CRHP has provided us the means of drawing it out of the well. We are like buckets filled with the water of knowledge at the CRHP. We take it and empty it in our villages, but come back regularly to replenish our knowledge.** We are taught in the formal sessions every week, but also when we come shopping in Jamkhed, we visit the hospital and we inquire if there is anything to learn at the clinic that day. When we bring sick patients to the centre, the nurses explain the sickness and get us involved in the treatment.'

The weekly training session began with a review of the previous week's topic. The VHWs then discussed problems they had encountered during the week and by consensus selected a new topic for discussion. This selection was based on how serious the problem was for the people, how prevalent it was in all the villages, and whether it could be easily managed by VHWs themselves. Once a baby died of diarrhea in Sarubai's village, so the group chose diarrhea as the topic of the week. Sarubai described how a one-year-old-child had developed diarrhea and later vomiting. The mother had followed the customary treatment: she stopped breastfeeding the baby, stopped food and water and she gave the child an extract of acacia tree bark. The child did not improve and died within two days. Sarubai described how the child's fontanelle was depressed, its eyes sunken and skin inelastic. Jeribai, who was trainer that day, asked the group what villagers normally did for diarrhea. They said that most people would do exactly as the baby's mother had done. Those who could afford a doctor usually got an injection and a few tablets.

Jeribai explained how water and salt are lost in the case of diarrhea. It was easy to compare the child to a seedling that withers away and dies due to lack of water and soil. Plants need a proper proportion of minerals and organic material in addition to water. If water is insufficient, the plant dies. Children with diarrhea need water, salt and sugar in the proper proportion to replace the fluid being lost. If a plant gets water on time, it can be saved. The same was true of the child. It is necessary to replace the lost fluid on time. 'But how can a child be given so much fluid?' was often asked. The amount that it has lost has to be replaced plus its daily need.

The VHWs learned to prepare the salt and sugar solution. They asked what to do if there was no sugar in the house. Then, we suggested, raw sugar could be used. If raw sugar was not available, then flour could mixed with water to make a thin gruel instead. The importance of starting the oral rehydration with the appearance of first loose bowel movement was stressed. Tasting the mixture to make

168

Village health worker with mother and child

sure that too much salt has not been added was also emphasised. The women laughed at that and said that they were all used to cooking every day and that salt was the commonest ingredient they used. It was rare that they would make a mistake with salt in food — the consequence could be a beating from their husbands.

The women broke up into small groups, each with a senior village health worker and discussed what they had learned. A CRHP team member would help facilitate the discussion. The senior village health workers clarified any remaining questions. Then they planned how to teach these new ideas to the village women. Sometimes they went to the hospital ward and with the help of the senior village health workers learned to instruct mothers in the ward on how to make the solution. Thus they got hands-on training.

Discussions were continued into the night. The senior village health workers shared their own difficulties and how they had overcome them.

The next morning, the session focussed on the causation of the disease: 'Why did that baby get diarrhea?'

Firstly we asked the women for their ideas. Many replied that in this particular month, there was always an epidemic of diarrhea. Then we explained the concept of germs. They looked at a drop of sterile water under the microscope and a drop of dirty water with bacteria.

The discussion then moved on to the bad sanitation in the villages. Children defecated on the street, then played on the same street, got the filth on their fingers and thus developed infections. Children's stools contain more pathogens than adult stools and thus it is important to prevent contamination of food and water and children's fingers from this source. The water also got contaminated as it drained into the streams and wells. This was another source of infection. Flies were also carriers of infection.

The women split up into groups again to discuss what they learned and how they could prevent diarrhea in their villages. After a couple of hours, they reassembled to share their ideas. They would talk to the mothers about the importance of clean water. The deep tube wells in most villages had safe water. They would ensure that drinking water was taken from these tube wells and teach the mothers not to allow their children to squat in the streets where others played. They would make flash cards to help mothers understand the cycle of infection and we would seek assistance from farmers' clubs to carry out their plans. There was a discussion on how to dig and construct soak pits for drainage of waste water.

Back in the village, they put into practice what they had learned and the following week, the first objective would be a discussion about their experiences. The teacher would make sure that everyone understood the subject before moving on to the next topic.

Understanding traditional beliefs and practices

A great deal of time was spent in identifying the women's beliefs and practices. Those practices that were good were encouraged and those that were harmful had to be discarded. We soon learned that many good practices were distorted by poverty. For example, a special high-protein food consisting of almonds, dates, and some tree resins was given to postpartum women. But the prices of these foods were so high that most people could no longer afford it. Yet instead of giving new mothers what was available and affordable, the mother was starved. We discussed the value of the tradition and identified protein-rich foods that were within economic reach, such as peanuts and pulses for replacing the expensive nuts. Also, the local diet was traditionally nutritious and balanced. All the villagers recognised the value of fresh vegetables, pulses and milk in their diet. But because of poverty, they could not afford them. They did eat many types of greens and never wasted any part of a vegetable, usually eating them with the skin on. When peeling gourds or pumpkins or other vegetables, they would make a special dish of the peels. They had special preparations made

170

out of bran, and whole wheat or sorghum was eaten regularly.

Once the women understood the importance of greens and other foods, they started identifying plants that they used to eat when they were young, or they asked their grandmothers for more information. They soon discovered that there were over twenty varieties of edible greens growing wild that could be included in the diet regularly. They also recalled that as children they used to eat many wild berries and other fruits while looking after the goats. These bushes and fruit trees could be grown. All this knowledge was added to their health education material. As one woman put it, 'All these years we had the treasure right in front of us, but we went looking for it elsewhere.'

The young urbanised middle class were slowly giving up the staple foods in exchange for refined foods and practising other customs imported from the West, such as bottle-feeding infants. Some of these practices were considered progressive, and a few rich villagers were following them as a fashion. We warned the poor village women not to follow these ill-informed semiliterate women, but to continue to identify the good traditions their grandmothers had followed.

Some traditions and taboos were harmful to health. These had to be identified and discontinued. Some of these beliefs prevented people from accepting medical care. For example, pregnant mothers were prevented from eating adequate quantities of food. The common belief was that too much food would harm the growing fetus, perhaps based on the fact that large babies caused difficulty in labour and even death to the mother. I explained to the VHWs that now we could deliver large babies safely. On the other hand, small babies were likely to die. Such discussions helped the village health workers to think rationally and accept new ideas.

Village health workers carry out an experiment

Village witch doctors claimed divine healing powers. They usually went into a trance during certain days of the week or phases of the moon. Hundreds of villagers sought help from them. Many village health workers had realised that these healers were fake, but some still believed in them. The village health workers decided to find out for themselves the truth about these healers. The witch doctors believed that they would be 'polluted' if touched by a menstruating woman; as a result, the goddess would not enter them and give them advice. A group of such healers were persuaded to come to the centre. The necessary rhythmic music was provided. Soon the healers were swaying to the music. As the tempo increased they went into a frenzy and started flinging themselves about. At the height of this frenzy,

171

the VHWs performed the necessary rituals. Coconut, turmeric and betel leaves with betel nut were placed on a plate along with a lighted wick lamp. Joss sticks were also lighted and placed on the plate. The plate would be moved in a circle in front of the healer, now in a trance. Turmeric and ochre powder were placed on the foreheads of the healers and of all those present. The audience fell at the feet of the healer and touched them. After this act of worship, they brought in a child who had polio and asked for healing. One possessed woman told them to sacrifice a few chickens and perform other rituals. Since the healers were in a frenzy and supposedly possessed, one of the VHWs poked her with a needle. The woman immediately screamed curses at her and moved away. If she had really been in a trance, the VHWs argued later, the healer should not have felt the jab.

After the healers left, we discussed the incident. The VHWs who had participated in the rituals were menstruating women. They felt that the goddess should have known better and not entered 'polluted' healers. Once convinced, they started creating skits that enacted this possession to explain to people how they were being duped.

To accept intellectually that some traditional practices were harmful and that science had some good things to offer was exciting to the VHWs. In practice, however, the village health workers needed a long time to internalise these new concepts. Each incident was discussed in detail by the women as they shared their experiences, yet each woman had her own doubts. The VHWs were seeing many snakebite victims coming to the centre and being cured. Yet when Asrabai, one of the village health workers, was bitten by a cobra, she instinctively ran toward the temple, then hesitated as she was torn between what she had learned at CRHP and her traditional beliefs. The village people, including her husband, urged her to go to the temple. Suddenly, she stopped short. 'Something clicked in my brain. Just as the key opens the lock, my confusion cleared; I had to get to CRHP as soon as possible and get the antisnake venom.' She tied a tourniquet on her thigh and started running towards the main road. The village people refused to take her to the centre, telling her that she needed to go to the temple but her mind was made up. She continued to run to the main road where she met a passing cyclist and begged him to take her to the hospital. The man tied the semiconscious woman to the back of the bicycle and brought her to the centre. After successful treatment and recovery. Asrabai became an ardent advocate of treating snakebite in the hospital.

Training strategies

Most village health workers were not used to sitting and listening to lectures, which often distracted them. Lalanbai recalls, 'The first day with the stress of sitting and listening to the lectures for a couple of hours, I got fever and became stiff.' They needed frequent breaks. Didactic lectures were replaced by dialogue and discussion. Because these women had observed most of the illnesses, frequently they would interrupt to share their experiences.

In addition to discussion and dialogue, we used pictures and models in our teaching. Initially, we procured commercially produced audio-visual charts and flannel graphs. But many of these depicted urban middle-class life. Symbols and colours we considered commonplace did not convey the same ideas to these village women as they did to educated people. Their perceptions differed greatly from our expectations. For example, to the VHWs, the colour red does not signify danger. Rather the traditional red dot on one's forehead signified how fortunate one was to have a living husband. Red blood also meant life. Nor did an arrow necessarily represent direction to them. Line drawings also did not always convey the intended message.

Thus, the women decided to develop their own teaching materials. They sat with Kachuru, the local artist, and instructed him to draw pictures that would explain the intended message more clearly. They made up the stories based on local sayings and experience.

A favourite was based on a local aphorism that a child has to cross twelve rivers before reaching its third birthday. They identified the rivers as the common causes of death in childhood. Then, they asked, why not build bridges across these rivers of death? These bridges were made up of breast milk, supplementary nutrition, immunisation, early treatment of minor illness and home remedies, with the mother of the family as the architect of the bridges.

The VHWs sat with Mr Wade, Mr Ganpat and Mr Khandagale, and health team members who taught them skills in health education and communication and composed many songs on topics ranging from nutrition to family planning. As the training continued the village health workers delved more deeply into the underlying causes of illness – poverty, the status of women, social injustice, illiteracy and other such factors that affect health. They spent half their time learning technical aspects of health; the other half was reserved for their own growth and understanding unjust social structures, prevalent value system and their effect on health.

The training included discussion of effective methods to promote the health in the villages. The VHWs prepared stories, songs or skits

173

on health topics. Many stories were based on day-to-day life. 'We feed the cow well in order to get plenty of good, rich milk. Then why do we starve the breastfeeding mother? We don't allow the baby to breastfeed the first three days of life, believing the mother's colostrum to be harmful, but babies drink the colostrum of cows with relish. The goat's kid is forced to suckle right after birth and the kid immediately starts prancing around.'

Lessons in anatomy

As part of the training a goat was dissected and the internal organs in the trunk and chest were used to study anatomy. This practice soon removed many misconceptions about human anatomy and physiology. Following tradition, the women believed that the placenta must remain attached to the baby and that it should not be severed until it was expelled from the uterus. They believed that if the placenta was separated from the baby it would go into the heart and kill the mother. By dissecting a female goat, we first showed that the uterus was a compact organ and then that diaphragm separated the heart from the uterus and other abdominal organs. We convinced them that the placenta could not leave the barriers of the uterus and diaphragm and get stuck to the heart. They also saw a Caesarian operation and we demonstrated how the human uterus held baby and placenta inside.

The women had previously thought that vasectomy meant castration like that practised on bulls. Villagers castrated a bull by crushing the testes between two metal plates, making it impotent. In the operating room they were able to watch a vasectomy being performed. They saw that a small piece of the vas deferens was removed and that the testes were not even touched.

Value based training

A basic value system undergirded the training. Universal values of integrity, honesty, concern for others, forgiving wrongdoers, sensitivity to other people's problems, equality and justice were considered essential to the development of village health workers. These issues were openly discussed without preaching. The practical implications of the value system became evident in their work.

Asrabai Shinde tried to practise what she had learned. Tukaram, their neighbour, was a young strong man. His family shared a well with Asrabai, which was used to irrigate their fields. Tukaram refused to allow Asrabai's husband to use the well for irrigation and encroached on their land, creating constant enmity between the two

174

families. When Tukaram's daughter developed a chronic ulcer on her foot, Asrabai found that it was due to leprosy and went out of her way to treat the girl. Her husband objected to Asrabai's interest in the daughter of their 'enemy', but Asrabai told him that personal grudges should be overlooked. The girl was healed and was able to get married. Tukaram, grateful to Asrabai, apologised for having behaved in a disgraceful manner and restored their land and water to them. Asrabai learned that it paid to be good to each other.

Leelabai Amte had a son of marriageable age. The parents of the prospective bride offered Rs:5000 and a grand wedding as a dowry. However, Leelabai knew that the expenses would put the bride's family in debt. She therefore refused the money and agreed to a wedding without the dowry. Her husband was cross with her because he felt that they had many uses for the money. He did not speak to her for days. She stood her ground and subsequently he relented.

VHW training continues in the village

The training did not stop at the centre. The health team continued the training on their weekly visits to the villages. Anjanabai says 'The nurses helped me to examine a pregnant mother in the presence of many women. She asked me some questions and praised me for the correct answers. This was good. The village people realised that I had the support of the hospital and that I was improving my skills. One day I gave tablets for anemia to the wife of the Sarpanch. She was getting better. But the Sarpanch approached the doctor and asked for better medicine. The doctor asked me to bring my kit and took out the same iron tablets that I had given her. "There is no better medicine than this," he said. I was so happy and the village people respected me all the more.'

Salubai says, 'A woman in my village had obstructed labour. I advised them to take her to CRHP immediately. I accompanied the woman to the hospital, and indeed she needed a Caesarean section. The village people were grateful to me for the timely advice. The following week, I went with the health team nurse to the woman's house for a follow-up visit. The team members were offered tea in regular cups, but I was offered tea in a broken vessel especially reserved for Dalits[1].' By this time, Salubai had acquired enough self-respect to feel insulted by this. She pretended that she did not drink tea and politely refused the cup. The nurse noticed this and told the women of the house that none of the team would drink tea since Salubai would not. By then, the men of the household came to see what was going on. When they heard how the women had behaved

175

with Salubai, they reprimanded them saying that it was not the way to treat a woman who had saved their daughter's life.

The visible support of deliberately training the VHWs in front of the community legitimised their role in the village. A doctor's reinforcement of her treatment as the best treatment increased her confidence. The village health worker was treated as an equal by and shared equal responsibility with the team. The health team's weekly visit improved her skills and her record-keeping.

Anjanabai says, 'In the eyes of the people, CRHP is like a tent. We village health workers are like the ropes holding the central pole.'

Problems

Though Mabelle and I were convinced that a woman from the village would be effective, our nurses, ANMs and other team members were not sufficiently convinced. When the ANMs realised that village health workers were replacing ANMs in the villages, they felt that their territory was being encroached upon, even though they were not willing to stay in the village. They did not want to accept them as equal members of the team, but would treat them as servants. These attitudes were frequently discussed in the weekly team training. Change in attitude could be brought about only by our own example and ensuring that the VHWs were not given chores that would be looked upon as menial in this caste ridden society. The VHWs were not made to sweep and wash the floor or cook and including them in social functions along with other members of the health team also helped to bridge this gap.

They often said, 'CRHP is the only place we are treated with respect. Even in our mother's house we do not enjoy such privileges.'

The training is slow and requires patience and innovations. We could not always get trainers with empathy and willingness to demystify medicine.

Although the majority of village people accepted them, in the beginning the VHWs faced many problems from the villagers, especially the women. Vatsalabai says that village people used to ridicule her and sarcastically address her as a big doctor. Often mothers-in-law prevented young women from accepting her advice. Asrabai wanted to deliver her friend's daughter's baby. Her friend refused; she did not trust the new techniques Asrabai had learned. When Asrabai tried to go near the mother, she beat her up with a broom and sent her out of the house. A dirty sickle was used to cut the cord and a few days later the baby died of neonatal tetanus. Asrabai wept that she had not been able to convince her friend to allow the safe delivery.

Muktabai was concerned about a few malnourished children. The grandmother would not send them to the nutrition programme. Every time she went to convince her, the grandmother would close the door on her. Although the village health workers were volunteers some women would not listen to them saying, 'You must be getting paid for your work. You are doing it for your own benefit. Why should I listen to you?' They found role models in the doctors and health team, who had also faced insults from village people and learned to ignore such comments.

Yamunabai, the Brahmin VHW, was prevented by her family from entering the Dalit houses and used to shout instructions from the courtyard when a Dalit mother was in labour. She overcame the opposition and served the whole village. On the other hand, Salubai, the Dalit VHW, was not allowed to enter the high caste houses. Both these women persisted in their efforts to overcome caste barriers. Usually the breakthrough came by saving a life of a mother during childbirth or of an infant with some acute illness. Within a few months of becoming village health workers, the women were given opportunities to show their midwifery skill or treat a child for fever or diarrhea. CRHP stood by them and properly managed patients they referred for emergency care. It took six to eight months for the village health workers to establish their credibility in the villages. Many of these village health workers have served their villages for over fifteen years.

The reason they did not give up was that they were supported by the farmers' clubs who encouraged them. They were also finding the weekly training very interesting and they were learning many ways to improve themselves. They realised the value of such training. When they came to the weekly training sessions they were given a chance to share their problems. This was something they had never experienced in normal life. They had always been told that it was a woman's lot to suffer and that it was her fate. Now they were learning otherwise.

Some women could not continue as village health workers. The brother of one VHW felt that his sister was bringing shame to his family by going about in the village. In spite of her husband's support, she was forced to leave the village for her own safety. The brother of another VHW was scared that because she was now enlightened and worked for the rights of the poor, she would also demand her own right to property from him. He accused her of immoral behaviour and forced her to leave the village. Janabai worked as VHW for over twelve years. She had to leave her village for the sake of her daughter's education. She left Sakat and settled in Jamkhed. Sometimes husbands became very jealous of their wives because of the popularity they enjoyed. The farmers' clubs had to spend consider-

able time in counselling these men. A few health workers went over-
board with the freedom they had acquired. They neglected their families
and children. In one instance, the farmers' club tried to counsel the
VHW and finally advised that she be discontinued. Another worker
was chosen instead. The VHWs had access to food materials intended
for community kitchens. A couple of women were tempted to pilfer
the supplies. Two women were found misusing drugs and selling them
at a high cost. Such problems were discussed collectively by all the
village health workers and the farmers' clubs. They reprimanded their
colleagues, punished them and reinstated them. Some of these errant
village health workers are among the best health workers today.

Another VHW in a big village became popular as a midwife. She
took undue advantage of her popularity and joined with an 'un-
scrupulous village doctor'. She made pregnant women take unnecessary injections and tonics from him. The village health workers found
her behaviour too far outside the standards of the health movement
and therefore she was expelled by them.

In a few villages when the communities did not support the village health workers, they were not able to function adequately and
decided not to work for the village. In one village two religious groups
became polarised. The village health worker who belonged to one
group was not able to serve the whole village and therefore she decided not to continue working there. After a few years the two groups
have reconciled and the VHW is back serving her village. In some
villages factions between two groups led to community disharmony
that CRHP efforts could not reconcile, so the work was stopped.

Some villages were far away from the centre and there was no
regular bus service. The VHWs could not come regularly for the training
and during the monsoon season they were further isolated. They lost
contact with other VHWs and lost interest in the programmes. Constant contact and support is needed in the beginning.

But in most villages the VHWs had good support from their leaders.
This support kept their morale up. Over 75 per cent of the VHWs
continue to serve the villages.

Some agencies have faced the issue of the VHW herself becoming an exploiter, keeping the health knowledge to herself and doing
'private practice'. There is the danger of the VHW perceiving herself
as another health worker and beginning to align with the professional
health workers rather than being a representative of the community.
We faced this problem when the government Community Health Guides
(CHG) formed a union and wanted to become regular employees of
the government. The CHGs wanted to get the Jamkhed VHWs to
join the union. Unlike the CHGs the CRHP VHWs are true volun-

teers and had nothing to do with the CHGs. We realised the danger of their monopolising the knowledge and skills and using it for their own ends and means as we in the medical profession have done. The very objective would then be lost. We overcame this problem by organising women's groups called Mahila Vikas Mandal. Instead of just the VHW attending the classes, every week a couple of women from the Mahila Vikas Mandal also came to the class. Soon we had several women in the village with skills and knowledge. These women's groups started sharing the responsibilities. Why have these women continued to serve in the villages for over eighteen years? They were selected by the village leaders or health committees such as the farmer's clubs. These committees have continued to support them. Especially in the initial stages, these farmers clubs helped the women to be accepted by different factions. Then the women's own commitment to the village won them support in the village. Their curative skills helped the poor women and children in their illnesses and saved them from paying exorbitant fees to the doctors in town.

The CRHP taught them to think for themselves. They were not taught like parrots nor treated like servants but as responsible adults or equals. An atmosphere was deliberately created to allow them to share their knowledge and experience of health and social customs freely and without being ridiculed.

There was an atmosphere of learning together. They chose what they wanted to learn. They had access to knowledge. The centre staff was ready to answer any questions at any time.The health team supported them by further training them in the village and increasing their confidence in their work. The women had free access to the hospital staff and felt themselves to be part of the health team. Their decisions were respected, especially when they recommended free or concessional treatment for poor patients. The patients they referred received priority care, which strengthened their standing in the village. As they learned to deal with social and cultural issues, they became leaders in integrating curative, promotive and preventive services from the villages to the centre.

Opportunities were available for the VHWs to share with one another and they formed lasting friendships, often visiting one another's villages. They also experienced a social transformation in themselves. They first learned to cast away the irrational caste system. Then they organised themselves to fight male domination.

It was not easy to impart these skills and commitment. We needed patience and had to constantly overcome the numerous irritations that arose. We believed in the women's innate capabilities and built up trust so that we were able to work with them. We believed in

Village health worker teaching leprosy patient care of hands and feet

what we were doing and transferred the vision to the poor illiterate women.

The CRHP helped them gain a sound financial base. Social workers helped them to take advantage of government programmes aimed at the poor. They learned to get credit from the bank and start their own enterprises. During the training they were also given business skills and information. Their standing in the village made them credit worthy. They were not unduly dependent on CRHP for a salary and therefore did not consider themselves as employees. Yet they felt part of a movement that CRHP was creating.

As soon as the VHWs acquired new knowledge and skill, they took on new challenges. This continuous dynamic process of adding to knowledge and improving skills eliminates the boredom associated with listening to the same messages over and over again. The depth of their knowledge has also improved over the years. Their horizon has expanded beyond health to human development. They have developed an understanding of the social structure and effective ways to overcome the oppression inherent in such a structure. As a result they have been transformed from nobodies to self-confident dignified individuals.

'We are like rough rocks lying in the field,' they sang. 'Come,

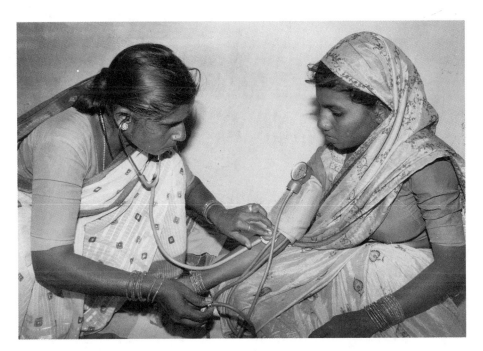

Muktabai taking blood pressure

let us gather these rocks – cut them and shape them so that we together may build rock upon rock – a temple worthy of our creator.'

1 The Dalits were not allowed to touch the vessels in the house. Most high caste households reserved a broken plate for this purpose. The Dalit was expected to use this special vessel, wash it and put red hot coals on it to purify the vessel.

CHAPTER 14

The Mahila Vikas Mandal

MABELLE

Health does not exist in a vacuum. It is dependent upon sociocultural and economic factors. In most societies, women are the keepers of health in their households and therefore their status, knowledge and attitudes influence health.

Women's struggle for survival

Health problems for women start even before birth. Advanced biomedical techniques allow *in utero* sex determination which could result in termination of the female fetus. The birth of a girl is heralded as a bad omen. As a child she is poorly nourished because she, like her mother, is restricted to food left over from the men's meals. She is given fewer opportunities for schooling. Then comes early marriage, coupled with all the risks of teenage pregnancy. As the village health workers discussed each health topic, the relationship between women's status and health became apparent. They also realised how much their own lives had been affected by the social pressures and norms imposed on them. Salubai was particularly vocal when she described her own experience:

'I was married when I was child. I got pregnant when I was fourteen and as is the custom, I came to my mother's house in Rajuri for delivery. I was in labour for three days. Finally a dai arrived and said that the baby was too big, I would not be able to deliver normally and the only way to save my life was to remove the baby piecemeal. She then proceeded to dismember the various parts of the baby and take it out. I was so terrified and also in such agony that thankfully I fainted and do not remember what happened afterwards. I was told that I remained unconscious for three days raging with high fever. I recovered but remained weak and ill for months. During

182

that time I never heard from my husband. Later he sent word that he did not want a woman who could not produce a living child. As a woman left by her husband, I became an outcaste looked down on by society. I was not wanted, uncared for, living at the mercy of my brother.

'Why did all this happen? All because we women have no value in society. Because I was a girl my parents were interested in getting me married off as soon as possible. I was only fourteen, not old enough to bear a child. Then like a piece of property I was thrown off by my husband.'

Asrabai replied, 'At least you lost your baby. My daughter has two healthy children. She needed a Caesarian operation and now her husband has sent her away. He feels that she may not be able to do hard manual labour and carry heavy loads because of the operation.' Asrabai welcomed her daughter home and worked on changing the attitude of the husband.

Most village health workers faced these social evils in their own families. They took care of their daughters and sent them to school. Anjanabai's husband and relatives wanted to get her 14-year-old daughter married. They kept pressing Anjanabai to take her daughter out of school, but Anjanabai resisted. She told them, 'When it comes to fruit trees, you know what to do. If the tree starts blossoming early, you remove the blossoms and allow the tree to grow strong and sturdy before it can bear proper fruit. So also with the girls, you must wait until the girl is old enough before getting her married. So often we see a girl married when she is too young and then she becomes pregnant before her body is fully grown. Then her body remains stunted. Her pelvis is not fully grown and she may need a Caesarean operation. I shall wait until my daughter grows up before she is married.' Despite community pressure, Anjanabai stood her ground and the daughter was married only after she attained the legal age of eighteen years.

The health of women, the VHWs knew, is also affected by the violence within the family. Husbands beat up their wives for trivial reasons like not cooking food on time. One of our first patients in Jamkhed was a woman who had been so badly beaten that both her legs were fractured. The reason: she wanted to visit her mother for a few days to celebrate a festival. Many burn victims were young women whose families did not provide enough dowry to the husband and mother-in-law![1]

The village women had many responsibilities, including bringing up their children. They were responsible for providing food and water and disposing of waste. They were the major workers in the field and took care of the farm animals. However, the men sold the milk and eggs in the market. They controlled the money and spent part of it on their own pleasures, like buying a watch or a radio or having a good time with their friends.

A major cause of malnutrition was the seasonal migration of the young families to the sugar factories. Women had to work hard in the cane fields and leave the children to fend for themselves. The result was severe malnutrition among their children.

Too oppressed to think for themselves

As the village health workers discussed the social causes of ill health, they saw the need to organise the women in the villages if major social changes were to occur. However, they encountered numerous difficulties in doing so. The women, in their isolation, were not open to change and seemed to be trapped in their own fatalism and superstition. Ironically, though the women had the most to gain, they were the ones who most opposed the health teachings.

Health surveys showed that women and children had the greatest need for health care. Most of the preventive programmes were directly related to them, but the village health workers encountered hostility in educating these women. Muktabai said that when she talked about solid foods for babies, one woman threw a broom at her. Others shut the door on her. The opposition came mainly from the older women. They did not like the idea of their daughters-in-law 'wasting their time', listening to new ideas about bringing up children or getting prenatal care instead of working either in the house or on the farm. These old women felt they knew enough to take care of their families' illnesses. Thus the daughters-in-law were powerless to take care of their own bodies or even talk about them.

The village women did not socialise and were fragmented by caste. Many were unwilling to break caste prejudices. After all, women were also the keepers of tradition in their society. Centuries of subservience had made them accept their secondary role; they were trained to suffer in silence. This attitude had to be changed. But how could a lone village health worker do it?

The need for a women's organisation

The village health workers expressed their conviction that other women in the village should experience the kind of liberation that they themselves had experienced. The farmers' clubs helped them in their work but the village health workers needed the support of the women too.

They felt that what was needed was a woman's group, a counterpart to the farmers' club to address issues specific to women. This idea germinated in one of VHW class sessions, and they decided to organise such groups. The farmers' clubs supported the idea and encouraged their wives and sisters or mothers to be part of these women's groups. They also persuaded other men to allow their wives to join the group.

The village health workers began to get together with women of their villages once every week or fortnight. In the beginning, only eight or ten women in a village were interested enough to meet for a couple of hours. They were never sure whether by coming together they would raise the wrath of their husband's family, so they always made sure to abide by traditional social customs. It was unconventional enough for women from different castes to meet in this fashion at all.

Who listens?

Mrs Ratna Kamble, one of the social workers, visited the villages regularly as part of the health team. She supported the village health workers as they began to form these groups. She says, 'It is individual flowers strung one by one that makes the beautiful flower garland. We had to get the women one by one. The village health worker would be able to convince just seven or eight women to get together. I often went with them. In the beginning, just these eight women would sit together and share each other's problems. All that we did was to listen to their difficulties. This was a new experience for them. The average woman is a complete slave in her family, at the beck and call of her elders. When she goes to her mother's house, even her mother does not listen to her problems. She is told that it is her fate and that she must learn to accept her difficulties. She is told not to complain. But in these meetings she was experiencing something new. She was finding someone willing to listen to her.

'The women liked to sing bhajans (religious songs). They also remembered lyrics they sang while grinding the grain by hand. Now the grain was ground in the flour mill, the home grinding was gone, so were the songs.'

The beginnings

Sarubai, one of the VHWs, organised women in her village. 'I was able to convince only seven women to come together in the beginning. We gathered together to socialise in one of the women's homes, to sing songs and listen to each other. In between, I taught them

185

child care. One day I was about to talk about child care, when one woman's husband came with a stick, ready to beat his wife. I pleaded with him, "Why do you object to your wife learning how to take care of your own son? I am just teaching her about his life." He thought we were gossiping. I invited him to sit outside and listen to our talk. He left without a word.

'As these gatherings became regular, more women joined the group. In spite of objections from their families, they gained courage as they found support in other women. Every week I shared with the women whatever I learned at the centre. I asked them to join me to improve the health of the village. I could not do it alone. Is it possible for a single bullock to plough a field? It takes six or more to do a good job. I told the women that we could do much to improve the health of our village. We only needed to work together. Each woman took responsibility for her own area. During the first week, they planned to teach every mother about how to treat diarrhea and fever in children. The mothers-in-law were curious. One by one they joined the group. Now the women's group had stature and the membership swelled to over fifty women.'

More and more women began to attend these informal meetings in different villages. They decided to call their informal groups Mahila Vikas Mandals (Women's Development Associations).

Organising around self-interest

Discussions on health and social conditions were not enough to hold the women's interest for long. The need for money was a constant preoccupation. Sometimes their children needed food or medicines. Older children needed books and uniforms. Every time, they had to request money from a husband or mother-in-law. What they really needed was their own income and control over the money. Therefore the Mahila Vikas Mandals (MVMs) began to think about income generating activities.

Building on own experiences

Traditionally, some village women participated in a self-financing credit plan called a Bhishi. In the Bhishi system, the women in the group each contribute a certain amount of money periodically. The contributions are pooled and the person whose name is drawn gets the total amount for that period. Ultimately everyone gets her turn. The MVM members decide to contribute an amount equivalent to one day's wages every week and make the pooled amount available to one or two members each week. Instead of drawing lots, they decided, the most needy would benefit first. Often the money was used to buy food or treatment for a sick child. Others used the money to raise poultry, market vegetables and dried fish or improve the farm. Organising women around their universal self-interest in earning money brought stability to the MVMs. The Bhishi system built a sense of trust and helped women to be sensitive to one another's needs. The MVM became a platform on which a village health worker built her health activities. As the members increased and attended meetings regularly, they began to realise that they had more power together as a group than as individuals. The VHWs gradually introduced social issues that had affected their health, especially that of women and girl children. They began to ask questions about why they treated their daughters differently from their sons, or why girls were not fed properly or sent to school like their brothers. They talked freely about alcoholism, wife beating and harsh treatment meted out to unwed mothers.

By 1978, thirty-one villages had Mahila Vikas Mandals. MVM members expressed a desire to attend the same training sessions as the village health workers. Each VHW brought two members from her village for weekly training at CRHP. Here members from different villages had an opportunity to interact with one another on health issues.

From income generation to health

The village health worker taught women in the MVM how to make oral rehydration solution, how to track woman's health during pregnancy, how to conduct safe deliveries. In each village three or four members shared the VHW's health activities. They did health work when the village health worker was away in training or on other business. The idea of one lamp lighting another lamp spread from village to village in the entire area. No longer there was just one worker; now there was a team headed by the village health worker to take care of the village.

Thirst for knowledge

The women's associations knew that the farmers' club members had seminars every three months. They too wanted to learn and participate in such activities. They wanted quarterly workshops to deal with issues related to women's lives. Women from different villages travelled by bus or bullock cart or walked miles to attend these quarterly gatherings. They stayed at the health centre for three days and two

Muktabai teaching women

nights. The attendance increased from fifty women in the first seminar to over two thousand women later. The gathering was a great
occasion for them to meet together and exchange ideas. They ate
together and slept together under a huge canopy. They composed
songs on social evils like alcoholism and exploitation and discussed
issues such as the status of women, their poverty, dowry, atrocities
inflicted on Dalits and corruption rampant in the society. Through
these songs they exhorted women to unite to end untouchability, to
control their own lives and to work constructively to improve village
communities. They often talked through the late hours of the night.

Professionals interested in the betterment of women addressed
these meetings. Most speakers were experts in their fields and had
grass roots experience working with women in non-governmental
organisations. Lawyers, social workers and other professionals explained, in simple terms, how the laws guaranteed women certain
rights regarding property, marriage, and wages. They explained how
to find help to solve one's own problems. Officials from the government agricultural department talked about kitchen gardens, veterinarians
explained how to raise chickens, goats and sheep. They also explained
what kinds of subsidies and bank loans poor women could get for
starting such enterprises. Each talk was followed by small group dis-

cussion. In these groups, women shared their successes and failures. They also planned how the information could be used for their own betterment and that of the village.

These seminars raised women's awareness and provided information that helped them improve their livelihoods and health. The women met face to face with government officials; the officials became more sensitive to their difficulties. The government officials were pleased to attend the seminars as they did not have other opportunities to address such a large number of women and achieve their given targets.

Empowering Mahila Vikas Mandals

Women used to be afraid of government workers in the villages. They feared the local village government functionaries like Talathi and the policeman, who would rather exercise their authority than serve. They were terrified at the thought of entering the court, police station or other government offices. For village women these officers were the Government, the rulers. Various strategies were adopted to remove these fears. We arranged for the women to meet with high level police and revenue officers, local judges, jailor, bankers and others. Contrary to their expectation, they found that these well-educated officers were cordial and showed real interest in their work and welfare. They not only spoke to the women respectfully, but offered them chairs and shared tea and refreshments. Experiences of this kind helped the women to be bold and confident and to understand their own worth in a free democratic society. This exposure to high officials exploded the myth that the village government employees were the rulers. Now the women understood that these workers were there to serve the village people.

Taste of power

The women soon had opportunities to deal with these local bosses. Most banks in India are nationalised and controlled by the Government. Bank officials in the villages treated women in a condescending and derogatory manner. They were used to providing credit to rich businessmen and farmers and they did not want to bother even with the paperwork for small loans to scores of women. The Government had a special programme of extending credit at low interest rates to women and marginalised people. The Mahila Vikas Mandal members in Rajuri were the first to apply for such credit. They knew the rules and were sure they had met the criteria. At first, the village bankers refused to give the loans. They used many excuses: the women had no property and therefore no collateral security and they were illiterate. They harassed the women through their bureaucratic procedures, but the women did not give up because they knew they were eligible for the loans according to government policy. They asked Mr Arun Londhe to accompany them to the bank for moral support. After reaching the bank this group of women firmly with one voice told the banker that he was unnecessarily harassing them. They would not leave the bank till he made a decision to either grant them the loan or give in writing his reasons for refusal. Sensing the power and determination of this organised group, the manager relented and granted the loan. These women triumphantly shared their story with women in other villages, at their regular gatherings. This success made other bank managers take these poor people seriously and not slight them.

The members of the Mahila Vikas Mandals became the advocates for the poor among the villagers. Leelabai was the secretary of the MVM in Halgaon. A bank was being opened in her village. Politicians, government and bank officials arrived from the district headquarters. They made speeches about how the new bank would provide credit to poor villagers. Leelabai, along with other women, was sitting right in front. She addressed the crowd of nearly three hundred people. She told the officials that it was almost impossible for the poor to get loans because of the corruption and inefficiency of the village level bureaucracy. If the dignitaries really meant what they said in their speeches, they should look into streamlining the process without undue harassment to the women. The villagers cheered as she concluded her speech. Impressed by this outspoken woman, the district officials promised to look into the matter and later ordered the village functionaries to issue the necessary documents without undue harassment.

In the meantime, the informal credit system of Bhishi continued to be popular among the MVMs. The success stories from Rajuri and Halgaon encouraged women to get loans from the banks. A group of thirty to forty poor women would come together, identify the most enterprising women, and encourage them to start their own businesses. These eight or ten women then went to the bank and secured loans and started their own business. After this group of women repaid the money, the next group would be selected for loans. The women not only selected who would receive loans but kept a tab on the repayments in order to establish a credit rating for the group as a whole. Because of peer pressure, the women had to pay back the loans but in genuine instances when repayment was impossible, the MVM paid on their behalf and kept the their credit rating with the bank. By this rotation system, the women started getting larger loans. Repayments were followed by larger loans and a real improvement in their credit standing. Eventually the Mahila Vikas Mandals throughout the project area had no trouble procuring loans from the banks. They had scored a victory!

Women as entrepreneurs

The women used loans to enhance their incomes. They bought chickens and goats for breeding. Others went into small businesses, buying and selling bangles, dried fish or vegetables. Some improved their farms by digging wells for irrigation or buying a pump set or a pair of bullocks to help in the farming operations. One woman bought a small canopy, a loud speaker, microphone and a record player, which she rented out for functions like weddings, elections and the numerous festivals that take place in the village. She was able to repay her loan in six months. Lalanbai leased fruit trees that grow by the roadside from the Government. During the season she sells the fruit and makes a profit of Rs:1000 to 2000 every year. Many women undertake this activity.

Access to credit made the Mahila Vikas Mandals very popular. Over the years, these successes helped women gain self-confidence. Over three thousand women who had never had any hope of getting out of poverty took out loans and improved themselves economically. Their performance attracted the attention of top bank officials at the state headquarters and the women were invited to a series of workshops to share their experiences with bankers in other parts of the state.

Tackling social issues

As they gained economic independence, the women began asserting themselves in all spheres of development. They applied their new found knowledge to everyday problems. Often, for example, women were cheated by bus conductors. The conductor would not issue the ticket or return the change. Anjanabai says: 'I got onto the bus and gave the conductor a two rupee note. He did not give me a ticket, nor did he give me the change. I asked him for it. He ignored me so I went on asking him. He told me to get off, saying he did not have the change. "What about my ticket?" I asked. "I am not going to leave the bus until I get my ticket and change." The other people on the bus asked me to keep quiet, but I persisted. The bus conductor soon realised that I meant it and gave me the ticket and change. You know, it works. We should have more knowledge about these things.' Anjanbai recounted her experience to the others with great relish. Soon, most bus conductors in the area knew they could not take advantage of the women.

Young women were often cheated by petty traders buying their farm produce, such as eggs or grain, at a low price. The MVM bought these commodities at a reasonable price and arranged to market them. This way, women were trained to practise social justice on their own level.

The MVM members often accompanied the village health worker to the local primary school when she gave health talks to the school-children. In some villages they found that the teachers were not attending the school regularly. They dealt with this problem with the relevant authorities.

A few years ago the primary school teachers went on strike and schools were closed for many weeks. Women like Lalanbai with other MVM members collected the children and arranged for classes. Since most women were illiterate, they themselves could not teach, but they could manage the classes. They selected children from the higher grades to teach the lower grade children. For the higher grades they found high school students or others to help the children review their lessons. They also organised cultural activities and used the time for health education. The children had a marvellous time in the informal setting.

Managing health programmes

From individual enterprises, the MVMs turned to some joint programmes for improving the health of the community. Health was a continuing concern. The Mandals developed various methods of achieving this goal, based on their own needs. Many carried out joint activities to raise money for their health related programmes.

An ICCO grant of Rs:5000 to 15 000 ($160–$500) was made available to each MVM to strengthen their movement. Many of the MVMs used the money as capital to start joint activities; others used it as a credit fund. The Mahi Jalgaon Mandal was given an initial grant to start a business of renting a PA system and a canopy for public functions. From the proceeds of this business and from voluntary labour, they built two rooms on land donated by the Panchayat.

One room was used to run a pre-school programme. The members took turns in running the under five programme and supporting the community kitchen. The other room was used for a 'fair price shop' for such essential commodities as food grains and oil. Special licences are granted by the Government to run these fair price shops.

The Government supplies the commodities at a controlled price; then the goods are sold at a reduced price to cardholders only. The quantity sold to each customer is also fixed, but in practice, there is a great deal of corruption in these shops and often the poor do not get their legitimate supply of food grains.

The Mahila Vikas Mandal at Mahi Jalgaon applied for a licence to run such a shop. The women faced a lot of difficulty from the previous owners of the shop. The officials scoffed at the idea of the village women running such a shop since most members were illiterate. But the women persisted and went to meet the district officials. They met the District Collector, told him their difficulties and obtained a licence to run their own shop.

The Mahila Vikas Mandal fair price shop was a huge success. The district authorities agreed to grant licences to any other Mahila Vikas Mandals willing to take on the responsibility. Thus the MVMs were able to make food grains available to the poor villagers.

Encouraged by the success of the MVM in getting permission for a fair price shop, Sathyabhama of the Kuldharan MVM decided to open one. The women had to raise enough capital to keep the levels of stock in a fair price store as prescribed by the Government. The women were from the poorest families in the village and could not obtain credit to get started. They pooled all their resources, sold their goats and raised the money they needed. Other Mandals are now negotiating to set up similar shops.

Other group income-generating projects included renting a winnowing machine to farmers during harvest time. The seed money provided to the MVM was used to buy the winnowing machine. This business is lucrative because sorghum and wheat have to threshed and winnowed. Traditionally, threshing was done by a pair of oxen trampling on the grain after which the women stood on a platform on a day with plenty of breeze and poured the grain down. The chaff was blown away by the wind, leaving the grain on the floor. The work was tedious and they often had to wait for days before a strong wind blew. With a diesel operated thresher, the work could be done faster. The MVM was paid one-tenth of the grain threshed and winnowed. They took contracts well in advance and were kept busy during the season. Out of this profit, the MVM supported tuberculosis patients and anyone else who needed help.

Preventing seasonal migration – a cause of child malnutrition

In some villages, the Mandals set a goal of introducing enough employment to reduce seasonal migration, an important cause of malnutrition and suffering for women and children. Like most Jamkhed villages, Kusadgaon was a poor village. The land did not yield enough. The poorer families had to migrate to sugar factory areas 200–300 kilometres away to cut sugar cane with sickle, load the trucks and bullock carts. While the parents cut sugar cane, their children were often left alone. The only food they received was sugar cane juice. These children came back to the villages severely malnourished. The women also suffered from malnutrition and anemia. The Mahila Vikas Mandal of Kusadgaon, led by Mrs Shashikalabai, started a broom-making business. Shashikala herself had been a beggar girl in Jamkhed. Her parents had died and Shashikalabai, who was ten, had been married to a man twenty years older. Shashikalabai learned how to make brooms out of date palm leaves and taught the other women to make the brooms. They found a good market for brooms in Ahmednagar. Contacting the forest department they obtained a licence to use the palm leaves from the whole Jamkhed block. Today, this Mahila Vikas Mandal has forty families making brooms and earning enough money so that they do not have to leave their homes every year in search of jobs. Their children get enough to eat and are no longer malnourished. The MVM later organised a water scheme for the village.

Programmes sponsored by the Mandals included learning social values. The importance of integrity, hard work and cooperative effort were emphasised. As women became more and more aware of their status, their actions together kept building their self-confidence and self-esteem. New knowledge and income helped empower them. They began to take part in the decision-making process in their homes. As Yamunabai said, 'When men go to get a loan of five hundred rupees, they come back with only three hundred. They bribe the officials, or so they say, and they spend some money for their own entertainment. In the end, it is us women who have to work hard to pay back these loans. Now we know all this is not necessary. We walk to the bank so that we do not have to spend bus fare. We know exactly what is required and submit the necessary documents. We go as a group and the official is forced to give us the certificates without a bribe. We bring all the money home and use it for the benefit of the family.'

As the women gained self-confidence, they started participating in village affairs. They worked closely with the farmers' clubs. They were now in a position to tackle some of the real barriers to health in the social structure.

A few villages had a problem of alcoholism. The men would get drunk, come home and beat their wives. They would take the money meant for food. The Rajuri women decided to put an end to this

194

injustice in the village. One day, a man got drunk in Rajuri. He started beating his wife. The woman screamed for help. Forty of the Mahila Vikas Mandal members came running. They caught hold of the man and pushed him into the house and locked the door from the outside. When the man came to his senses, he realised that he had been put to shame by a group of women. He had lost face. They made him promise that he would not do it again or the consequences would be worse. This kind of solidarity helped decrease the harassment of women.

Many programmes initiated by the Mahila Vikas Mandals were later incorporated by local government in their development programmes. Some Mahila Vikas Mandals began adult literacy programmes. Village health workers, like Leelabai Amte and Vatsalabai of Halgaon introduced the programmes in their own villages. They did not allow their own illiteracy to deter them. The MVM members contributed 25 paise (1 US cent) a week to buy chalk and slates. They asked a schoolgirl to help them in teaching. The village health workers also attended literacy classes at the centre when they came for their health education. During the lunch break, the village women practised the alphabet on the back of the metal baskets they used to carry earth at their work sites. Leelabai, illiterate all her life, did so well that she was chosen as a teacher for the government adult literacy class. She even received the best teacher award in the district for teaching illiterate women to read.

Mahila Vikas Mandal women learning to read

Child to child programmes

The Mahila Vikas Mandals also saw the importance of teaching 8 to 10-year-old girls to read and write. Most girls in the villages did not go to school. They had to look after their younger siblings or the farm animals. In these new programmes every evening, after these girls came home, they were taught not only to read and write but also about health.

One member of the family, usually a child or woman had to spend time every day looking for firewood for cooking. Over the years, most trees have been cut down to supply timber for houses and firewood in growing towns. In villages women face a shortage of firewood for cooking; scarcely 5 per cent of the village population can afford to buy firewood in a commercial market. Most women cook with twigs and dried cow dung cakes. Even these twigs are hard to come by. To deal with these shortages, the Mahila Mandals decided to jointly plant more trees. In the last eight years, five million trees have been planted! The women have also developed plant nurseries. They identify fallow land and plant the trees. These trees could not have been preserved without the cooperation of the whole village. Goats, cows and children had to be kept away from them. As one MVM member commented, 'Our eyes are the fence for these trees. Who can dare to cross such fence? We have struggled to keep these trees alive. When they were young saplings, we had to carry water on our heads to water them all through the nine dry months for over two years. We cannot watch them being destroyed.'

The Government of India recognised the effort of the Mahila Vikas Mandals in growing trees and reforesting in many villages and conferred on them a National Award; 'Priyadarshani Friends of Trees Award' in 1988. The social forest department officer, Mr Patil, said to me, 'You know, working in Jamkhed block is different from other blocks. People have a sense of justice here. They talk about right and wrong. Women are eager to plant trees. In addition to what you are doing through the Mahila Mandals, individual women have taken contracts from me to supply saplings to the Government. This year, I have bought most of the saplings from the women's nurseries.'

The Mahila Mandals have become well known in the district. Various government departments request them to arrange seminars that discuss the social and economic issues to help set development targets for the Government. One target is that at least 30 per cent of loans granted have to be given to women. The government department officers arrive at a central place along with the bank managers. The MVMs know the rules and are ready with the necessary certificates.

The loans are sanctioned with little effort on both sides.

Women who were once poor, marginalised and weak have been empowered to determine their own lives. Increased food production, safe drinking water and increased access to money and earning capacity were their primary needs. The MVMs had begun with a focus on income and health, which widened into the areas of social and ecological development that make healthy lives possible. Now with progress in these areas integrated into the women's lives in the villages, the MVMs used their empowerment in activities to directly improve health.

With funds from their cooperative enterprises, the MVMs increased the support of the village health worker. They took more and more responsibility about health in the village. In many villages the farmers' club gave over most of the health responsibilities to the MVM.

Sarubai explains how the women's groups are involved in health in Jawalke. 'We have divided the village into four sections and one MVM member is responsible for the health of her section. She ensures that all the children are immunised and that all the pregnant women are receiving prenatal care. The other women in her section help her in the activities. Then, we have trained three women to be

Village health worker with Mahila Vikas Mandal

in charge of the deliveries. They have attended all the deliveries that I have conducted and also attend the classes at Jamkhed. When I am not around, they will conduct the deliveries.

'Every year we conduct a house-to-house survey to find out the health and economic status of the village. Both the Mahila Vikas Mandal and the farmers' clubs participate in this. The survey helps us plan our programmes and understand what we have to emphasise.'

The MVM have 'keep the village clean' drives. They destroy allergenic weeds that are harmful to people, they construct drainage pits and encourage the use of toilets.

As well as helping the village health worker follow up on patients with tuberculosis and leprosy, they assist in the rehabilitation of these patients and their families. Tuberculosis patients need adequate nutrition in addition to medicines. Often such patients starve in the village, since they are unable to work. The Mandal members take turns in providing the patients with eggs, vegetables and grains, based on their need.

In villages, women suffer the most when they are sick. When they have tuberculosis, they are not welcome and are forced to leave the house and return to their parents' village, where they may or may not be welcome.

In Halgaon, Gopinath came back from Bombay with extensive bilateral tuberculosis. His wife Radhabai and two girls also contracted the disease. After he died of this disease, his parents drove Radhabai and her daughters out of the house. The Mahila Vikas Mandal intervened and helped his wife get her rightful share of the land from the family. They built a small hut for Radhabai, helped in regular treatment and supported the family until she was strong enough to work. Later, they found a job for her, looking after the nursery plants owned by the Mandal.

Most of the Mahila Vikas Mandals are involved in helping patients with chronic disease. If any deserving patient needs surgery, the Mahila Vikas Mandals collect contributions and CRHP further subsidises the treatment.

Mandals members assist with health education. They plan the programmes according to their needs and invite health personnel to guide them. In the beginning, the ANMs had to go from house to house and ask mothers to take prenatal care. Now, the women are knowledgeable enough to invite health personnel when necessary.

Some health concerns can be dealt with more economically through mass programmes. The Mahila Vikas Mandals plan and carry out these special programmes based on their own health surveys. Mahila Vikas Mandal have organised eye camps in their villages. They take care of the publicity, identify patients and make all the arrangements for registration, facilities and food. The health personnel only have to provide technical services. Many Mahila Vikas Mandals also arrange for diagnostic camps for tuberculosis and other diseases. They arrange for whole population immunisation with tetanus toxoid since those working in the fields are in greater danger of getting the disease.

The women's organisations have been successful though progress has been slow. In the beginning, problems were plentiful. Most village women had never been to school. They had never been involved in decision making. Someone else had always controlled their thinking and their time. Now, they are beginning to think for themselves. They also have learned to work together to share responsibilities and to trust each other.

In the initial stages the MVMs had many problems. Many were due to the women having worked on a cooperative basis and never having been in decision-making positions. In one village the MVM started a milk cooperative and bought cows with credit from the bank. The programme was doing well. However the leader of the cooperative got over ambitious and began helping herself to the bank dues she collected from the members. Action had to be taken.

In some villages there was a struggle for power between the VHW and the emerging women leaders in the village. The feud kept simmering until other members had to step in. They removed both the VHW and the MVM member and installed a new VHW. In another village, the community was divided between two strong groups along political lines. Each group tried to use the MVM for political gain. The leadership within the MVM fell prey to this and split the group. The village women dissolved the MVM and established a new one.

Sometimes MVMs would get carried away by programmes offered to them by government and development organisations, but which were not relevant or feasible. In Rajuri the government development organisation sold the idea of rearing an exotic breed of Jersey cow. The MVM did not study the project and its implications. It was only after they bought the cows they realised that they had no means of feeding them. They were stuck with the animals and a huge loan to be repaid. This led to frustration. However their findings were documented and later they were able to induce the banks to provide them with loans for raising goats.

In one village, the Mandal took a loan for a poultry cooperative. The men were upset at the women's enterprise and brought division among them. They also cheated the women in the marketing of the chickens. The Mahila Vikas Mandal got discouraged and the whole venture was abandoned.

In other villages some ambitious women tried to take advantage of the group for their own improvement; the rest of the women became disillusioned. But they learned to weed out such women from their organisations. The biggest problem was men. They would try to persuade women not to pay back loans on time, and even attempt to take away the money from their wives. The members therefore have to pledge that they will control every penny of the loan or face expulsion from the group. These problems were always discussed openly in the MVM meetings and also in the larger seminars and appropriate action was determined. Almost always the women were asked to pay back their loans and often others members helped them do so. This sharing of the failures and success was a learning process for the entire group.

In most villages, after the birth pangs and setbacks were over, the MVMs blossomed into effective village organisations supporting the village health workers as they sought to bring health for all.

Instilling values of cooperation, team spirit and trust take time. The Bhishi proved to be invaluable in building trust. Only a small amount of money was involved, but investing one rupee, every week, trusting that the others would keep it up regularly was a test of trust in each other.

The CRHP has acted as a catalyst for the various development activities introduced into the area. It has also functioned as an information bank for the women. Health alone would not have sustained the women's long-term interest. But the Mahila Mandals' wide range of activities have kept the Mandals alive and enthusiastic. In the words of Salubai, the Rajuri village health worker, 'For good health, one needs the combination of an active Mahila Vikas Mandal and farmers' club, combined with constant activity and education.'

Every Mahila Mandal has its own history. It has its own individuality, created by the uniqueness of each of the women who make up this vital vehicle for social change.

1 Devendra, Kiran. *Status and Position of Women in India.* Skhti Books, Vikas Publishing House, New Delhi, 1985

CHAPTER 15

Organisation and expansion

MABELLE

Extending to other villages: the people's role

It took three full years from the time we entered Jamkhed to establish services in the area, win the confidence of the people, organise them into farmers' clubs, and find suitable village health workers for each village. By 1975 we were working in thirty villages, covering a population of approximately 30 000 people. In each of these villages we had first started a curative clinic, held village meetings and organised the farmers' club.

During one of the regular quarterly seminars, the farmers' club members and village health workers expressed their desire to visit surrounding villages and expand health and development activities.

Badam said, 'The other day I visited my sister in Aggi and was surprised at the amount of sickness there. I have been there so many times, but now I notice the dirty streets and the need for programmes like ours. Aggi is hardly 8 kilometres from Bavi and the village people have not taken the benefit of CRHP.'

Shahaji added, 'People do not change just by seeing other villages develop; they need someone actually to go and organise them, otherwise nothing will happen. They are so sceptical and sleeping. They have to be woken up. Just because our village has improved, it does not mean that these messages will automatically filter or spread to neighbouring villages.'

'Yes, that is true. We took so long to wake up. We from Bavi had to convince Madhukar and others from Khandvi, otherwise they too would have been like Aggi.'

'Why don't we get together and go from village to village and organise the village people and get them into the CRHP programme? We have relatives or friends in most of the villages. We can go and

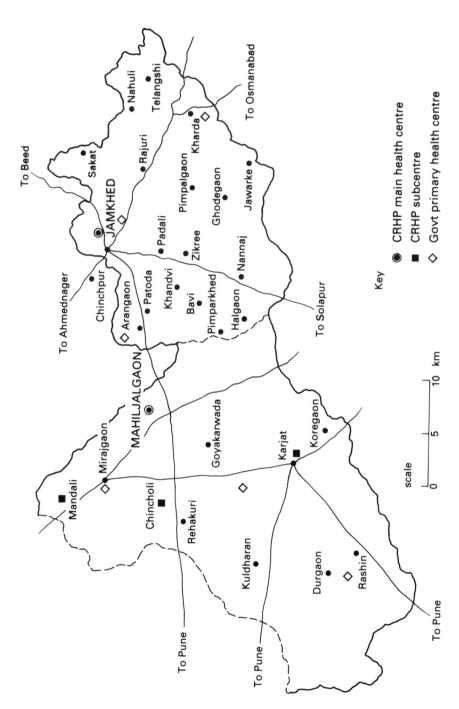

Sketch map of Jamkhed and Karjat blocks

stay there for a couple of days and tell them how we have improved our health. I am sure many of the villages would be interested.'

Badam from Bavi, Madhukar from Khandvi, Shahaji of Ghodegaon together with other members of the farmers' clubs and some village health workers thus developed a plan to extend the project into the surrounding villages. They established initial contacts through their relatives and friends and especially through the girls from their villages who were married and now lived in these villages. A group of three or four men and women would go out to a village and stay with the community for a couple of days. During this time, they shared their experience of improving health and agriculture, they encouraged the formation of farmers' clubs and they introduced the idea of selecting a health worker for each village.

These volunteers from CRHP were accepted readily by the villagers, because they spoke on equal terms and freely voiced their concerns or doubts. Indeed, these messengers of new ideas became honoured guests in the new villages. They were treated respectfully and their ideas taken seriously.

This group of three or four people represented men and women of different castes and this in itself demonstrated the importance of overcoming caste barriers and treating women with respect. The group did not take a package of services or a set of ideas or particular promises to the villages. Individually and as a group, they had different experiences and different expertise to share.

Lalanbai and Salubai had experienced liberation from caste prejudice, poverty, and discrimination against widows. They shared their difficulties in gaining acceptance by their own villages, and they told how different castes worked together and contributed to village development. Shahaji Patil of Ghodegaon reinforced their story by talking about the Dalit Sarpanch in his village and about how he had brought prosperity there. Bayadabai and Anjanabi spoke about diagnosing and treating leprosy patients and subsequently integrating them into the village community. Asrabai Shinde emphasised how harmful superstitions and traditions damage health. As a group they talked in a leisurely way with the villagers, often late into the night. In such a relaxed atmosphere they were able to exchange ideas openly and honestly.

Each CRHP project village was unique. The interests of farmers' clubs had varied according to their needs and topography. Some had excellent community kitchens, some were good in leprosy control and rehabilitation, and others excelled in social forestry. Because different groups and individuals emphasised different programmes according to their needs and capabilities, the entry points into new villages were also different.

As time went by, Mahila Vikas Mandals were formed and the women, too, got involved in the expansion programme. They were able to contact other women in the new villages. No matter what caste or class they belonged to, all had suffered equally under the male dominated society. Thus they quickly focused on the difficulties of day-to-day life such as feeding and schooling children, gathering water, and caring for animals. Over time, these women helped to form new Mahila Vikas Mandals and organise income-generation programmes.

The newly formed farmers' clubs and MVMs were invited to visit the ongoing programmes and exchange ideas. This way the villagers themselves expanded the programme from 30 to 175 villages and recruited over 150 village health workers. In all, over 300 volunteers gave their time and energy to expand this programme.

Indeed, the programme was no longer organised solely by health professionals like us, but it became a People's Movement. The health team accompanied the village volunteers to explain technical details of a particular health programme such as family planning or medical treatment of leprosy. Once the village selected its village health worker and organised the farmers' club/Mahila Vikas Mandal, the mobile health team started going to the village on a regular basis to work with health and development programmes.

Since the volunteers became the guests of the village, they received hospitality. CRHP was responsible for their transportation and other incidental expenses. Costs were therefore minimal and as project staff we did not have to have to spend time establishing our credibility as we had been obliged to do to in the first few villages. People from the new villages could visit the older villages and see the different programmes for themselves.

Depending on volunteers for expansion does have some limits. At first, volunteers could only go to those villages where they already had personal contacts, so the pattern of expansion did not follow regular geographic lines.

Networking with other non-governmental organisations

A Coordinating Agency for Health Planning in India was formed, to be an advocate for basic health care among the non-governmental organisations involved in health care. Raj and other like-minded doctors drew the attention of NGOs to the health needs of the rural poor. He was a founding member of the Voluntary Health Association of India (VHAI) in 1974 (VHAI is an offshoot of the Coordinating Agency for Health Planning) and remained its president for several years. VHAI staff travelled throughout India and stimulated interest in providing basic health care to the rural poor. In the formative years of VHAI (and the state voluntary health associations), Jamkhed became the venue for informal training. VHAI also sponsored numerous workshops for NGOs at Jamkhed. Over the years VHAI has continued to promote primary health care.

Health by the people

In 1973, the executive board of the World Health Organisation commissioned a joint WHO/UNICEF study to reappraise the health situation in developing countries. As part of this study, four health experts, under the chairmanship of Dr Djukanovic, came to Jamkhed, visited the villages and studied the CRHP programmes. The results of this case study were published in two books: Alternative Approaches to Meeting Basic Health Needs in Developing Countries, edited by V. Djukanovic and E. P. Mach, 1975, and Health by the People, a WHO publication edited by Dr K. Newell, 1975. As a result, our experience in primary health care, especially with community participation and the village health workers attracted the attention of health professionals. The WHO/ UNICEF sponsored senior teachers of obstetrics from developing countries who came to observe PHC in action. We were invited to participate in seminars and workshops both in India and abroad and had opportunities to share our experience in primary health care with professionals around the world.

Indeed, our success with women village health workers to provide basic health services greatly influenced the Government of India. They introduced the community volunteer scheme in 1977. In this plan, village people selected a person from their own community to be trained as a community health worker, later known as a village health guide (VHG) or community health guide (CHG). The goal was to have one VHG for every thousand people throughout the country.

Ahmednagar District – a challenge

The government plan to train VHGs all over the country was facing difficulties. The criteria for selection, the insistence of minimum education, poor training facilities and an inadequate number of trainers in government services contributed to the inadequacies of this plan. At this point the Central Government of India approached us to select and train community health guides on behalf of the government primary health centres in each of 1800 villages in Ahmednagar district.

We agreed to do so on condition that some of the flaws in the

VHG programme be eliminated. We emphasised that the worker should be a woman because the most pressing health activities related to women and children. Secondly, we requested that a minimal level of education not be required, considering the poor literacy levels among women in the district. If the worker were to be a true representative of the village poor, she too would likely be illiterate and poor. Though we realised what an enormous task it would be to suddenly scale up from a micro-level programme, heavily dependent on community participation, to a large programme needing a large work force to select, train and follow up workers for a period of five years, we agreed to take on the responsibility of preparing these VHGs for the Government. The Swiss Development Cooperation funded the programme and the Voluntary Health Association of India evaluated and monitored the progress. We took up the challenge mainly because of the support from our trained village health workers and over three hundred volunteers from the FCs and MVMs in the villages.

These volunteers gathered at Jamkhed for several days and discussed the strategy for covering the entire district and selecting the VHGs. They were divided into fifteen teams of twenty people each. Each team was supported by a member of CRHP staff. These selection teams first visited the community development block headquarters and met with the block development officer, primary health centre staff, teachers and other government workers and explained to them how primary health care was practised at CRHP. The VHWs shared their own work and discussed what was expected of the village health guide, the criteria for selecting these VHGs and their training. The selection team was joined by village representatives who took them to their respective villages. The team then moved around the village talking informally to the people, particularly in the poorer sections, explaining the purpose of the visit and the need to select a proper woman as village health guide. The Jamkhed VHWs explained that the women selected would be trained like themselves at CRHP in Jamkhed. They usually stayed overnight in the village to complete the selection of the village health guide.

The selected VHGs then came to Jamkhed with the volunteers for training. The CRHP veteran village health workers stayed with the newly selected women at Jamkhed for a week, helping in their orientation and guiding them in their training. In the second week three to four trainees were taken by a CRHP village health worker to her own village and stayed with her for one week. During this period, the trainee got hands-on experience in providing primary health care to the village. This exposure gave the trainees a concrete idea of what their role in their own villages would be. Now they became

206

enthusiastic. They then spent a final two weeks at the training centre in Jamkhed.

Throughout the training period, members of the FCs and the MVMs helped the trainees understand the extent to which they could teach village people to participate in health programmes.

Following this initial programme, training teams visited each new trainee once every three months in her village and also met her once a month at the government primary health centre to which she was attached. During these visits they helped the new VHG solve her difficulties in the village. This follow-up continued for over five years. Once a year for three consecutive years, the community health guides returned to Jamkhed for refresher training. After intensive training and monitoring for five years these CHGs were handed over to the Government.

Grass root workers need support

The VHGs expected the same kind of support from the staff at their primary health centres as the village health workers enjoyed in Jamkhed. But the government PHC staff are not trained or even inclined to provide support or consider VHGs as learners and competent equals. To overcome this problem we identified about twelve non-governmental organisations (NGOs) in the district, that were willing to support these VHGs and provide regular training. The nurses and social workers in these organisations also helped to form Mahila Vikas Mandals to support them. These NGOs continue to support the government VHGs.

The Government did not make monetary provisions for ongoing refresher training of the VHGs and did not have facilities for overnight accommodation. The involvement of NGOs thus ensured proper training and monitoring of village guides throughout the district.

Village people as trainers

The mobilisation of the village people and their participation in the health programmes was considered one of CRHP's major strengths. The Maharashtra State Government requested that their district training teams, district health officers and primary health centre doctors attend workshops at Jamkhed for reorientation to primary health care. The members of the farmers' clubs and Mahila Vikas Mandals together with the village health workers again played an active role in the discussions and shared their experiences.

Later the Government of Maharashtra invited representatives of the farmers' clubs and Mahila Vikas Mandals and village health workers to participate in workshops for doctors working in rural areas at their regional family welfare training centres. The village people accepted this challenge and over a period of three months enthusiastically travelled hundreds of kilometres and spent several days at these centres. A team of ten village men and women accompanied by a CRHP social worker participated in each workshop. It was a new experience for the medical officers to have to listen to 'illiterate' village people expound on the components of primary health care. The villagers pleaded with the doctors to demystify medicine, so that ordinary villagers could grasp the essentials of basic health. An average villager, they demonstrated, was intelligent enough to learn new ideas and practices. They argued that if the doctors would get rid of the belief that villagers are ignorant and trust their capacity to make decisions, community participation would be vigorous. Then the doctors would be successful in achieving their health goals.

After WHO identified Jamkhed as a model for innovative health programmes, many organisations visited the area. These organisations included the Mandva project headed by Dr N. H. Antia and the Wadu project of KEM Hospital in Pune. The most significant contribution we made to these projects was demonstrating the training and empowerment of village health workers and successful community participation. Initially most doctors and administrators from these programmes were sceptical about training illiterate village women and about meaningful and dynamic community participation. There was considerable exchange of ideas and they have incorporated many of Jamkhed's principles on training, integration and community participation into their programmes.

Beyond Maharashtra – reaching out to the world community

During the 1980s, CRHP conducted a large number of workshops on community health and development for non-governmental organisations, both in India and abroad. Several international workshops on primary health care were held in Jamkhed, with participants from almost eighty countries. In these workshops the village health workers, the Mahila Vikas Mandals and the farmers' clubs participated freely. These workshops also exposed the staff of CRHP and the village people to many new ideas, which further enhanced the capabilities of the teams and the village people.

Several documentaries on Jamkhed and the CRHP communities helped spread the philosophy and principles of primary health care. In the mid 1970s Dr and Mrs Mook made a documentary, 'Open My Eyes,' on the training of village health workers using Shantabai's work as an example. It served as a teaching aid for many non-governmental groups involved in primary health care.

Lalanbai's work in Pimpalgaon was documented in 'A Way to the Village'. This film is being shown in cinemas in India. Later, the Family Planning Foundation of India produced 'Triumph Over Rock', as part of a series depicting women's participation in health and family planning programmes in India. The BBC also produced a documentary called 'East of Bombay', which showed the hard life of rural women and demonstrated empowerment of women through Salubai's work as a village health worker. Through all these documentaries, the work at Jamkhed has had far-reaching effects and has contributed to the primary health care movement worldwide.

CRHP's impact has not been confined to health alone. The multisectoral approach and the socioeconomic changes in Jamkhed attracted officials in other sectors of development to CRHP. The success of the women's income-generating programmes and credit trustworthiness led the National Agricultural Bank for Rural Development (NABARD) to invite the Mahila Vikas Mandals to six national seminars for block development officers and bankers. These village women were able to articulate the needs of rural women and persuade them to provide loans to women for income generation activities.

The Mahila Vikas Mandals' success in afforestation also drew attention to the role of women in the development of plant nurseries and in the overall national social forestry programme. The Jamkhed philosophy is not confined to a few villages. The village people have demonstrated that the key to development is the possession of appropriate and relevant knowledge and skills, and not necessarily formal university degrees. Possessing, sharing and using this knowledge has empowered them. This empowerment gives them self-confidence to share boldly their experiences with formally educated professionals.

Ordinary village women like Lalanbai, Parubai and Muktabai have travelled all over India and shared their views on health and development with planners, policy makers and health professionals. Many have addressed international conferences and thus made a significant contribution to the primary health care movement far beyond their own villages.

CHAPTER 16

Monitoring, evaluation and achievements

MABELLE

Village surveys

Assessment of the health needs of the community and evaluation of how those needs are being met is traditionally considered the prerogative of the health care provider. Usually public health personnel are involved in this exercise. At Jamkhed, over the years, this skill has been shared with the people. If people are to be involved in the decision making, planning and implementation, they need to assess whether their programmes are working towards the objectives they have set.

Since the assessment is community based, it is so simplified that only necessary information based on the objectives and priorities of the project is collected. In this process the community and the CRHP staff together collect information, analyse it and plan strategies. It is a learning process for all those involved, namely, the village people, village health workers and the health team. The information is not a set of figures to be sent to a distant administrator but a tool for monitoring the programme and for improving on the services of the village health worker and the health team at the village level.

Because the information system utilises the local village people, costs of collecting information are minimised. House-to-house surveys, participatory rapid appraisal, and focus group discussion are some methods used to collect information.

After the village curative clinics were established in the early 1970s, the health teams, including the ANMs, nurses like Jeribai and paramedical workers like Vasant Jadhav and Uttam Thorat, were taught how to carry out a house-to-house health survey. This survey not only established baseline data on the health of the community but also introduced the health team to every family in the village. It helped members of the team understand the health priorities and health needs in the community. The survey identified target populations for such health priorities as the under-five children, women for prenatal care and those with chronic diseases such as leprosy and tuberculosis.

Assessment of crude birth rates, family planning practices, mortality and causes of death were included in the surveys. Firstly the village leaders were contacted and involved in the surveys. Since they did not have time to participate, they identified a few people to help us in our task. Usually the village Kotwal, or watchman, was appointed to accompany the team. Village Kotwals collect and store information on births, deaths and migration in the villages and therefore they know every family. Having the Kotwal along was an advantage to the team. He provided details such as the names of the head of the household, caste and other information, so that when the interviewers went into the household they could greet the person by name and make appropriate comments, such as sympathising if there had been a recent death in the family or offering congratulations for a recent birth. If they encountered an illness they first gave appropriate treatment before proceeding with the survey. Meeting primary needs helped establish rapport between the health team and the village people. Despite this friendly attitude, people were sometimes reluctant to talk to us 'outsiders' about sensitive issues like death or the practice of family planning and abortion. Nine villages were surveyed initially.

Here are some results:

Population	7819	
Infant mortality rate	176	per 1000 live births
Crude birth rate	40	per 1000
Crude death rate	16	per 1000
Children under five		
Immunisation -		
DPT and polio	0.5	%
Malnutrition weight for age	40	%
Maternal services		
Prenatal care	0.5	%
Deliveries by trained birth attendants	less than 0.5	%
Couples practising family planning	less than 1	%

Later as the farmers' clubs were formed, they participated in the house-to-house health surveys. This learning process helped the village people to have a clearcut health picture of their village.

The Bavi farmers' club conducted one of the first surveys. Badam, one of the FC members recalls: 'Five or six of us were involved in the first health survey of my village along with the CRHP team. We were told that this health survey would enable us to understand some of the health problems in the village and it was necessary to have accurate and complete information. Well, if it was for our own good, then we should do it. Each of us took one area of the village and collected all the preliminary information. No family was left out.

The questionnaire was not difficult to answer. There were questions about immunisation of the children and whether they had been ill in the preceding two weeks. We were to report any child death in the past twelve months and details of how the child had died. We learned to assess the nutritional status of the child by measuring the arm circumference. Children with 'sparse brittle light hair' were pointed out to us as children eating food lower in protein. To our surprise, many of the children we thought had severe illness turned out to have just lack of adequate food! There were questions on pregnancy and family planning. Because of our presence, village women did not mind answering sensitive questions. We also helped Uttam Thorat and the others to examine everyone for leprosy. Some people would be away at the time of the survey. We would visit them at their convenience and complete the survey. We could contact the people at their convenience as we were from the same village.'

Thorat and Jadhav helped the farmers' club to analyse the survey. The results provided many topics for discussion in club meetings.

Badam continues, 'The survey revealed that over 40 per cent of the children were malnourished. Thin scrawny children were commonly seen in Bavi, but we had accepted the situation as our fate. While few of us were discussing these concerns at the beginning, slowly over forty men joined us. The whole group was interested in reducing this malnutrition. We decided to organise a community kitchen and appointed a few members to be in charge.

'Donated food would be used till the drought was over. We learned to weigh the children every month and record the weights on the "Road to Health" cards.'

Another action emerging from the survey was improvement in sanitation. Many village people had experienced repeated attacks of fever and chills. Diarrhea was common. Madhukar Walunjkar says, 'We discovered that 80 per cent of the families suffered at least three episodes of fever with chills, which we presumed to be malaria, in

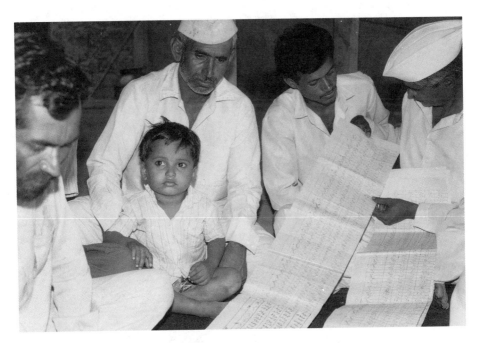

Farmers' club members discussing socioeconomic survey

the year. We were told by CRHP that if we got rid of the puddles made by the waste water and composted the rubbish heaps, the mosquitoes and flies would not breed so fast and that would reduce the frequency of diseases. With each attack we spent close to Rs:10 to go to the doctor. That meant Rs:30 per year. Our village has a population of approximately six hundred people. That means at least Rs:14 000 was being spent for diseases that we could prevent! Moreover, we were told that even if we did have such illnesses they did not need injections and expensive medicines to cure. So why not try cleaning up the village? Mr Arun Londhe showed us several methods of draining the waste water. The soak pit, with water draining underground, appealed to us most. We mobilised the whole village to build soak pits. Most families showed interest. We farmers' club members dug the pits and the owners provided the filling of sand, broken bricks and a wooden plank to place over the pit. It certainly drove away malaria from our village.'

The surveys further brought out that whooping cough affected almost every child. Measles with its complications contributed to the high morbidity and mortality among children. Pregnant mothers did not receive any care.

As the surveys continued, participation in collecting information became an important aspect of CRHP. In 1973 village health workers

Weighing a child for the 'Road to Health' card

were incorporated into the programme. As they became knowledge-able, the VHWs were also involved in the information system. Later, the newly formed Mahila Vikas Mandal also joined in the surveys.

Gathering health information from house to house has become an annual feature. Members of the farmers' club and the Mahila Vikas Mandal and representatives of the village health workers meet with the mobile health team. They design questionnaires according to their interests and compare them with programmes of the previous year. They have so simplified the form that a semi-literate person can handle it. The health team works with the village people to analyse and discuss the results of the survey. They provide technical help wherever required.

The house-to-house survey serves several purposes. It is an instrument to help village people periodically to assess their health status. It helps them plan new programmes. For example, in 1973 prevention of blindness was added to the health priorities because surveys showed that many persons had vitamin A deficiency and elderly persons were blind due to cataract. People initiated a programme to provide vitamin A capsules regularly and encouraged mothers to cook food rich in vitamin A. They requested CRHP to teach women how to diagnose cataract and bring those persons with mature cataract for surgery.

Another purpose is to identify the impact of health education on the community. Knowledge, attitude and practice questionnaires are developed and administered to village men and women from time to time.

The yearly survey helps the VHW to target her activities on priority groups. Muktabai Pol explains the procedure. 'One of the farmers' club members like Madhukar Sastare helps me extract the information. The list of all the children under three is made. I have a notebook divided into different sections for the different priority groups. There is a section listing all the children needing immunisation, malnourished children and any other special problems. In another section I have the list of pregnant mothers with details of each woman's pregnancy and if she is high risk. All couples eligible for family planning are listed along with the method of contraceptive practice. Then there are the lists of tuberculosis and leprosy patients and those with eye problems.

'During the year I update the information in my book. This enables me to understand what programmes need my attention. A symbol is used to attract my attention. An empty O indicates that work is to be done. For example, the child has not had immunisation, or a pregnant woman is not taking prenatal care or a person is suspected of having tuberculosis or has been diagnosed and is not taking treatment. O means high priority. Work needs to be done. A+ means that the intervention is under way, but not complete. For example: The child is being immunised but has not completed the doses. The same symbol is used for a mother having prenatal care or a tuberculosis patient taking treatment regularly. I just have to follow up such people and see that the action is completed. Then those whose have completed treatment or the immunisation or have had a permanent method of sterilisation will have a (+), meaning the action is complete. In the beginning I needed the help of an FC member or relative to fill my records. Now I can do it on my own.

In addition to the data collected through the house-to-house survey, the village health worker maintains a record of her daily or weekly activities, including a record of births and deaths in the village. During her weekly training session at the CRHP centre, each death is thoroughly discussed. This verbal autopsy includes discussions on cause

215

of death and whether it could have been prevented. Sometimes a preventable death in a village results in introducing a new programme. For example, a 13-year-old girl who was injured got tetanus and died in Pimpalgaon. This girl's family had always refused immunisation. The village health workers and Mahila Vikas Mandals realised that there was no immunisation programme for adults and older children, though they are prone to injuries. The MVMs organised tetanus toxoid immunisation programmes for the men and youth in sixty-four villages.

The health team systematically collects and stores the information extracted from the health surveys. The information system at the centre level is a collation of all the village surveys with the various health priorities. Team members divide the responsibility of keeping the records at the centre. Registers are kept for the various programmes, such as tuberculosis, leprosy, prenatal care, deliveries, immunisation and so on. The records are updated throughout the year and the yearly survey helps to cross check and add new information. The trends in infant mortality and birth rates and the utilisation of services such as prenatal care and safe deliveries are discussed with FCs, MVMs and VHWs.

Because information from the annual surveys is shared by the farmers' clubs and the Mahila Vikas Mandals, the village health workers

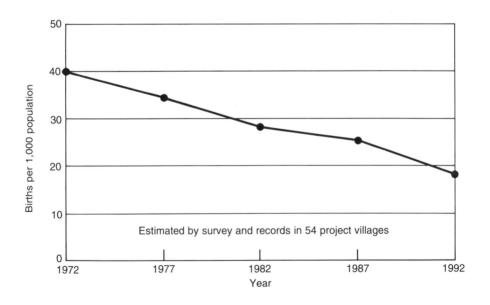

Crude birth rate; project villages 1972–92

and the mobile health teams, all of them can review the work done and plan programmes.

Each village has its own priorities for development activities. Through the networking at the centre, common objectives and plans are formulated for health. Each village tends to emphasise its own interests, which often depend on the problems there. Some villages have more leprosy patients than others. In Bavi the farmers' club found over twenty patients suspected of having leprosy. So eradication of leprosy became their main objective.

From health to development

The entry point of CRHP into the community was with health activities. It has evolved from merely a health service activity to a comprehensive development programme. The non-medical aspects of the programme were evaluated in 1983. Representatives of the farmers' clubs, Mahila Vikas Mandals, village health workers and the social workers got together and decided how they would go about the evaluation. The group was familiar with house-to-house surveys. They decided to use that as the main method. In addition, they planned on having focus group discussions to find out the attitudes of village people toward women and caste.

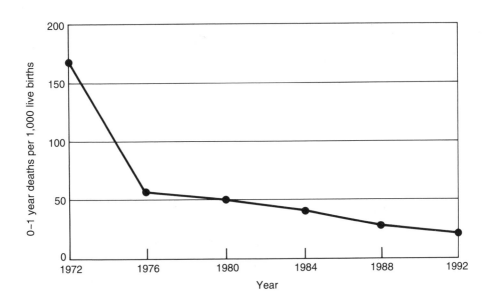

Infant mortality rate; project villages 1972–92

217

Questions ranged from technical knowledge on agriculture and animal husbandry to the environment. Behavioural changes were determined by a variety of questions such as, 'Are you afraid of the village government functionaries or village power brokers?' – a question that only a villager would think of! Villages were also asked for information on how much money they borrowed from money lenders and to what extent they knew about various government development programmes and how many had benefited from them.

The evaluation group set their own criteria for economic classification, based not on money but on availability of basic necessities of life, namely, food. They arrived at three categories of economic status, as given in the table below.

Economic class	Criterion
1. Well off	Those assured of food twelve months of the year
2. Average or poor	Those assured of food nine months of the year
3. Indigent	Those assured of food less than nine months of the year

Focus group discussions and observations were led by members in villages other than their own. The Dalits and women also gave their impressions. The evaluation group developed criteria which they considered important as indicators of change.

The analysis was done by the village people and tabulated by them. Some of the results are:

Villages surveyed	57
Families interviewed	5634

Family in this survey was the joint family – those living under one roof. All those families present in the village at the time of survey were included. Of the respondents 75 per cent were women although whole families generally participated.

Economic status of families surveyed:

Well off	24.5 %
Poor	41.0 %
Indigent	34.5 %

Distribution of villages according to years the village has had a functioning farmers' club/Mahila Vikas Mandal.

A	Above 5 years	17 villages
B	2–5 years	24 villages
C	1–2 years	16 villages

Results:
Number of respondents: 5364

Topic	Economic status:	Duration of village programmes		
		above 5 years A	2–5 years B	1–2 years C
Knowledge of	Well off	90 %	70 %	30 %
agricultural techniques	Poor	83 %	66 %	18 %
	Indigent	80 %	52 %	6 %
Knowledge of animal	Well off	86 %	87 %	55 %
husbandry	Poor	90 %	73 %	35 %
	Indigent	94 %	72 %	33 %
Knowledge of	Well off	83 %	85 %	46 %
forestry	Poor	89 %	85 %	80 %
	Indigent	90 %	86 %	52 %
Knowledge of	Well off	75 %	80 %	43 %
government	Poor	95 %	68 %	22 %
and bank programmes	Indigent	89 %	87 %	7 %
Fear of government	Well off	0 %	2 %	66 %
functionaries etc	Poor	6 %	6 %	92 %
	Indigent	2 %	7 %	87 %

Changes in attitude and practice towards caste and status of women were judged by observation, impressions and discussions in focus groups conducted by the farmers' club and the Mahila Vikas Mandals.

Criteria for caste problems
1. Are Dalits allowed to draw water from the common well?
2. Do people of different castes help each other?
3. Is there subtle pressure applied? (a negative answer is given a score of 2)
4. Do all children of all castes participate in the nutrition programme?
5. Do people of all castes eat together at weddings?

Each positive answer is given a score of 2 points (score of 2 indicates that majority have a positive attitude or practice): the possible total score is 10 points

Caste problems

Score	Number of villages in each category		
	A	B	C
0	–	–	–
1	–	–	–
2	–	–	1
3	–	1	4
4	–	5	4
5	4	11	3
6	4	6	2
7	4	–	1
8	5	1	1
9	–	–	–
10	–	–	–
	17	24	16

Criteria for women's status
1. Are women allowed to speak to leaders?
2. Are women allowed to come to public places?
3. Do women participate in village affairs?
4. Do women participate in literacy classes?
5. Do women participate in the decision making in the family?

Again, each positive answer is given a score of two points: the total possible score is 10 points.

Women's status

Score	A	B	C
0	–	–	–
1	–	–	–
2	–	–	2
3	–	3	3
4	1	3	7
5	1	5	3
6	4	7	1
7	6	5	–
8	5	1	–
9	–	–	–
10	–	–	–
	17	24	16

Following this exercise, several changes in strategy were suggested. These arose mainly from the focus group discussion. More participation in the seminars would be possible, it was proposed, if they were decentralised. Clusters of villages could hold a seminar. More women could participate if it was within walking distance of their village. This suggestion was adopted and the seminars were organised in the peripheral villages. The survey showed that people knew less about raising poultry than other livestock and that more training was needed.

One conclusion was that people take a long time to change and accept new ideas. In villages where MVMs had been working for two years or less, people were not sufficiently empowered. We learned that it takes almost three years for the people to organise. More than five years are needed for lasting changes to take place.

Improving the quality of life

Tremendous visible changes have occurred in the Jamkhed villages. Children are not malnourished. Infant mortality is now 18–20 per 1000 live births. Most deaths occur in the neonatal period. Significantly, the birth weights have increased by 0.75 kg. Despite the drought in 1992, children in the project area did not lose weight. Attitudes towards family planning have significantly changed. Women are interested in having fewer children. In some villages in the project area, over 70 per cent of couples are practising family planning. Oral contraceptives are also popular in the project villages. The preference is for sterilisation after a male child, but this is affecting the male:female sex ratio. In the under fifteen population the ratio is 1000 males to 715 females indicating a further need to change the attitudes that prefer male children. Acceptance of the female child would further reduce the birth rate. As women become more empowered such attitudes will also change.

Acceptance of preventive health programmes has increased over the years. Results of the surveys in 1992 are:

Preventive health programmes

Children under five	
Immunisation DPT and polio	92 %
Malnutrition weight for age	5 %
Maternal services	
Women having prenatal care	96 %
Deliveries by trained birth attendants	98 %

221

The extent to which mothers have health knowledge is studied from time to time by asking village women about whether common misconceptions have been removed. A sample of such a questionnaire is given below:

Knowledge attitude and practice survey

	% correct answers	
	1973 (baseline)	March 1985
I. Maternal care:		
1. Food restrictions	5 %	89 %
2. Food restrictions soon after delivery	4 %	78 %
3. What instrument would you use to cut cord?	3 %	99 %
II. Child care:		
1. When should you start breast feeding the baby?	1 %	98 %
2. When should solid food be introduced to the baby?	2 %	95 %
3. Home remedies for diarrhea?	3 %	99 %

The socioeconomic survey was conducted in 1990. The questionnaire was developed by 25 farmers' club members and the Mahila Mandal members along with CRHP staff. All families belonging to the lower socioeconomic groups were interviewed by the farmers' club members.

Number of villages surveyed:	12	
Number of families:	930	
Dalit	38.2 %	(355)
High caste	41.4 %	(385)
Other castes (Muslim, Tribes)	20.4 %	(190)

222

Results of socioeconomic survey

A LIFESTYLE	Status at the beginning of project		Present status	
1. Housing				
Thatched huts				
Dalits	42.2 %	(150)	5.6 %	(20)
High caste	15.1 %	(58)	2.6 %	(10)
Other	23.6 %	(45)	6.3 %	(12)
2. Clothing				
Rags				
Dalits	51.5 %	(183)	0.56 %	(2)
High caste	36.6 %	(141)	0.78 %	(3)
Other	38.9 %	(74)	0.00 %	
3. Food				
One meal a day – (The remaining ate two or three times a day)				
Dalit	50.4 %	(179)	0.28 %	(1)
High caste	32.2 %	(124)	0.00 %	
Others	40.5 %	(77)	0.00 %	
B Loans				
Loans from Moneylender				
Dalit	60.3 %	(214)	0.84 %	(3)
High caste	47.3 %	(182)	0.52 %	(2)
Others	58.4 %	(111)	1.6 %	(3)
Bank loans				
Dalits	10.4 %	(37)	62.8 %	(223)
High caste	18.7 %	(72)	62.9 %	(242)
Others	7.4 %	(14)	68.9 %	(131)
CRHP loans				
Dalits			35.8 %	(127)
High caste			13.8 %	(53)
Other			22.6 %	(43)

Benefits received through CRHP Interventions

	Families	Benefited
Bank and Government schemes	63.2 %	(588)
Agricultural development schemes	49.3 %	(459)
Seeds and fertilisers	45.5 %	(423)
Agricultural implements	21.8 %	(203)
Wells and land development	34.5 %	(321)
Check dams	26.5 %	(246)
Afforestation	31.9 %	(297)
Poultry	36.8 %	(342)
Goat keeping	43.2 %	(402)
Animal husbandry	23.7 %	(220)
Dairy	27.3 %	(254)
Health	77.1 %	(717)

Women's status	Percent with positive response	
Changed attitude toward women	97.6 %	(908)
School enrolment of girls	98.9 %	(920)
Own adult education	26.7 %	(248)
Women involved in financial decision making	94.7 %	(881)
Women attending meetings and seminars	93.5 %	(870)
Have seminars increased knowledge?	91.9 %	(855)

Change in attitude towards:	Percent with positive response	
Caste system	79.6 %	(740)
Helping others	83.7 %	(778)
Self-esteem	69.0 %	(642)
Attitudinal changes attributed to:		
Village Health Worker	76.5 %	
MVM / FC	61.0 %	
CRHP Seminars	76.7 %	

CHAPTER 17

Leprosy: integration into primary health care

MABELLE

Raj and I were in the outpatient clinic at Jamkhed. A 14-year-old girl in rags came in, hungry and wanting food. She had nodules on her forehead, her ear lobes were thickened and red and one of her fingers was deformed – all signs of leprosy. I asked her where her home was. She said she had no home but was an orphan girl staying with her married sister. A leprosy 'doctor'[1] had come to her village and had told her sister's family that she had leprosy. As soon as they heard the word leprosy they had told her to get out of the house and not stay anywhere near the village. The leprosy doctor should not be seen visiting their home. With no where to go, she had wandered from village to village begging and finally reached Jamkhed. This is the fate of many a leprosy patient.

The stigma of leprosy

From time immemorial leprosy has been known to humankind and yet lack of understanding of the disease by the general public has resulted in leprosy patients being ostracised and segregated. It is a stigma to have leprosy. It is thought to be a divine curse and the whole family is socially isolated. The disease tends to occur where there is overcrowding and in poor families. The medical profession in large measure has contributed to this misunderstanding. Even after the character and cause of leprosy has been understood, leprosy patients, although no longer treated in sanitaria, have still been made to attend separate leprosy clinics. Leprosy control programmes are separate and are not incorporated into other health systems. It is a vertically administered programme. By isolating the leprosy patients

225

we were endorsing the myth that leprosy was too contagious to be treated along with other patients.

The integration of leprosy patients

Both Raj and I were inspired by Dr Brand's approach to the leprosy patient, which involved admitting them to the general surgery ward and performed surgery to restore function. Persons having leprosy often bore the deep scars of segregation, and the family also suffered as they, too, were ostracised. The girls could not get married and even close relatives did not socialise. This social stigma prevented patients from being detected early as they preferred to hide the disease and not take treatment for as long as possible rather than be seen in a leprosy clinic or have a leprosy worker come home. Not only the patient and the families suffered, but the paramedical workers in leprosy found themselves being ostracised.

Vasant Jadhav, who came to us as a leprosy paramedical worker from Vadala says, 'As a leprosy paramedical worker, I found that I had no friends. People were scared to come near me as they feared that they would be mistaken for taking treatment for leprosy from me. When I went to the village people shut their doors on me. It made the work difficult. There was no job satisfaction.'

Another problem we observed was that most of the paramedical workers were men. Leprosy patches on the skin often occurs in the covered parts of the body. Women would not allow the men to examine them and so were not detected early.

We felt that integrating the leprosy programme with the rest of the health strategy would help overcome most of these problems. It has been argued that health workers involved in other health activities would give low priority to leprosy and neglect the disease. We felt that with proper orientation and management the leprosy control programme could be well integrated.

CRHP integrated the leprosy programme with the other health activities and the American Leprosy Mission have supported the leprosy control programme over all these years.

The first opposition to integrate the programme with other health activities came from the nurses. Raj and I saw quite a few patients with leprosy in the clinic at Jamkhed. We treated them along with the other patients. Akka was upset. 'How can we treat leprosy patients along with the others in the general clinic?' Akka was not against treating them, in fact she was the one who devoted hours removing maggots from the nose of a leprosy patient. But her training came in her way of accepting the leprosy patient in the general

226

clinic. She wanted to isolate these patients and hold separate clinics for them. Traditionally that is what is done in most hospitals if they care to treat patients with leprosy. Raj replied, 'Why can't you treat leprosy patients in the clinic like anyone else. They are human beings aren't they?

You treat tuberculosis in the clinic. It is also caused by the same family of bacteria, *Mycobacterium*. Yet you have not objected to treating tuberculosis patients. In fact tuberculosis is more infective than leprosy. We have no difficulty in treating these other infectious diseases such as typhoid and cholera and other highly contagious diseases. It is unscientific to isolate the leprosy patients. It is not so easy to get leprosy you know.' 'But what about the village people. Will they accept leprosy patients coming to our clinic?' was another fear expressed by the nurses.

I replied, 'It is up to us to teach patients and village people about leprosy. It depends on how we behave with the patients. We must take the fears away. Today leprosy patients are being shunned. They are treated badly by their families. They are losing their dignity and have to take to the streets to beg. We have to help these patients get back into society and lead normal lives. The first thing is that we ourselves have to change our own attitude. We know that casual contact with a leprosy patient does not give the disease. By having a separate clinic we are telling people to keep away from those with leprosy.'

'ANMs must be involved in this programme' I told her. 'As you know, the diagnosis depends on finding an anesthetic patch on the body. Women do not allow the male paramedical workers to examine them and so are missed out in the examination. The result is that few women get diagnosed early. When the hands start getting deformities, their relatives realise it is leprosy and send them away. They end up as beggars in the cities. This must be prevented.' Akka as always would make a feeble objection and then comply. She would sigh and say 'After all this, "the project", and every day we are learning new things.'

Sometimes leprosy patients came with high fever and chills and 'in reaction' with severe joint pains and other symptoms which needed hospitalisation. We admitted them to our makeshift ward. Others came with ulcers on the foot. They too were admitted. Most patients came to the general clinic and took medicine as anyone else did. Once in a while when there was a patient with obvious leprosy sitting in the outpatient clinic. A villager would ask us about the disease and why we did not send him to another clinic. He would readily accept our explanation and say 'if you do not think it is harmful to us we have no objection.'

Leprosy was discussed in detail in the Tuesday classes. The ANMs

227

and the other paramedical workers learnt to look for the anesthetic patch, for thickened nerves and other signs of leprosy. Over the years eight men and women were sent to a nearby institution for a six-month course in leprosy. Apart from training in leprosy, each of them acquired other skills. None of them could be singled out as a leprosy paramedical worker.

The village health workers recognised the part they had to play in leprosy control work. They wanted to learn all about the disease, and so were taught how to examine persons for leprosy. They learned to look for symptoms such as the typical skin patch having no sensation, less hair and change in colour, wasting of the small muscles of the hand, thickening of certain nerves, nodules and thickening of the ear lobes. We taught them to find leprosy in the early stages of the disease so that effective treatment could be started and deformities prevented. They took the help of the farmers' clubs and Mahila Vikas Mandals in this control programme. As a result of community involvement the leprosy control programme became a community programme.

When people themselves are involved in detecting the patients, they are able to comprehend the extent of the disease in their own villages. They get interested in its control. For instance in Bavi, the farmers' club noticed that there were quite a number of people with early signs of the

Village health worker examining for leprosy

228

disease. They took special interest. Firstly they had educational programmes, developing skits and dramas on leprosy. Following the educational programmes they conducted the surveys themselves. In the words of a village woman, 'When we look for leprosy we keep our eyes open. Always alert for tell-tale patches. As we walk down we observe people who are bathing at the well, swimming in the pond. Our surveys are more complete. When the health team comes from outside, people who have skin patches go into hiding. But we know who is in the village. They may hide from us a couple of times, but not forever. We can see them anytime, day or night. That's why we find more leprosy patients than the health teams do.'

One of the farmers' club members adds, 'We found twenty-two patients with leprosy in our village. We convinced all but one the importance of treatment. Shanthabai our village health worker followed them up regularly. Only one of the patients refused to take treatment. He said it was a visit from a goddess. We started putting pressure on him.' They said they would ostracise him not because he had leprosy but because he would not take treatment and thus encourage the spread of the disease to their children. It took more than one year and a severe reaction of the disease to convince the person to start treatment.

Every year leprosy detection is part of the multifaceted survey conducted by the village health workers, the Mahila Vikas Mandals and the farmers' clubs. New cases are referred to the health team when they visit the village and once the diagnosis is confirmed they are started on treatment. Since the village health worker is dealing with a number of health problems, her visiting the house for follow-up of the leprosy patient is not suspected. As the village people learn more and more about the disease, it is not necessary to keep its appearance a secret.

The village health workers found different methods of looking for the disease. In the village there are divine healers who claim to have a cure for numbness, tingling and loss of sensation. The village health workers recognised that some of this numbness and tingling may be due to leprosy. They kept a watch on the people who went to the local divine healers who specialised in numbness and tingling symptoms. Later they would approach the person and find out if he or she had any signs of leprosy. Anjanabai's son was such a divine healer. People with symptoms of numbness and tingling went to him for advice. Anjanabai told her son to call her during the ritual. She would go round and if she saw anything that looked like a patch she would sign to the son to advise the person to take medicine from the clinic as well. As people came to know more about the disease they stopped going to the divine healer. Anjanabai's son later stopped his

229

practice. Thus without confronting the healers, the leprosy patients were gradually convinced to take treatment from the village health worker or the health team.

One of the methods of looking for leprosy is the school health survey. Every year quite a lot of time was spent conducting school health examinations. Most children with health problems were from poor families and were not in school. They were the ones who would often be missed out as they were not at home but in the fields grazing their animals, or playing. In 1978 a special effort was made by the village health workers to reach these children by going out to the fields and other places such as the streams where they may be swimming. The result was that sixty-three children with early leprosy were diagnosed in the seventy villages that were in the project area at that time.

Once diagnosed the patient is given the choice to take treatment through the village health worker or to go to the general outpatient clinic at Jamkhed. The village health worker keeps a record of the regularity of the treatment. Over 80 per cent of the patients kept up the treatment. In fact when we stared the multi-drug treatment which is short term, most patients did not want to stop it as they feared that deformities would occur and the new found lease of life would come to an end.

The prevention of deformities is important in leprosy. Once the village health workers understood the reasons for deformities they made the health teaching relevant to the local life-style and work. How can a woman with leprosy cook without injuring her fingers? How do you bake the local bread on the fire with the common utensils available in the home? Use the pair of tongs or the pipe with which you blow the fire. How do you hold the plough or the spade while weeding? These are some of the questions answered for the village people.

Anjanabai says, 'I used to visit the leprosy patients every day in the beginning to find out how they took care of their hands and feet. I taught my patients to use their eyes and look at what they are doing to prevent injury or a burn. I did that till the patients really understood the importance of looking after their hands and feet. I taught them how to massage their fingers and keep them straight. Many of the patients were poor and they could not afford footwear. Soft shoes without nails are needed for these patients. There was a cobbler at the centre who made these shoes out of old car tyres. I took the measurements and we made shoes just like the village ones so that these patients were not singled out.'

Merely finding the patients and treating them is not enough to break down the social stigma of leprosy. We taught the village health workers the nature of the disease. Most of the problems of deformity, infection and fingers and toes falling off is not directly due to the disease, but to injury because the patient cannot feel the pain sensation. We told them that when an affluent person has an ulcer as a result of neuritis as in diabetes, the person is not ostracised. But when a leprosy patient has a similar ulcer he is shunned, because of the stigma the disease bears, and the fact that it is commoner among the poor and marginalised. Both ulcers, however, are caused by the same lack of sensation. If a leprosy patient goes to a shop with a few pennies the shopkeeper may chase him out. But if he went with a wad of rupees then any one would do business with him. We took advantage of this weakness of human nature and decided to help leprosy patients earn get a good income.

The farmers' club and the Mahila Vikas Mandals were consulted. Raising goats was considered a lucrative business. The farmers, clubs and Mahila Vikas Mandals helped look after the goats. They prevented others taking undue advantage of the patient and buying the goats at a cheaper price. Those who had difficulty tying the goats or grazing them were helped by one of the members of the farmers' club or the village health worker. This programme was a success.

Many of these leprosy patients did well. One example is Vasant Sathe, who had no land and he was not able to work on the field. He was given eight goats in 1972 and by 1975 he had repaid them. The male kids are sold for meat and the females are kept back. He went on to buy a cow. His wife became a member of Mahila Vikas Mandal and raised chickens. In 1987 Vasant Sathe bought land for farming, and was completely accepted in the village.

Says Bhagwan of Bavi village, 'I noticed a patch on my leg and an ulcer on my foot. It was not healing and was confirmed as leprosy. The village farmers' club reassured me and on their advice I took treatment regularly. I was given eight goats, and was able to sell the kids for a good price and also drink the milk. My family and children were not left to starve. I gained a new lease of life. As the patches started disappearing I was able to proudly hold my head up and walk in the village. My farm also needed help. Through Food for Work programmes my fields were levelled. The farmers' clubs recommended me for a bank loan and I was able to get a pump set. Even though people in my village know I have leprosy, they wanted me to stand for the village election and elected me as a village council member. I, a Dalit with leprosy am now living in dignity. With the new drugs I do not have to take the medicines anymore. When I started prospering I gave eight goats to another leprosy patient and so the help continues.

I am actively involved in going around and telling people about leprosy – that I had it once and that it should be eliminated by everyone taking treatment.'

Women too have been rehabilitated. One has to be careful in treating a woman as often she may be expelled from her home by her husband. The village health worker knows the character of the individuals in her village. She knows which family should be told and when. Paraigabai and her sister have a step-mother. Both of them used to get severe reactions with leprosy and were not kindly treated at home. Muktabai, herself ostracised for tuberculosis, understood their problems. For over ten years the two girls were followed up by the village health worker. Today the younger sister is married. Paraigabai herself became a member of the Mahila Vikas Mandal, often taking the village health worker's place. She obtained a loan, learnt tailoring and supports herself. She also looks after her father's farm as he is getting old and she has no brothers. Often the village health worker has to give treatment to a woman without the knowledge of her husband's family. This is possible because leprosy is treated along with other health problems. The village health worker's kit contains many other medicines in addition to the anti-leprosy medicines.

With the advent of medicines like rifampicin and clofazimine, the treatment of leprosy has became simple. Formerly these patients had to take treatment for life but now it is stopped within six months to two years. But now a close watch has to be kept on the persons to look for any signs of relapse.

This is easily possible with the help of the local community organisations. They do house-to-house surveys every year and thus keep a surveillance on the patients with leprosy. Today, in most villages, persons having leprosy are well accepted, and people publicly admit that they have the disease. The ultimate acceptance of the disease is marriage. Many of the patients have been able to get married.

What about Indubai Powar the beggar girl? She was treated in the health centre. When she turned eighteen we asked the farmers' club members to find a husband for her. One of the villages responded. They found a young man with a few acres of land. The club members decided to help with wedding expenses. They made all the arrangements. Other clubs pitched in and provided the band for the ceremonies. The dignitaries and leaders of Jamkhed were also invited to the wedding. The farmers' club built a small house for the couple. Indubai has two children now. She lives in dignity. Over the years the number of new patients being diagnosed is gradually coming down. In villages where there were over twenty patients, today there are only three or four left.

By demystifying the nature of the disease it has been possible to work towards its eradication. That leprosy should be eradicated is

232

no more a goal of CRHP than it is of the people themselves. Because of their participation it has been possible to detect patients at an early stage of the disease. They have been rehabilitated in their own villages. Their migration to the cities to end up begging on the streets has been prevented.

Often leprosy patients are sent to the city to learn trades such as furniture making, tailoring and other occupations useful in the city. They are uprooted from their own culture. On their return they are not readily accepted by the people. It is better to rehabilitate these patients in their own villages in occupations they are used to. The need for family support is also important and the psychological problems seen in individuals who have been uprooted from their families can be avoided.

Over the years, over two thousand leprosy patients from the neighbouring areas also come for treatment. Among them are people from all walks of life. There are businessmen, professionals and administrators. They pay for their treatment. Most of them come because they do not have to go to a segregated leprosy clinic. There is no loss of dignity.

In the 175 villages, 2026 patients have been diagnosed and treated in the last twenty years. Only 403 patients are now on treatment. The number of patients being diagnosed is gradually diminishing. Those newly diagnosed are people with early signs of the disease. Vasant Jadhav also has developed. In 1970 he came as a leprosy paramedical worker. Today he is the coordinator for all the health activities in Jamkhed block. He says, 'Today, when I go to the villages, people welcome me and invite me in. They talk to me about their farms and their problems. They are knowledgeable about health and ask for their children to be immunised. They know about leprosy and if they suspect they call us in to have a look. The village health worker is there and so are the members of the farmers' club and the Mahila Vikas Mandal. They find the patients; they bring the children and mothers. We do not have to go from house to house begging people to listen to us. It is so satisfying. I too have learned to look beyond leprosy, beyond disease, at the human face, the person, the family, the community behind the disease.'

Leprosy can be effectively brought under control in the context of primary health care. It is more acceptable and more cost effective. With such an approach we can dare to think of eradication of leprosy as a possible goal!

On indigenous practitioners

From the time we came to Jamkhed we attempted to incorporate all systems of medicine in our work. Though there are many indigenous practitioners, most of them were involved in magic and goddess possession. There were a few herbalists and bone setters. We had many discussions with them and found out what they did. They showed us a few herbs which were effective and these we incorporated in the home remedies. In particular was the medicine for hepatitis. Crab soup boiled with liquorice proved to be effective as were other herbs identified by the local healers. There were also many herbs used for ordinary cough, skin infections and scabies.

We also employed Ayurvedic and homeopathic trained doctors. However we found that they did not have any regard for their own system of medicine and tended to practise allopathic medicine. We also found that the Ayurvedic medicines are commercialised and are as expensive as modern medicine and there was no advantage in prescribing such drugs.

In some parts of India, particularly Kerala and Punjab, homeopathy and Ayurveda are popular. It may be because herbs are difficult to find in this drought area of Jamkhed that these herbal types of medicine are not so popular.

1. Generally in leprosy control programmes, leprosy technicians survey the villages for leprosy.

CHAPTER 18

Resource mobilisation: towards self-reliance and sustainability

From the very beginning we had the objective of developing a sustainable and viable health programme. Jamkhed block is chronically drought prone and was considered one of the poorest areas in Maharashtra State, so to work towards this self-reliance presented a challenge.

Resources

Human resources, materials and money are essential for health and development programmes. Money and material resources are limited in areas like Jamkhed. However, precious human resources are abundant and untapped. We mobilised the people to be involved in the health activities and ultimately this strategy turned out to be most effective. As the project evolved into a more holistic multi-disciplinary approach, many non-medical interventions were introduced. Finances were then divided into programmes that are conventionally considered as medical interventions, such as primary curative care, the mobile curative clinics, secondary and tertiary care including the hospital at the health centre level, and programmes considered non-medical interventions. These include programmes addressing the environment, water and sanitation, socioeconomic development and programmes related to agriculture. The cost of health care may be divided into primary health care at the village level including the work of the mobile team, and the secondary care and support services provide by the health centres.

Investing in human resources for primary health care

Human resources are crucial for primary health care. Ordinary village people have been organised, trained and continually supported in technical matters for their health and development. Initially, money is required to bring together hundreds of village people for training and demonstration. Though they come as volunteers, the CRHP has to provide them with accommodation and food and also provide for the experts in different fields of health and development to share their knowledge. These initial costs may seem considerable at first. However, an analysis reveals that in terms of per capita cost and long-term investment, the expenses are moderate and perhaps within in the range of most countries' resources. Take, for instance, the village of Pimpalgaon, with a population of approximately 1000 people. The initial investment for the initial three years was:

I. Human resource development:

Training VHWs, organising and supporting YFC and MVM

1. VHW training, travel, food	$800
2. Quarterly seminars (6–10 persons)	$1 500
3. Matching grant for FC	$200
4. CRHP staff visits to Pimpalgaon to organise and strengthen FC	$800

Total costs for three years — US $3 300

This is an investment of $1.10 per capita per year for a period of three years for training and empowering people in health care and development.

II. Investment in non-medical interventions:

1. Water: 2 tube wells	$1 500
2. Watershed development, improved agriculture, land levelling, afforestation	$23 000
3. Nutrition programmes	$6 500
4. Rehabilitation	$700

Initial development costs (three years) — US $31 700

or approximately $10.50 per capita per year for three years.

III. Medical interventions:

Initially, the backlog of immunisation coupled with higher incidence of disease required more inputs. Figures include staff costs and travel.

Weekly curative clinics*	$2 500
MCH and FP services	$400
Treatment of TB and leprosy	$1 400
Health education, etc	$200

Medical interventions costs 3 years — US $4 500

or approximately US$1.50 per capita per year.

---

* Does not include treatment of all episodes of illness in the village.

236

In 1974 surveys revealed that 29 per cent of the population did nothing for their illness. Only 25 per cent sought modern medical treatment.

$1500 per year or $1.50 per capita investment for medical interventions in addition to other capital costs included jeep and other medical equipment at approximately US $1 per capita over a period of 10–12 years. In the first three years of starting the project CRHP spent approximately $13.5 per capita for developing the primary health care programme in the villages. Not included in these costs are the hidden costs such as the time and effort of the village people.

These costs however, fell dramatically as the morbidity decreased and the immunisation backlog was cleared. As village health workers became knowledgeable and efficient, weekly clinics were no longer necessary. Interventions such as safe drinking water and health education have made a difference in the incidence of illness. This fall in morbidity patterns has been documented. In 1974, an average 7.6 per cent of the population reported an illness per month. In 1992 a year-long study showed that in the same villages the morbidity has dropped to 3.2 per cent per month.

As communities became more empowered, more and more responsibilities of primary health care were taken over by the village people. The cost of care was discussed with the people in focus groups, using the data of the morbidity surveys carried out in 1992. The results of the discussion in Bavi were as follows.

Bavi had a mid-year population in 1992 of 1014 people.

During the year, three persons in Bavi needed surgery (one Caesarian, one hysterectomy and one acute appendicitis). Two women delivered in the hospital and three others were admitted for medical conditions. The village people calculated the total health costs that the village had needed.

1. Consultation and treatment of episodes of illness by primary care	$300
2. Treatment of TB and leprosy, including rehabilitation	$250
3. Preventive programmes, MCH, FP, sanitation incurred by government or village	$150
4. Mobile team expenses, quarterly seminars, etc.	$400
5. VHW support and continuing education	$150
6. Secondary care hospital costs	$500
Total cost of health care	$1750

The village people of Bavi needed to spend approximately directly or indirectly $1.75 per capita for their total health care.

A similar exercise in other villages revealed that most village people are spending approximately $1.75 to $2 a year for their health care. These villages have a crude birth rate of 19 per 1000 population and an infant mortality rate of 17 per 1000 births and they enjoy relatively good health. Studies in other parts of India, such as that carried out by Duggal and Amin in Jalgaon district, show that people spend on an average Rs 154/($5.1) per capita per year for curative care alone. This does not include the cost of preventive and promotive services which they may or may not be availing themselves of. Morbidity studies in Jalgaon have indicated a morbidity rate of 16 per cent per month in the population studied. In contrast, the low morbidity rate of 3.2 per cent per month in Jamkhed may be attributable to increased health awareness as evidenced by people's willingness to spend money for promotive preventive programmes such as routine Pap smears, glaucoma detection and immunisation.[1]

The cost of secondary health care

A simple forty bed health centre with diagnostic and surgical facilities supports the primary health programme in the villages. Special efforts have been made to keep the cost of secondary care within the reach of the village people.

Principles to reduce cost of care

We have always followed certain principles to achieve this end. We involved the community leaders, farmers' clubs and Mahila Vikas Mandals in planning, implementing and evaluating programmes. As a result, the people were totally involved in each stage of a programme. As far as possible, initial resources were generated locally and external funding was sought for capital expenditures and for seed money to initiate crucial programmes. It was agreed that recurrent operating costs would be kept so low that the village people could afford the services. Various forms of funding were discussed with the people, most of whom felt a fee for service form of payment was best suited to their needs.

Paying for medical care

From the beginning we used a programme planning, budgeting and review system. Costs are constantly reviewed in relation to the objectives, such as reducing infant mortality and maternal mortality and providing basic health care services, rather than in relation to maintenance of institutions such as a hospital or subcentre. For example, when it was found that the subcentres at Koregaon and Chincholi were not contributing significantly to the medical objectives, they were discontinued. Instead, primary care through VHWs was strengthened and the subcentre at Mahi Jalgaon was upgraded to a hospital which supports the Karjat Block. The community leaders in Koregaon and Chincholi felt that the subcentre buildings could be utilised for education.

Constant vigilance in the use of scant resources leads to the cost effectiveness of each programme. If the programme is not cost effective, we discuss it with the people and either modify or discontinue it. For example, school health programmes were started in the villages. For the amount of time and resources spent on the programme, it was not cost effective at all. The children who were marginalised were out in the fields looking after the goats and other farm animals. A school health programme was of no use to them. The school health programme was discontinued and replaced by a programme where the village health workers went to the fields and grazing grounds and examined the children for specific conditions such as leprosy, nutritional deficiencies and other common conditions that could be effectively treated or prevented.

Appropriate personnel

To counteract the usual high proportion of costs for personnel, we have found it effective to mobilise community resources to provide and train personnel and to concentrate on efficient use of appropriate personnel. One factor in the rising cost of medical care is the plethora of specialists. Apart from their own expensive training and high salaries, they require expensive equipment and other assistants. We studied the health problems in Jamkhed and found that the diseases were so simple and repetitive that only 6 per cent of health problems need the expertise of a trained physician. Specialist services are needed even less often. Such specialists, if employed, cannot be utilised to their fullest potential and so become dissatisfied with their jobs. Furthermore, in order to justify their position, procedures beyond those necessary are introduced, thus increasing the cost of care to the patient. The effect is similar to using a machine gun to kill a cockroach! We therefore used the principle of training and delegating higher responsibilities to personnel with fewer academic qualifications. As experience in many parts of the world has proved, such workers are stimulated when they are given responsibilities beyond their own expectations and they strive to do the job well.

Another principle we used is overlapping job responsibilities. When personnel are trained in multiple skills, their time is utilised efficiently. Covering vacations and absences does not require employing extra personnel because there are adequate persons with overlapping skills. For example, there may not be enough work for a full-time X-ray technician, but with additional training a person like Moses can effectively work both as an X-ray technician and in the artificial limb programme. In addition to reducing costs, personnel have a more holistic understanding of the organisation and are aware of the various programmes in the project as a whole.

In the conventional hospitals, a larger proportion of personnel work as maintenance or support staff. Often it is necessary to employ more supervisory staff to supervise these people. But in CRHP, the relatives who accompany patients to the hospital are trained and help support staff. Relatives cook, clean and help in nursing the patient, so there is no need for extra employees. Patients too are more satisfied with such services because they get more concerned and caring help from their loved ones than from paid workers. This practice is also in keeping with the local culture.

In most medical models of care, salaries constitute 60 to 80 per cent of the expenditure. We have constantly attempted to keep personnel costs below 25 per cent of the total budget. When specialist services are needed, they are carried out through mass campaigns or through the 'camp' approach. For example, an ophthalmologist visits Jamkhed twice a month. All eye surgery is performed on those specific days, so specialised services are required for a limited time because village health workers take care of the common eye dieases and screen for more complicated problems such a glaucoma.

The low-cost hospital at Mahi Jalgaon caters to the Karjat block population. The hospital has twenty beds and facilities for surgery. Elective surgery, such as hernias, hysterectomies and other gynecological surgery, is performed twice a week. The total staff consists of a doctor well trained in general and gynecological surgery, one assistant doctor, three ANMs and one multipurpose worker who serves as receptionist, record keeper and X-ray technician as well as doing rudimentary laboratory work. In addition, two women are employed to clean the operating room and labour room. On operating days the operating room staff from the main health centre at Jamkhed and a part-time anesthetist go to Mahi Jalgaon. It is not cost effective to have more full-time staff at Mahi Jalgaon. Patients who need more laboratory tests are referred to Jamkhed, which is 27 kilometres away. As a result, major surgery is affordable to patients; it can be performed at a total cost to the patient of $50 to $100.

Appropriate technology

A second aspect of reducing the cost of medical care is using appropriate technology. In India, as elsewhere, there is pressure to use newer and higher technology. Increased commercialisation in medical practice in India results in unnecessary use of higher technology for the sake of prestige. The poor often emulate the rich in demanding such technology, even though the prices make them paupers. These demands are discussed with the village people. Is there a need for this equipment and personnel; or is the technique a status symbol? Can equipment be maintained? What will the procedure cost the patient? If the equipment is used rarely, and in cases where a patient really needs the procedure, it is cheaper to refer the patient to a reputable institution in the city. For example, the use of endoscopies has been discussed. It was concluded that a cystoscope was appropriate equipment to introduce for transurethral resection of the prostate. Such a procedure saves considerable time and expenses both to the hospital and patient. On the other hand, equipment for angiograms are not necessary because the poorer populations experience little need for them.

The cost of medicine is reduced by using medicines from the essential drug list of WHO and buying them in bulk from reputable firms selling generic drugs. It is important to manage the pharmacy with proper inventories so that optimum supplies are kept in stock. At primary care level, the village health worker uses simple home remedies or tablets that cost less than one cent each.

The services provided are in keeping with the culture of the people. Much of the cost in hospitals is due to providing 'hotel' services and maintaining external appearances that make a facility marketable to richer clients. Such hotel facilities are intentionally not provided in the CRHP hospitals. The main health centre of CRHP at Jamkhed is known as the 'tin shed hospital.' It does not have a sleek appearance but its aluminium construction reflects the heat in summer, thereby minimising the cost of cooling the building. The absence of luxuries prevents the well-to-do from utilising the facilities; otherwise, they tend to take advantage of low cost care meant for poorer patients. Scientific sterile technique is not sacrificed at any point in such facilities.

In primary health care, continuous technical support and training is important, as is contact with the people. In developing countries transport is expensive because petroleum products are expensive. We have found that diesel/petrol-run vehicles are necessary for communication when distances are great and roads are poor. Bullock carts and bicycles are slow and valuable professional time is spent on the road. Every year, 16 to 18 per cent of the CRHP medical budget is spent on transportation costs.

Where the money comes from

Income for the medical programmes has been generated through patient fees. Discussions with farmers' clubs and Mahila Vikas Mandals have enabled CRHP to set patient fees that are within the ability of the poorer sectors to pay. About 10 per cent of patients cannot pay for the services. The clubs identify such persons and work out ways of meeting the costs. The community may meet the cost through contributions or an arrangement may be made to contribute labour in some form. Total free care is often not respected and valued, and usually the provider of such care is not considered competent enough to charge fees. How often we have seen expensive free medicines thrown away in favour of an injection of distilled water or B complex! Every patient, therefore, is expected to pay at least a token of the cost. Approximately 50 per cent of the community can pay a little more than the cost of treatment to offset those whose treatment is subsidised.

As we were first establishing the curative services, we used seed money from the United Church of Christ and the Disciples of Christ in the USA to subsidise medical care services. Four years later the medical aspects of the programme were being met with funds generated from the community, the Government and a few local donors. From 1975 onwards, apart from a few special programmes such as leprosy and tuberculosis control which have been assisted by the American Leprosy Mission and Lutheran World Relief, little external funding has been utilised.

External funding has been used to initiate programmes, which are later absorbed into the general budget. When the village health worker programme was initially introduced, seed money from OXFAM was used for two years to defray the expenses of training and developing the educational materials. Then the VHW expenses were absorbed into the general operational medical budget and are no longer subsidised.

Initially, new programmes have to be promoted. For such 'promotion', external seed money is needed. Immunisation, family planning and other services are examples of such promotion in the early 1970s. Now local awareness has grown to the extent that if these services are not available through government sources, the community pays for them. Recently, many villages decided to do mass tetanus immunisation for the adult population. They collected money and held the immunisation campaign.

In some instances the problem is so prevalent that external fund-

242

ing is necessary initially. Funds from the Christoffel Blindensen Mission in Germany helped initiate the Blindness Control Programme in 1976. The backlog of cataract operations and widespread vitamin A deficiency were treated and village personnel trained. Within two years, the external source of funding was no longer needed. This programme has now been incorporated into the general medical budget and is met by local resources.

Non-medical interventions

In starting programmes which change conditions that affect health and help villages with development, we followed the same principle of using initial seed money. Often this initial input was followed by a much larger mobilisation of resources from the Government or local resources. Provision of safe drinking water to the villages required a large initial investment. To drill 100 wells cost approximately $70 000, whereas the health centre building and equipment cost only $35 700. Because a good well serves a community for over twenty years, the investment is less than one tenth of a cent per capita per year. The benefits of a safe drinking water supply reduce morbidity and mortality in the population by over 50 per cent.

Most of these non-medical interventions have brought far-reaching economic and agricultural development. Single interventions, such as drilling tube wells, were funded initially by OXFAM and Christian aid and later by ICCO as the programme expanded. Because the community has to maintain these wells, its village people are trained to do so.

In many instances initial investment through CRHP has resulted in mobilisation of government resources in the area. The afforestation programmes were initially subsidised through Food for Work programmes. The success demonstrated by these models led to mobilisation of resources from the social forestry department to continue the programme.

The formation of Mahila Vikas Mandals also needed initial grants for training, literacy programmes and strengthening their organisations. Lutheran World Relief contributed to the development of Mahila Mandals in the early stages of the Mahila Vikas Mandal movement.

As the project expanded from 70 villages to 175 villages, the major external source of funds for socioeconomic development came from ICCO in the Netherlands. With investments of approximately $8 per capita for socioeconomic and agricultural development, village communities have worked to wards self-reliance. They are able to mobilise more and more resources from within the community and from government agencies and bank loans.

243

Sustainability

Sustainability is often viewed in relation to the survival and continuation of a programme or an institution such as a hospital. However, sustainability should be seen in terms of goals and objectives rather than of individual programmes. Therefore, CRHP views sustainability in terms of continuing improvement in the quality of life and continued reduction in measurable health parameters such as infant mortality. As the development process proceeds, many programmes become irrelevant or redundant. New priorities emerge and new programmes need to be undertaken. Therefore sustainability does not mean finding alternative funding agencies for the same programme for many years. It does not mean handing over the programme to the government. Sustainability means empowering communities to choose their own objectives and find their own solutions. It does not mean survival of the institution that enabled the programme.

Through the work at Jamkhed many communities, especially those with active Mahila Vikas Mandals, have become self-reliant. They depend on CRHP only for technical support and networking. For example, in 1971, supplementary nutrition was an important programme because more than 40 per cent of the children were malnourished. Over the years, the comprehensive approach of addressing the root causes of poverty, the social status of women, and health and nutrition education led to a great reduction in malnutrition. Soon the village people decided that such a supplementary programme was no longer necessary. In the more than ten years since supplementary nutrition has been stopped, the village children continue to be well nourished, despite a couple of years of drought.

Since 1989, CRHP has been gradually withdrawing, as many of the community organisations have become self-reliant. Many Mahila Vikas Mandals are functioning well, mobilising resources on their own. For example, the Mahila Vikas Mandal at Mahi Jalgaon has started many income-generating activities for women and is running a pre-school nursery. They organise health camps and continue to monitor the health of children in the village. They work closely with the government ANM and ensure that women get proper antenatal care. The primary health care activities are continuing through these Mahila Vikas Mandals. The CRHP now remains as a networking organisation, providing the secondary and tertiary support services whenever needed. Our experience shows that investment in the building of self-reliant communities is crucial to sustain improvements in health and needs to be stressed in the development of primary health care.

Although the initial costs for primary health care are expensive, the cost of care is effectively reduced when people are empowered and enabled to have equitable health care they can afford. Sustainable health care can be a reality when people become co-partners with the health care system to provide health care.

1   Duggal R and Amin S *Cost of Health Care: A Household Survey on an Indian District*. Foundation for Research in Community, Bombay, 1989.

CHAPTER 19

Equity, integration and empowerment

In this span of twenty-three years since we came to Jamkhed, many changes have taken place. The harsh realities of life where there is poverty, lack of knowledge, superstition, fear and injustice have been brought home to us over and over again. The present programme at CRHP bears little semblance to the small project we originally planned at Johns Hopkins School of Hygiene and Public Health. Through the years we practised and worked in Jamkhed, we learned to build on successes and turn failures and crisis situations into opportunities for improvement and correction. We share with you some of the lessons we learned.

The perceptions of poor and marginalised people are different from those of the elite and educated.
Health is not a priority as marginalised people struggle for survival. The basic necessities of life such as food, water and shelter are more important priorities. Lack of these important necessities contributes to more than 50 per cent morbidity and mortality in poorer communities. It is necessary for health professionals to acknowledge these needs and convert them into health programmes for nutrition, provision of safe drinking water and clean environment.

Academic and project planners often set the reduction of infant mortality as a goal. How do village people perceive infant death? In 1970, infant mortality in the CRHP area was over 176 per 1000 births. With a birth rate of 40, approximately 8 infant deaths occurred in a year in villages for every 1000 population. Six out of these eight deaths often occurred among the poor and marginalised. Although the death of male children is mourned, the death of the female children may even be welcomed! Unless attitudes towards girls changes, conscious or unconscious neglect of the female child, female

246

infanticide and female feticide will continue to be a factor in high infant mortality rates. Social injustice and the status of women and children need to be addressed as well.

It is not hard technology but often social action that improves health. CRHP does not have a sophisticated pediatric unit. Infant mortality has been reduced because of better nutrition, cleaner environment, better status of women and community participation. The birth rate fell because communities realised that female children are as precious as male children. The status of women has been raised by empowering them with skills, knowledge and income generating programmes. Availability and promotion of different methods of family planning to already knowledgeable communities have motivated couples to practise family planning.

The input of social sciences in primary health care must be emphasised. Medical workers must recognise the role of social science in primary health care. Social inputs are necessary to organise communities to deal with social injustices such as caste and class structures and the status of women and children. The practice of social medicine has a greater impact on rural health than do technical inputs such as injections, medicines and expensive diagnostic procedures. At CRHP, mobile teams and grass roots workers spend over 50 per cent of their time on learning the social aspects of health. The health worker should have an intimate knowledge of the community and how to cope with the problems of poverty.

Health education should be related to the resources and culture. The knowledge shared with the people should be appropriate to the resources and culture of the community. Middle-class lifestyle should not overlap on scientific facts. For example, commercially prepared baby foods or infant formulae should not be advocated to take the place of scientifically proven superior breast milk.

Rural communities are capable of planning and maintaining their own health. Rural communities around Jamkhed acquired skills to collect and analyse health information and support health workers. They can contribute to health care substantially provided:
a. They are taken seriously and not treated as ignorant people. Village people's ideas need to be taken seriously. They speak out of experience in adverse conditions. CRHP staff entrusted health services to the people and got them involved in different health programmes.

247

The attitude of superiority was replaced by a feeling of equality and working towards a common goal.

b. Medical knowledge and procedures are demystified.

Medicine needs to be demystified and knowledge should be shared freely with people so they can attain and maintain good health.
CRHP demystified surgical procedures like Caesarian sections and sterilisation operations by inviting people into the operating room and explaining the different procedures. This kind of demonstration removed many misconceptions about sterilisation and delivery of the placenta. Knowledge is freely shared at all levels of care.

Self-confidence must be promoted at all levels of the health team.
The process of enabling, developing and empowering others and sharing knowledge and skills can only occur if the facilitators, health professionals and the team have developed self-confidence and self-esteem. Hierarchical attitudes have to be replaced by a team spirit and equality. The realisation that knowledge not only gives power, but that sharing knowledge also increases self esteem is important in the development of a team spirit. Health workers who were nobodies gain status as they successfully provide useful services to the community. Self esteem has to be developed to the extent that the facilitator is ready to receive, enjoy and synthesise the ideas of the group (group/co-workers/partners) and to return those ideas to the group as recognisably their own, so that the creativity is theirs.

Community participation does not mean confrontation.
Indian villages have a tradition of inequality and exploitation of the poor and marginalised people. As these marginalised groups are empowered, efforts at reconciliation and cooperation among different groups are emphasised. Since health is dependent on the village community as a whole, it involves interconnected aspects of life which the individual often can affect only when there is cooperation among the members of the community for the benefit of all. Health is then a fundamental reason for community involvement and also provides a reason for community involvement and cooperation which everyone can easily see as valid. Small events which cannot be manipulated or theorised, can lead cumulatively, to profound changes in society, such as changes in collectively held beliefs which previously limited the abilities of people to act on their own behalf for their own benefit. Accepting treatment for snakebite and exposing the devrushis are but a few examples. This, coupled with continuous dialogue on issues such as the caste system, providing women with opportunities to improve

248

their socioeconomic conditions, and the inculcation of values of respect helped communities to come together. Confrontation only alienates and drives communities apart, leading to hatred and violence and away from a state of positive health.

Taking advantage of community enthusiasm leads to progress.
Community interest waxes and wanes. When the leaders of Jamkhed showed their enthusiasm to have a health programme, the opportunity was seized and the project was started promptly and decisively before the enthusiasm could wane. Crisis situations such as drought were turned into opportunities for gaining the confidence of the community by responding to needs for food and water.

It is essential to train grass root workers who are culturally acceptable, available and accessible.
Health is influenced by socioeconomic factors, many of which are well knit into the social fabric of the society. It is only persons from within the community who can really understand the practices and beliefs that exist within the community. Only a person from the community is readily available and accessible at all times at a cost the community can afford. CRHP took a bold step in training illiterate village women as health workers. The very limitation of reading skills led to the system of continuous weekly training and support which has resulted in their learning progressively more and more skills and thereby keeping them motivated.

Planning needs to be flexible.
When people are involved in planning and implementing their programmes, flexibility and innovations are needed. Constant review and evaluation led to changes in the programme. When ever failures were noticed immediate corrective measures could be instituted. The failure of the ANM to be the link in promotive and preventive programmes led to the development of the village health worker. This flexibility is important for the success of health programmes.

There should be a balance between curative, promotive and preventive health services.
Poor communities have a large backlog of morbidity and disease. People look for solutions for their immediate medical problems. It is necessary to have curative services to respond to this need. These curative services increase the credibility of the health professional. They also can act as a springboard to introduce preventive programmes. Jamkhed had many patients with tetanus. Successfully treating these

249

patients led to the acceptance of tetanus toxoid immunisation.

Primary health care needs the support of secondary and tertiary services.
A good support system in the form of secondary and tertiary care is necessary. The village health worker must have the confidence that she can approach a secondary or tertiary care centre for help when needed. Preventive programmes will be effective only if backed up with appropriate support programmes. Antenatal care without a back-up service for Caesarian section will soon lose all credibility. It is important to have a good onward referral service to tertiary care hospitals in the city. From time to we have referred village people for open heart surgery and other specialised services.

Scientific knowledge must be applied to develop technology appropriate to the needs and resources of the community.
Poverty and isolation of the village people make it difficult to practise expensive sophisticated technology. The delivery pack used by the VHW ensures that sufficient sterile technique during delivery is eliminating infant and maternal infection. This pack is inexpensive and can be used by any mother in the village. The Jaipur foot is another example of a simple prosthesis based on the life-style of the people.

Accept the slow pace of development.
Professionals and donors want quick results. The pace in the village is slow. Poor people weigh all options before choosing a particular course of action. Patience is needed as people take their time in decision making. However, when communities do show enthusiasm it is necessary to act promptly.

The primary health care approach is dynamic and encompasses a wide range of health activities.
It is not limited to mother and child health programmes, family planning or nutrition programmes or immunisation. Priorities will depend on the needs of the people. In successful programmes the priorities do not remain the same. As immunisation and good nutrition become universal, village people are addressing issues such as cancer and diabetes. At CRHP, through the PHC approach, communities are involved in physical, social and economic rehabilitation of persons with leprosy and tuberculosis. They are addressing the issue of HIV/AIDS and cancer. In the national context, problems such as leprosy seem enormous and unsurmountable. However, when these problems are reduced to the smallest community unit they become

manageable. In a village perhaps only three or four persons have tuberculosis or leprosy that needs special care. Communities when motivated can take care of these problems.

Role of non-governmental organisations.
The government should have the basic responsibility of providing basic services. However, non-governmental agencies have an important role in primary health care. The success of PHC depends to a large extent on community participation. It is difficult to elicit this participation, particularly from those who need the services most, namely, the poor and marginalised. NGOs are in a position to act as the interface between the government and the people, training and empowering people so they can become co-partners with the government in PHC activities.

The PHC approach calls for a multi-sectoral approach to health and development. The NGO can act as catalyst in bringing these different sectors of development together at the grass roots level.

The NGO is in a position to be flexible and should be innovative. Apart from countries like China and Cuba, the components of the Alma Ata declaration were mainly tried out by NGOs in micro-level projects around the world. NGOs should not merely replace the government activities by acting as contractors for the government. Rather they should complement the government's activities.

The problems in rural areas are so vast and the government has such meagre resources, and therefore there is little possibility of duplicating the government activities. The NGO should not be perceived as working in competition with the government.

Integration.
One of the most important aspects of CRHP has been the development of totally integrated services. Not only have the preventive and curative health services been totally integrated, but non-medical intervention and social and economic aspects of development also have been well integrated into all the programmes. Doctors, nurses, paramedical workers, social workers and others work together as a team. They are trained together and learn to respect each other. Hierarchy has been replaced by a sense of belonging to a team. Learning to share with each other becomes the climate. Undergirding this continuous training is the development of values of service, sharing knowledge, respecting each other and concern for other members as equal partners. Trust in each other and an optimistic attitude toward fellow village people have helped communities to accept each other and form strong cohesive groups.

Equity in health care.

Equity implies that every man, woman and child, no matter where he or she lives, has the right to enjoy good health and deserves to have access to health services. Equity then means to seek out those who are poor, forgotten, marginalised, wherever they are. CRHP works with the 50 per cent of people in the rural communities who live below the poverty line. Health teams ensure that the Dalits, women, widows, nomadic tribes and those shunned as criminal tribes are sought out. CRHP has made sure that the infrastructure and facilities created to serve these groups are not snatched away from them. The drinking water tube wells were placed in the Dalit section of the village so that the Dalits would have access to the well.

Empowerment.

Primary health care means empowerment. Human beings, regardless of their station in life have innate unlimited potential within themselves. People have been empowered through a process of discovery, experimentation, trial and error, rerouting when necessary, and by being non-dogmatic in sharing values and skills. Rural communities have been empowered through information, training, and imparting medical, economic, and social skills. Communities are empowered by way of organisation of farmers' clubs and Mahila Vikas Mandals. Through these processes individuals and communities have gained in self-esteem and self-confidence and have realised that they have the capacity within themselves to determine their own lives.

Looking to the future.

For the past four years we have not been actively involved in the PHC work at Jamkhed. While we spent two years at Johns Hopkins School of Hygiene and Public Health in Baltimore, writing this book not only did the work continue, but the project expanded to a tribal area over 200 km distant from Jamkhed. Groups of village men and women from Jamkhed went to Bhandardara, stayed with the village people, observed their customs and organised Mahila Vikas Mandals as well as identifying village health workers. Yamunabai and other village health workers went and stayed in the Bhandardara villages to help with the organisation and training. Of her experience Yamunabai says, 'The tribal people are very poor and they live in thatched huts. They are friendly and they invited us to stay with them and share what they had. It was difficult for me because there was no water and there was filth and flies all around. Almost every family had scabies and skin infections. We had no choice; we had to stay in the overcrowded huts. I, a Brahmin, have never eaten meat. The only food they had was dried fish and rice. The odour of the fish soon overcame me and I could hardly keep the rice down. Then I remembered that once upon a time we too had filth in our village and there was scabies. All of us from Jamkhed determined to first get rid of the scabies just as we had done in Jamkhed. Water had to be fetched from a long distance. This did not deter us. We worked with the people and in three months we got rid of the scabies. We encouraged the women to be involved in health activities, identified and trained women to become village health workers. Despite the physical hardships it was a rewarding experience.'

With a minimum staff of doctor, social worker, ANM and paramedical workers, together with village volunteers, the primary health programme has progressed rapidly in the Bhandardara area.

In India, many NGOs have successful primary health care programmes. There are also many examples of similar experiences around the world.

Recently we have had opportunities to visit and share our experiences with marginalised communities in several countries in Latin America and Africa. We have been met with enthusiasm as people in these communities perceive that these principles of PHC can be applied to their own situations.

Despite these successes, medical education continues to emphasise training medical graduates in more and more highly specialised areas of medicine. There is little emphasis on addressing the basic health problems of the poor and marginalised people who form more than 50 per cent of our country. There is a need for workers to be trained in community based primary health care.

Encouraged by the sustainability of its approach at Jamkhed, CRHP wishes to share its experiences with those interested in the health of marginalised people. Village people also agreed to participate in new training activities. An institute for training in community based primary health care is underway. The unique feature of this institute is that 50 per cent of the training will be given by the village people themselves.

As we have had opportunities to travel and to share these principles and our experiences, a number of people, especially those in more 'developed' regions and countries, have said to us, 'But Dr Arole, but Mabelle, but Raj, you make it sound easy. Surely there have been crises that were hard for you personally to face, times when you doubted strength to go on?'

Yes, of course there have been such times. Perhaps the gifts of our own particular temperaments and the support we have had always for each other lead us to make less of these difficulties (such as seasons

253

of drought) than others may feel. We began with a hope, a vision, that has continued to sustain us. But most importantly, we have learned over and over that empowerment is not a one-way process. It is not that we, that one set of people 'provide' empowerment for others who receive it. Rather, like water from a well dug in a fortunate spot, the power flows in many directions and sustains those who may set the process in motion as well as those disempowered for such a long time. It is a dynamic process which once set in motion transforms us, persons and communities.

So from the beginning, we ourselves have been given power by the very processes and people involved in realising the vision. We have firmly come to believe that through a process of recognising and sharing the resources and potential of everyone, communities claim their right to health. Only people empowered and empowering others for the common good can find and keep the respect, cooperation and peace so much needed in this world.

REFERENCES AND SUGGESTED READINGS

Antia, N H and Bhatia, Kavita (eds). *People's Health in People's Hands.* The Foundation for Research in Community Health, Bombay 1993

Arole M. A comprehensive approach to community welfare: growth monitoring and role of women in Jamkhed. *Indian Journal of Paediatrics* 1988; 55 (Suppl): S100–5

Arole R. *The Role of the Private Sector in Primary Health Care.* International Health Counference; The National Council for International Health, 1979: 7–10

Bang, Rani. Nurses: the cursed women in the medical system. In: *Health Care which way to go?* Bang, Abhay and Patel, Ashvin, J. (eds). Voluntary Health Association of India, New Delhi 1982

Berman, Peter and Khan, M E (eds). *Paying for India's Health Care.* Sage Publications 1993

Bichmann W, Rifkin S B, Shrestha M. Towards measurement of community participation. *World Health Forum* 1989; 10 (3–4): 467–72

Bryant J H. *Health in the Developing World.* Ithaca Press, NY, Cornell University 1969

Burkey, Stan. *People First: A guide to Self Reliant Participatory Rural Development.* ZED Books Ltd, London, New Jersey 1993

Caldwell J C. Routes to low mortality in poor countries. *Population and Development Review* 1986; 12: 171–220

Chambers, Robert, *Rural Development: Putting the Last First.* Wiley and Longman 1986

Cernea, Michael M. *Putting People First: Sociological Variables in Development.* A World Bank Publication. Oxford University Press 1991

Devendra, Kiran. *Status and Position of Women in India.* Vikas Publishing House, New Delhi 1985

Desai, Neera and Krishnaraj, Maithreyi. *Women and Society in India.* Ajanta Publications (India) 1990

Devasia, Leelamma and Devasia, V V. *Girl Child in India.* Ashish Publishing House 8/81 Punjabi Bagh, New Delhi 1991

Fendall N R E. *Auxiliaries In Health Care.* The Johns Hopkins University Press, Baltimore MD and London 1972, reprinted in 1979.

Gatkin, Davidson R et al. *Can Health and Nutrition Interventions make a Difference?.* Overseas Development Council, Washington, Monograph No. 13

Government of India, 1946, *Report of the Health Survey and Development Committee,* (Chairman, Sir J. Bhore) Volumes 1–4, New Delhi; Suptd of Government Printing.

Halstead S B, Walsh F A and Warren K D. (eds) *Good Health at Low Cost*. Proceedings of a conference sponsored by the Rockefeller Foundation, 29th April–3rd May 1985, at Bellagio, Italy.

Harnar R *et al. Teaching Health Workers: A Guide to the Process*. Voluntary Health Association of India, New Delhi 1978

Hawes H and Gayton J. *Child to Child*. Macmillan, London 1979

ICSSR. *Health For All: An Alternative Strategy*. Report of the ICSSR/ICMR Study Group, New Delhi 1980

Illich, Ivan. *Limits to Medicine*. Penguin Books Ltd. Middlesex, England 1976

Jeffrey R. *The Politics of Health in India*. University of California Press, Berkeley and London 1988

King M. *Medical Care in Developing Countries*. Oxford University Press, Nairobi 1966

Mckee, Neill. *Social Mobilization and Social Marketing in Developing Countries*. SouthBound, 9 College Square Penang, Malaysia 1992

Mckeown T. *The Role of Medicine*. Preston University Press 1980

Madan T N. Community involvement in health policy. Socio-structural and dynamic aspects of health belief. *Society, Science and Medicine* 1987 **25** (6): 615–620

Mahadven K and Sumangala M. *Social Development, Cultural Change and Fertility Decline*. A study of fertility decline in Kerala. Sage Publications 1987

Mayfield, James, *Go to the People*. West Hartford, Kumarian Press 1986

Morley, David. *Paediatric Priorities in the Developing Countries*. Butterworth, London 1973

Morley D, Rohde J and Williams J (eds). *Practising Health for All*. Oxford University Press, Oxford 1983

Morley, David and Woodland, Margaret. *See How They Grow*. Macmillan, London 1979

Pandey, Shashi Ranjan. *Community Action for Social Justice*. Grass roots Organizations in India. Sage Publications, India 1991

Rifkin S B, Muller F, Bichmann W. Primary health care: on measuring participation. *Society, Science and Medicine*. 1988; **26** (9): 931–40

Rao, Sangeetha R. *Caste System in India: Myth and Reality*. India Publishers and Distributers, New Delhi 1989

Seipp, Conrad (ed.). *Health Care for the Community* Selected Papers of Dr John B. Grant. Johns Hopkins University Press, Baltimore, London

Stampar, Andrija. *Serving the Cause of Public Health*. Selected Papers of Andrija Stampar. Ed. M. D. Grmek, Zagreb 1966

Taylor, Carl E. and Associates. *Child and Maternal Health Services in Rural India Vol. 1 and 2*. The Johns Hopkins University Press, Baltimore and London 1983

WHO/UNICEF. *Primary Health Care*. Report of the International Conference on Primary Health Care, Alma-Ata, USSR, Geneva 1978

WHO *Health by the People*. Newell, Kenneth W. (ed.). WHO, Geneva 1975

Werner, David and Bower, Bill. *Helping Health Workers Learn*. The Hesperidian Foundation, Palo Alto California 1991

GLOSSARY OF INDIAN WORDS AND ABBREVIATIONS

Akka	older sister; a nurse is generally addressed as akka
ANM	auxiliary nurse midwife
Bai	suffix added to woman's name as a form of respect (in Maharashtra)
CHG	community health guide
CRHP	Comprehensive Rural Health Project
Dacoit	armed robber
Dada	older brother; as a suffix to denote respect
Dalit	oppressed person; a person belonging to the lower castes of the caste hierarchy.
Dai	traditional birth attendant
Devrushi	traditional spiritual healer
Dharmashala	a building where travellers can rest for the night. In villages it is usually a simple structure with three walls and a roof and mud floor.
FC	farmers' club
ICCO	Interchurch Organisation for Development Cooperation
Kotwal	the village watchman
Mahila	women
Mandal	organisation or group
MVM	Mahila Vikas Mandal; Women's Development Organisation
NGO	non-governmental organisation
Panchayat	the village council of elected members
Panchayat Samiti	the council of representatives from villages of a block
Patil	landlord; currently used as a form of respect.
Purdah	women wearing a veil to cover their face to screen themselves from men; literally means curtain
Sabhapaty	chairperson of the Panchayat Samiti (Block council)
Saheb	placed after a name as a form of respect
Samiti	Council
Sari	traditional garment worn by Indian women. Consists of 5–9 metres of cloth wrapped around the body.
Sarpanch	chairperson of the village council; mayor
Shamiana	canopy used for functions
Taluk/taluka	administrative division of district which forms the unit for local administration
VHG	village health guide
VHW	village health worker
Zillah Parishad	the council of elected representatives at the district level

INDEX

(Page numbers in **bold** refer to illustrations.)

abortion 33, 152–3
adult literacy: and MVMs 195
afforestation programmes 91, 119,
    209, 243
Aggi 201
agriculture 10, 105, 122
    improvements 14, 28
    seminars for 108, 120
Ahmednagar: city 16, 24, 56, 79
    District 1, 33, 48, **51**, 78, 93
    VHGs for 205–7
alcoholism 118, 194–5
Amte, Leelabai 175, 195
ANM, Auxiliary Nurse Midwife 40, 42,
    45, 76, 78, 83, 93, 113, 135–45
    and leprosy 227–8
    and VHWs 176
appraisal: rapid, of surveys 210
Arole, Raj and Mabelle: early life
    16–23
    in USA 35–48
artificial limb manufacture 102
Ashta 75–6, 107, 116, 148
attitudes: changes in 224
Aurangabad District 78, 93
auxiliaries, role of 39–40
    see also ANM
Ayurveda 234

Bavi 107, 110–11, 115–16, 126, 131,
    148–9, 161, 201, 203, 228, 231
    health costs in 237–8
beliefs, traditional 170–1
    and harm to health 171–2
Bhandardara: dam 35
    primary health care in 252–3
Bhanushali, Ravikant 103
Bhid 48
Bhishi system 186–7, 190, 200
Bhore, Sir Joseph 41, 43
    Committee 41–2
birth rate, crude 43, 211, **216**,
    238
Brahmins 11, 67
Brand, Dr Paul 22
bureaucracy: problems of 52, 55,
    65

caste 16, 52, 67–8
    discrimination 2–7 *passim*, 10, 14,
        110, 121, 123, 125, 127–8, 133,
        203, 219
    and health 106–8
    and VHWs 149, 150, 177
cataracts, eye 6, 75, 117, 133, 243
Chande, Parubai 7–9
check dams 99, 110, 131, 132
CHG, Community Health Guides 178
child: health care 121–6, 162–3, 211,
    212, **214**
    mortality 6, 13, 43, 54, **217**
    nutrition 112–13
    status of 14
    under five clinics 40–1, 45, 135
child-to-child programme 129–30, 196
Chincholi 7, 134, 239
Chinchpur 124
Christian Medical College,
    Vellore 19, 21
clinics: under five 40–1, 45, 135
    weekly 73–4 *passim*, 77, 84, 135,
        157, 237
communication: oral 15
community: cooperation 110, 111, 248
    and cost of health care 238
    Development Blocks 52
    and health 38, 248
    interest 249
    kitchens 112–13, 127–8, 129, 203, 212
    participation 44–5, 77, 105–20
    resources 234
    selection of, for health project 50–5
    skills 247
    structure 67
Community Volunteer Scheme 205
contraception 28
    oral 6, 12, 162, 221
costs: of health care 237–9
credit: for women 189–90, 191
CRHP, Comprehensive Rural
    Health Project 1, 88, 134
    advisory board 95–6
    benefits through 223
    expansion of 201–9
    flexibility of 145

impact of 209
inauguration in Jamkhed 63–4
and MVMs 200
and self-reliance 244
cultural adaptation: and VHWs 167–70
curative care 36, 43, 249
cost of 37
and preventive treatment 33, 44,
62, 74

dacoits: gangs of 16, 80, 118
Dalits 2–5 *passim*, 10, 11, 59, 61,
67–8, 111, 117, 134, 149, 150, 231
discrimination against 68, 123–4, 252
leaders 73
poverty of 71–2
and VHWs 166, 175, 177
Dalvi, Bayadabai 148
death: records of 215–16
delivery (birth) 163–5, 187, 198
development: agencies 46
and health 217–21
overall, need for 75
slow pace of 250
Dharmashala: in Jamkhed 59, 62,
84
diet, local 170–1
disease 30, 166
documentaries: on Jamkhed and
CRHP 208–9
drought 11, 121–6, 249, 254
Durgaon 111

economic status 218, 219
education 15, 17
see also under health
employment: and famine 121, 130–2
empowerment 15, 69, 117–19, 209,
221, 237, 248, 252, 254
of MVMs 189
equality: sex 14, 15
equipment, appropriate: for health
centre 99
equity: in health care 252
environment: clean 158
expansion: of health care 201–9
eye camps 117, 133, 198, 240
EZE grants: for health centre 99

family planning 6, 12, 27, 33, 37,
42, 58, 59, 139, 183, 221
and VHWs 160, 162
famine 126–32
farmers' clubs 105–20, 127, 135,
138, 203, 204, 207–9 *passim*, 252
cooperatives 110, 111

and Food for Work programmes 130
grain banks 110
and health education 116–17
and health surveys 113–15, 212–14
passim, 216
and leprosy 228, 229, 231
and MVMs 184–5, 198
seminars 108–9, 120, 187–9, 201
and VHWs 147, 156, 159, 177–9
passim
and village development 110–12
Fendall, Dr N.R.E. 40
feudal structure 52–4
focus group discussions 210, 217,
218, 221
food 105, 171, 223
common feeding programme 128
shortage, and drought 126–32
Food for Work programmes 130–2,
231, 243
funding: of health care 27, 236–9, 242–3
future: of primary health care 252–4

Gaikwood, Murlidhar 80
Gavhale, Angadrao 10
Ghodegaon 9–14, 106, 110, 115,
118, 203
maps of 12
Ghodke, Helenbai (Akka) 25, 79, 83,
86, 87, 136, 142
and leprosy 226
and VHWs 160
Goyakarwada 7–9 *passim*
Grant, Dr John 38, 41
guinea worm infection 12, 52
Guram, Moses 102, 103, **104**

Halgaon 107, 110, 148, 161, 190, 198
Hambirao, Shantabai 149
'healers' 29, 34, 37, 116–17, 171–2
and leprosy 229–30
health: care system 28, 39, 40, 44,
83, 197
centre, in Jamkhed 95–9
education 36, 37, 81–3, 102, 198,
229, 237, 247
insurance 37
officials 55
surveys 85, 91, 113–15, 198, 210–24
teams 45
Health for All **2**, 41
herbal medicines 29, 234
hierarchy: breaking 80–1, 100, 251
holistic approach: and medicine 33, 235
homeopathy 234
hospitals: costs of 37, 58, 240, 241

resources for 41, 42
housing 222

illiteracy 159, 192, 193, 206
illness 14–15, 173
  home treatment 19
immunisation programmes 27, 73,
  115, 133, 156, 199, 212, 237,
  242
income: for women 186–7, 193, 209
indigenous practitioners 233–4
infant mortality **217**, 238, 246
institute: training, for health care 253
integration 15, 251
irrigation 28, 130, 132
IUDs, intrauterine devices 28, 33

Jadhav, Vasant, leprosy technician 80,
  89, 90, 92–3, 160, 210, 212, 226,
  233
Jamkhed 2, 48, 131, 201–9 *passim*,
  235, 252
  choice for community work 56–64
  community participation 59–64
  map **202**
  as model 208
  water shortage 124
job satisfaction 93
Joshibai, Mrs 141, 146, 147

Kadam, Lalanbai 2–7
Kamble, Ratna 185
Kapse, Girjabai 161
Karjat **202**
Kark, Dr Sydney 39
Khandagale, Prakash 91, **92**, 173
Khandvi 91, 110, 115–16, 160, 201,
  203
  farmers' club 112, 119
Khansaheb 96
Kharda 16, 91
knowledge: extent of 222
  relevance of 209
  sharing 179, 187–8, 248
Kolar hospital 24
Koregaon 239
Kothari, Bansilalji 33, 35, 48, 56, 58,
  62, 66, 80, 96, 98
Kshatriyas 67
Kulkarni, Yamunabai 11–14 *passim*
Kusadgaon 194

leaders, village: attitudes 66–7, 74
  cooperation from 65–77
learning: oral way of 165
leprosy 13, 22, 32, 36, 42, 43, 45,

52, 54, 90, 91, 113, 119, 160,
  180, 216, 225–33, 250–1
  holistic care for 92
loans 32, 191, 223
Londhe, Arun 120, 156, 160, 190, 213

Madhukar 201
Maharashtra State, India **47**, 48
Mahi Jalgaon 192–3, 238–40 *passim*,
  244
Mahila Vikas Mandal (MVMs)
  women's groups 182–200, 243,
  252

  empowerment 189–200
  expansion of 204, 207–9 *passim*
  and health 192–3
  and leprosy 229, 231
  self-reliance 244
  and village surveys 214, 216
malaria 42
malnourishment 112, 127, 212, 244
  and migration 184, 193-4
Mandlik, Shri Gulabrao 116–17
Marathi Mission 24, 48, 50
marginalisation: and health 246, 248,
  252, 253
mass health programmes 117, 133,
  198
maternal: mortality 30, 43
  services 211
Mathkuli 125
medicines: cost of 241
  demystification of 248
Mishrilalji, Shri 95, 96, 99
Mook, Dr Telfer 48
morbidity 14–15
  fall in 237, 238

Nahuli 149
Narangwal, Punjab 40, 138, 142
NGOs: and CHRP 204–5
  and community 251
  and VHGs 207
night blindness 153
Nikam, Usha 139–41
Nimbalkar, Hon. Shri Abasaheb 64–6
  passim, 96
Nimgaonkar, Meena 143, **144**
non-medical interventions 243
nurses: clinical challenges 87–8
  recruitment 78
  responsibilities of 85–7
  see also ANMs
nutrition 158
  lack of 30, 81
  programmes 27, 113, 127, 129, 163, 244

oral rehydration solution 167, 168–9, 187
Osmanabad 48, 50
  District 52–4
outcastes 2
outpatient clinics: in villages 27, 84

Panjabi, Dr 18–19, 29
paramedical workers 113
Patil, Nanasaheb 8, 9
Patil, Shahaji 9, 203
Patoda 88
payment: for medical care 238–9
personnel: appropriate 239
Pimpalgaon 2–7 passim, 106, 209,
  216, 236
  health survey 6
Pimparkhed 116, 124
Pol, Muktabai 1, 149, 154, 155, 177,
  181, 188, 215, 232
polio 133
poverty: and chronic starvation 105
  and disease 159, 166
  and exploitation 30–1
  and health care 30–1, 34, 38, 43, 83
  round Jamkhed 57
  understanding 81–2
Powar, Indubai 232
prenatal care 30, 45, 88–9, 133, 139
preventive treatment 28, 30, 33, 59,
  115, 166, 221
  and curative service 62, 74
  and ANMs 137, 141
primary health care 38, 41–3,
  centres 42, 45
  flexibility of 249
  future of 252–4
  resources for 235–45
  support for system 250
  and VHGs 206–8
  and water provision 125–6
public health training: in India 34

quality of life 221–4
questionnaires: for village
  surveys 212, 214

Rahuri 16, 17, 20, 55
Rajuri 110, 131, 148, 189, 194–5, 199
  wells for 122–3
reforestation: and MVMs 196
relatives: as partners in healing 84–5,
  97, 240
resources: for health care 235–45
  human 235–8
responsibilities: delegation 85–6, 239–40
  sharing 84, 94, 105

road-building workcamps: and health
  education 133
Road to Health programme 114
rural health: planning for 43–6
rural indebtedness 117

Sakat 76, 118, 131, 139–41
  VHW in 146, 147–8
Sadafule, Salubai 148
salaries 240
Salbatpur 28
Sanap, Janabai 147
sanitation 14, 15, 30, 36, 44, 170, 212
Sastare, Madhukar 112
Sathe, Vasant 231
school health surveys: and leprosy 230
secondary health care 235, 238
self-esteem 248
self-reliance 235–45
  lack of, by village poor 69
seminars 221
  see also under farmers' clubs
Shinde, Asrabai 174, 203
Shrisunder, Jerus (Jeribai) 79, 83, 87
  field activities 89
  and VHWs 160
Shudras 67
skills: development of 93–4, 247
small-pox 42
soak pits 116, 213
social: change 117
  issues, and MVMs 191–2
  medicine, role of 247
  values, and MVMs 194
soil conservation 130
Solapur 48, 50
Sole, Kisanro 13
Sonawane, Vatsalabai 148
spirituality: active 14
Stampar, Dr Andreja 39
starvation, chronic 112
  and poverty 105
sterile techniques: for operating 64
sterilisation 6, 12, 28, 37, 138, 144
stoves, smokeless 8
survival: and health demands 75
sustainability 244–5, 253

talents, local: use of 95–104
Taylor, Dr Carl 40
teaching materials 173
team: breaking hierarchy 80–1
  expansion 93
  finding workers for 78–94
  spirit 81, 84
  training 84, 89, 94

261

technology: appropriate 46, 99, 102, 241–2, 250
Telengeshi 87, 118, 149
tetanus 58, 62, 84, 133, 199, 216, 242, 250
Thorat, Uttam 80, 210, 212
traditional healers: see 'healers'
traditions: harmful 146
training: continuous 241
    village people 32, 33, 249
    see also VHWs
transport 241–2
tuberculosis 31, 32, 36, 42, 43, 45, 160, 250–1
    and MVMs 198
tube wells: for water 97, 122, 124, 125–6, 170, 243, 252

untouchables 68, 123, 128
USA: Aroles in 35, 36–48
    grants from 27

Vadala 55, 79
    Mission hospital 20, 24–34 passim
Vaishyas 67
Varade, Ramling 96, 98
veterinary care 112
VHAI, Voluntary Health Association of India 204
VHG, village health guide 205
    for Ahmednagar District 205–7
    support for 207
    training 206–8
VHWs, village health workers 146–57, 159, 165, 173–6, 237, 242, 253
    and leprosy 228, 229
    and MVMs 187, 197
    selection 158, 159–60
    self-sufficiency of 156, 180
    training 153–4, 156–81
    and village surveys 214–16 passim
village: bondage 31–2
    community, structure of 67
    feuds 75–6
    life 23, 83
    health 25, 27, 29, 34, 84
    politics 76

surveys 210–24
visits to 70–3
vitamin A deficiency 54, 127, 215, 243

Wade, Sitaram 89–90, 136, 173
wages 132
Waibhat, Ganpat 96, 107, 99–102
    puppet drama group, and health education 101–2
water: cost of 82
    divining 123–4
    in drought 121–6
    at Jamkhed 57, 66, 96–7
    safe supply 7, 14, 15, 30, 36, 83, 105, 158, 170, 237, 243
    waste 115–16
weddings: community 118–19
    cost of 118
well: construction of 8, 124
    see also tube wells
WHO/UNICEF study 205
witchcraft: use of 25, 43
witch doctors 29, 166, 171–2
women, village: and drought 127
    empowerment 150–2, 189, 197
    as entrepreneurs 191
    hardship of 18
    illiteracy of 159, 192, 193
    leadership roles of 7, 179
    and leprosy 232
    and MVMs 179, 182–200
    oppression of 184
    organisations 119
    problems of 119
    respect for 203
    responsibilities of 183–4
    rights of 188
    status of 14, 21, 147, 182–3, 220, 224, 247
    and traditional values 158–9
    as VHWs 146–57, 158–81
work ethic 132
workshops: international 208
    for VHGs 208

Zikree 107, 122
Zillah Parishad 51, 59